Motivating Elementary Students
to Self-Monitor and Regulate Their Behavior

The Guilford Practical Intervention in the Schools Series

Kenneth W. Merrell, Founding Editor
Sandra M. Chafouleas, Series Editor

www.guilford.com/practical

This series presents the most reader-friendly resources available in key areas of evidence-based practice in school settings. Practitioners will find trustworthy guides on effective behavioral, mental health, and academic interventions, and assessment and measurement approaches. Covering all aspects of planning, implementing, and evaluating high-quality services for students, books in the series are carefully crafted for everyday utility. Features include ready-to-use reproducibles, appealing visual elements, and an oversized format. Recent titles have Web pages where purchasers can download and print the reproducible materials.

Recent Volumes

Social, Emotional, and Behavioral Supports in Schools:
Linking Assessment to Tier 2 Intervention
Sara C. McDaniel, Allison L. Bruhn, and Sara Estrapala

Family–School Success for Children with ADHD:
A Guide for Intervention
Thomas J. Power, Jennifer A. Mautone, and Stephen L. Soffer

School Crisis Intervention: An Essential Guide for Practitioners
Scott Poland and Sara Ferguson

Classwide Positive Behavioral Interventions and Supports,
Second Edition: A Guide to Proactive Classroom Management
Brandi Simonsen and Diane Myers

Family–School Collaboration in Multi-Tiered Systems of Support
S. Andrew Garbacz, Devon R. Minch, and Mark D. Weist

Overcoming Test Anxiety:
Tools to Support Students from Early Adolescence to Adulthood
Alex Jordan and Benjamin J. Lovett

Motivating Elementary Students to Self-Monitor and Regulate Their Behavior:
The SMARTS Program for Tiers 2 and 3
Aaron M. Thompson, Keith C. Herman, and Wendy M. Reinke

Trauma-Informed and Culturally Responsive Practices in Schools:
Building a Climate of Compassion
Isaiah B. Pickens

DBT Skills in Elementary Schools:
Skills Training for Emotional Problem Solving in Grades K–5 (DBT STEPS-E)
James. J. Mazza, Elizabeth T. Dexter-Mazza, Jill H. Rathus, and Alec L. Miller

Brief Counseling in Schools: 40 Techniques for Rapid Change
John J. Murphy

Motivating Elementary Students to Self-Monitor and Regulate Their Behavior

The SMARTS Program for Tiers 2 and 3

AARON M. THOMPSON
KEITH C. HERMAN
WENDY M. REINKE

gp

THE GUILFORD PRESS
New York   London

This publication is intended to provide helpful and informative material. It is not intended to
diagnose, treat, cure, or prevent any health problem or condition, nor is it intended to replace
the advice of a health professional. No action should be taken based solely on the contents of
this book. Always consult your physician or qualified health care professional on any matters
regarding your health and before adopting any suggestions in this book or drawing inferences
from it.

The author and publisher specifically disclaim all responsibility for any liability, loss, or
risk, personal or otherwise, which is incurred as a consequence, directly or indirectly, from the
use or application of any contents of this book.

Any and all product names referenced within this book are the trademarks of their
respective owners. Always read all information provided by the manufacturers' product labels
before using their products. The author and publisher are not responsible for claims made by
manufacturers.

Library of Congress Cataloging-in-Publication Data is available from the publisher.

ISBN 978-1-4625-5886-5 (paperback) — ISBN 978-1-4625-5887-2 (hardcover)

About the Authors

Aaron M. Thompson, PhD, MSW, MEd, is Professor and Director of the School of Social Work at the University of Missouri, where he also serves as Associate Director of the Missouri Prevention Science Institute. Prior to becoming a professor, he worked as an adventure therapist, juvenile court counselor, school social worker, and public school principal. Dr. Thompson is the primary developer of the Self-Monitoring and Regulation Training Strategy (SMARTS) program. He has authored over 100 publications on interventions and reducing risk factors in schools and has been recognized with the Gary Lee Shaffer Faculty Award from the School Social Work Association of America and the Faculty Award from the University of Missouri Alumni Association, among other honors.

Keith C. Herman, PhD, is Curators' Distinguished Professor in School Psychology at the University of Missouri, where he codirects the Missouri Prevention Science Institute. Previously, he worked as a school psychologist in an Oregon school district. A member of the Motivational Interviewing Network of Trainers, Dr. Herman presents nationally and has published over 190 peer-reviewed articles and chapters, as well as several books. Much of his research and applied work focuses on using motivational interviewing with students, teachers, and families to promote effective environments for youth.

Wendy M. Reinke, PhD, is Curators' Distinguished Professor in School Psychology at the University of Missouri, where she codirects the Missouri Prevention Science Institute. Previously she worked in a variety of school consultation settings, including as a school psychologist in an elementary school. Dr. Reinke developed the Classroom Check-Up, an assessment-based classwide teacher consultation model. Her research focuses on the prevention of disruptive behavior problems in children and increasing school-based implementation of evidence-based practices. She presents nationally, has published over 140 peer-reviewed articles, and has coauthored several books. Dr. Reinke is Director of the National Center for Rural School Mental Health.

Preface

If you are reading this book, then you are seeking new ways to empower and support students by teaching self-management and self-regulation skills. Before we describe for you how and why the SMARTS strategy can support positive change in your students, we thank you for engaging with these ideas and want to briefly introduce ourselves.

We have worked in many roles in education: as a counselor, educator, school social worker, and principal (A. M. T.), as a clinical therapist, school counselor and psychologist, and motivational specialist (K. C. H.), and as a clinician, treatment coordinator, school psychologist, and classroom behavior consultant (W. M. R.). Cumulatively, the three of us have over a half century of practice, service, and research experience in educational settings, studying practical strategies to facilitate healthy outcomes for students. With this knowledge and experience, we have spent the past decade at the Missouri Prevention Science Institute at the University of Missouri studying effective, school-based practices and programs that improve youth, educators, and school outcomes. This work has included observing student–teacher interactions, interviewing students and educational professionals, implementing promising practices and evidence-based programs, working across community sectors to design enduring and effective change for schools, collecting and analyzing data on these practices and programs, and working to disseminate these tools to the humans who engage in the daily work to support school success for youth.

Our experiences with students and schools have taught us an essential truth: there is not one behavioral support intervention that works for all students. Rather, success depends on selecting and tailoring a solution rooted in proven practices to address the underlying causes of behavior. So, although every strategy we discuss in this book may not be effective for every student, we believe the processes and procedures embedded in this work employ basic universal and supportive practices that can be tailored to meet an individual student's needs. To us, these practices are obvious and embody everything we do and teach others in our roles. To put it simply, these key practices include (1) using data to identify, select, monitor, and adapt both individual and team-based decisions about intervention supports; (2) engaging students and teachers through the intentional use of motivational language and conversational strategies that promote autonomy; (3) advocating for the direct involvement of students and teachers in the design and implementation of school-based interventions that impart skills and strategies to students; and (4) cultivating positive relationships with students and educational professionals to foster healthy outcomes. The aforementioned elements weave throughout everything we do at the Missouri Prevention Science Institute, and our research suggests that these foundational practices facilitate positive change for both students and teachers. Infusing these core practices into our daily efforts, we can help students learn skills that, over time and with practice, will help them in all facets of their lives at school and beyond.

In this book, we have joined basic autonomy support and motivational practices with using data and other strategies for teaching youth self-management and self-regulation skills. We have named this bundle of practices the _Self-Monitoring And Regulation Training Strategies_ approach, or _SMARTS_, as we affectionately call it. SMARTS was developed with input from so many students, teachers, and student-support personnel over the past few decades. SMARTS is grounded in theory and scientifically supported practices that, if used faithfully and with positive intent to support youth, will help you implement a self-monitoring intervention in your school building that meets the needs of a range of students and the various challenges they face. Challenges are inevitable in life; building resiliency, goal setting, self-monitoring, and self-regulation strategies are the keys to helping our youth met those challenges. So, let's get on with it here and start by answering the question posed in the title of the first chapter: _Is self-monitoring effective?_

Acknowledgments

This book reflects the dedication of many professionals committed to empowering young students to solve their own challenges. We deeply appreciate the special and general education teachers who helped develop the SMARTS intervention, contributing their expertise to create a meaningful and feasible tool for student growth. We also thank the school social workers, psychologists, counselors, teachers, and administrators who have implemented SMARTS with care and provided valuable feedback along the way. Most importantly, we recognize the countless number of young people who have contributed to SMARTS—your resilience and determination inspire us. We hope the strategies and tools from your SMARTS groups help you achieve success in school and beyond.

SMARTS has been shaped by countless individuals, including graduate students and research assistants at the Missouri Prevention Science Institute, whose dedication to school-based research has refined SMARTS. A few individuals provided exceptional input into SMARTS, including Anne Stinson, Ellen Wilson, Mary Beth Faulhaber, Dr. Tanya Weigand, Dr. Anna Kim, Mackenzie Dallenbach, and Will Spiller, whose contributions in editing, advising, delivering content, running focus groups, and problem solving were invaluable along the way.

Keith and Wendy would like to acknowledge Aaron for his passion and creativity that led to the development of SMARTS. SMARTS is rooted in Aaron's experience as a school principal and later in his work as a doctoral student. He has always been committed to making a difference in the lives of youth, and SMARTS is just one of the many ways he has accomplished this goal.

Finally, I—Aaron—wish to express gratitude to my coauthors, Keith and Wendy. Their partnership, mentorship, and leadership in founding the Missouri Prevention Science Institute—and welcoming me as a collaborator—made this journey possible. Together, we have built meaningful supports for educators and youth with compassion and prevention science. And, most importantly, all my work on SMARTS required substantial time and effort. As such, I want to dedicate this book to the four people in my life with more SMARTS than anyone I know—my partner, Josie, and our daughters, Olive, Esme, and Iona. Thank you.

Contents

7. SMARTS Phase I: Student Training Lesson Plans   130

8. SMARTS Phase II: Student Self- and Teacher Monitoring   178

PART I

BACKGROUND
AND RATIONALE FOR SMARTS

CHAPTER 1

Is Self-Monitoring Effective?

The short answer: *yes*. You picked up a book on self-monitoring, so obviously you are interested in the topic. In fact, many people are interested in learning more about self-monitoring. So, why all the fuss?

Anyone who has spent time in schools is well aware of the challenges educators encounter in supporting the development of many students, both socially and academically. Students come to school with a wide range of prior experiences, abilities, and motivation levels, and these levels may vary over the course of days, weeks, and months. One of the main tasks of our education system is to help all students be successful, but we all know that this is easier said than done.

If you eavesdropped on conversations in which educators express some of their frustrations with achieving this goal, you likely would hear some variation of the following statements. Maybe you have expressed some of these yourself:

"If only Miguel tried, he could be successful."
"Kyan is completely out of control. It's like she has no awareness of what's going on around her."
"Addison is always off task. It's impossible to teach her anything."
"Xavier just explodes anytime things don't go his way. How can I keep him in class when he's like that?"

These are examples of students who, compared to their peers, need additional support to reach their full potential at school and beyond. It is for these students that self-monitoring supports matter and can make a difference. More generally, it turns out that self-monitoring is a key life skill that can be beneficial for everyone wanting to learn and improve. In this book, we describe SMARTS (Self-Monitoring And Regulation Training Strategy), a self-monitoring and self-regulation skills intervention that was developed to address this need. It is a practical approach, designed specifically for schools to be implemented by school professionals alongside input from students and teachers, and our work has shown SMARTS to help a wide range of students overcome the challenges they face at school.

We begin this chapter by describing the compelling evidence that shows why self-monitoring is an effective and efficient approach to improving outcomes for students. Specifically, we will:

- Define self-monitoring and what activities make a self-monitoring intervention.
- Summarize the research base that supports the effectiveness of self-monitoring.
- Discuss the types of behaviors and students that self-monitoring works well with.
- Examine the neurological, theoretical, and motivational reasons self-monitoring works.

WHAT EXACTLY IS SELF-MONITORING AND SELF-MANAGEMENT?

First, self-monitoring is a *self-management*—hereafter referred to as SM—intervention. SM interventions are a collection of structured practices and skills that help people better regulate behaviors, thoughts, and feelings in a positive and productive way—including challenging behaviors that are disruptive to school and classroom settings. Though SM interventions are referred to by many names (e.g., self-control, effortful control, self-regulation), SM is defined as a set of practices that people are trained in to assess, monitor, and evaluate their own behavioral performances. But before we go into the science of SM, we would like to summarize the history regarding the study of SM. This story started in 1988 with a researcher named John W. Fantuzzo. Fantuzzo and some of his colleagues suggested that a successful SM intervention included a combination of 11 practices. These practices are listed in the left column of Table 1.1.

There are many independent, peer-reviewed scientific studies reporting the impact of SM practices over the past 56 years—so many that there are at least 21 separate systematic reviews that have attempted to summarize the effects of SM practices. Seven of

> **What Is It?**
>
> SMARTS is a self-monitoring or *self-management* (SM) intervention. SM interventions are a collection of structured practices and skills that help people learn to regulate behaviors, thoughts, and feelings in a positive and productive way, including challenging behaviors that are disruptive to school and classroom settings.

TABLE 1.1. Self-Monitoring Practices: Original Practices Compared to Revised SMARTS Practices

1988 list of SM practices	Descriptive of each practice	SMARTS practices
1. Self-selecting a target behavior	A student is directly involved in identifying a behavior that occurs frequently enough and is presenting a challenge to them achieving success.	1. Self-selecting the target behavior
2. Self-defining the target behavior	A student is directly involved in operationally describing the behavior in an observable and measurable way.	2. Self-defining the target behavior
3. Self-determining a performance goal	A student is directly involved in setting a SMART goal (*specific, measurable, achievable, realistic, time bound*) that would identify the selected behavior and decrease the occurrence of the negative behavior/increase an appropriate replacement behavior.	
4. Self-identifying reinforcers	A student is directly involved in selecting, from a menu of options, a reinforcing reward to obtain if they achieve their goal.	
5. Self-prompting a reflection of behavior	A student is directly involved in prompting/remembering to reflect on whether their behavior over a specified time frame met their targeted goal.	3. Self-observing the target behavior
6. Self-observing the target behavior	A student would observe whether their reflection of their behavior met the terms of the stated goal.	
7. Self-recording observations	A student would record their observation on a preformatted goal-monitoring sheet.	4. Self-recording observations
8. Self-charting observations	A student would mark their daobservations of their goal performance on a graph.	5. Self-evaluation of performance
9. Self-appraising performance	A student would determine if their observations met the criteria of their stated goal over time.	
10. Self-administering primary reinforcers	A student would select a primary reinforcer if they met their stated goal.	
11. Self-administering secondary reinforcers	A student would select a secondary reinforcer if they met their stated goal.	

Note. 1998 list of practices and descriptives provided by Fantuzzo and colleagues (1988).

these 22 systematic reviews were published prior to 2021 and examine the influence of the 11 SM practices listed in Table 1.1.

The first review of an SM intervention that applied the 11 SM practices to all studies was conducted between 1967 and 1988 and noted that only 9.6 of the 11 elements (88%) were used in all the studies reviewed. In fact, only 60% of those studies included all 11 practices (Fantuzzo et al., 1988). Later, Amy Briesch and Sandra Chafouleas (2009) led a follow-up review and reapplied the 11 elements from Fantuzzo's classification to SM studies published between 1989 and 2008. What Briesch and Chafouleas observed was that fewer of those steps were included in subsequent studies. Specifically, only 7.6 of 11 (range 4–11) practices listed in the left column of Table 1.1 were used in the studies reviewed—and this time, only 3% of the studies included all 11 practices.

Clearly, there was a decline in the use of Fantuzzo's SM practice framework over time. Why is this? With our experiences in school settings, we believe that Fantuzzo's original typology of SM practices was a bit cumbersome and did not reflect the reality of using an SM intervention in an everyday school setting. Simply put, some of those practices did not show up in subsequent studies because they were not practical or feasible. For example, it is good practice for students to be directly involved in identifying and selecting a target behavior; however, students can also benefit from the input and guidance of trusted adults in this process. The same goes for developing a goal that relies on SMART criteria (i.e., a goal that is specific, measurable, achievable, realistic, and time-bound). Also, it is not easy for us all to remember in the moment to reflect on the last

What Is It?

SMART goals are a widely used framework to help us all create clear and achievable goals. SMART stands for:

- **Specific:** Goals should be clear and specific and answer the questions What needs to be accomplished? Who is responsible for it? What steps should be taken to achieve it?
- **Measurable:** Goals need to be described in observable and measurable terms so that progress and success can be tracked. This involves using language to describe the goal that permits us to measure progress and outcomes and answers questions like How much? How many? How will I know when it is accomplished?
- **Achievable:** Goals should be realistic and attainable. While goals should be challenging to promote growth, they must also be accessible given available resources and constraints. This involves considering the skills, resources, and time available.
- **Relevant:** Goals must *matter* and align with broader objectives and expectations. Goals should be worthwhile and meet students' needs. Relevant goals are important to what a student wants to achieve in the long term.
- **Time-bound:** Goals should have a deadline or a defined time frame. Deadlines help motivate and prioritize tasks. Time-bound goal criteria answer questions like When will this goal be accomplished? What can be done today, next week, or next month?

What Is It?

Effect size: A way to communicate the size of a change or the difference between two groups. Imagine comparing the tallness of two groups of people. An effect size will tell you two things: (1) that one group is taller on average and (2) approximately how much taller by providing a standardized gauge.

- An effect size of 0.2 means the change or difference is noticeable only if you look hard.
- An effect size of 0.5 means the change or difference is quite noticeable yet modest.
- An effect size of 0.8 means the change or difference is obvious and unquestionable.

hour to determine if we achieved our goals. And who administers secondary reinforcers? Adults often do, and hopefully those reinforcers align with what students selected. All this to say that students need support in these areas.

In short, the later Briesch and Chafouleas (2009) study identified that, in reality, only 4 of Fantuzzo's 11 practices occurred most frequently in the studies they observed (i.e., selection of target behavior, defining the target behavior, observing the target behavior, and recording the target behavior). The most logical explanation for the reduction in the steps to successfully implement an SM intervention practice is "reality"; that is, in every busy school environment, few people have the time to realistically apply all of Fantuzzo's original 11 steps. However, and as shown in the right column of Table 1.1, SMARTS organizes the SM practices around the four key steps that Briesch and Chafouleas identified, plus one more step. This fifth step of *self-evaluation of performance*, listed in Table 1.1, describes an important feedback step for directly engaging students in reviewing their data and appraising or evaluating whether they met their stated goals, as well as considering challenges they may need to be considered going forward.

On average, considering the effects from 79 single-case or group studies, our conclusion is that SM interventions are effective at improving both challenging behaviors (effect size = 0.69) and academic outcomes (effect size = 0.58). The two effect sizes reported here correspond to a 99% and a 78% improvement on those outcomes when compared to the earlier baseline performance of the students in those studies, respectively. More specifically, when examining the effects of SM interventions on specific types of challenging behaviors, SM interventions appear most effective at helping improve students' ability to follow directions, followed by reductions in disruptive behaviors and increases in prosocial behaviors. When it comes to the effect of SM interventions on specific academic behaviors, SM interventions appear to

What Is It?

SMARTS can be used as a standalone intervention to support individual or small groups of students struggling with a multitude of challenging behaviors or as a targeted intervention within a broader program of multi-tiered system of supports in a school.

have the strongest positive effect on helping students complete schoolwork, followed by improvements in academic achievements.

In short, there is a tremendous amount of research by various investigators over a period of 50 years that strongly indicates SM interventions are effective at altering even the most formidable behavioral challenges. Although these researchers defined and combined the elements of SM differently, SMARTS is an SM intervention that coalesces the most effective practices extracted from the broad body of research in a manner that is feasible, effective, and efficient. SMARTS can be used as a stand-alone intervention to support students struggling with a multitude of challenging behaviors.

FOR WHOM DOES SELF-MANAGEMENT WORK?

The short answer: SM works for a diverse variety of students including all youth from different races/ethnicities and genders, those with and without disabilities, students with concentration and attentional problems, and students of all grades and income ranges. And here is the longer answer to that question.

Self-Management Works for a Variety of Student Challenges

Of the 22 existing systematic reviews summarizing over 90 single-subject, multiple-baseline, small-group, quasi-experimental, and randomized studies on the effects of SM interventions, 13 of those reviews focused on studies examining the effects of SM for specific student subgroups (see Table 1.2). In summary, each of these reviews report positive effects of SM interventions on each of these meaningful outcomes.

Self-Management Works for Students from Different Backgrounds

Other reviews examined the influence or moderation of student characteristics (race, gender, disability, age, setting) as well as self-monitoring elements (length, interval length, goal, goal percentage, use of reinforcements) on the effectiveness of SM. In short, the effect of SM outcomes did not differ by student characteristics, and the strategy appears to work effectively for all students from different socioeconomic, racial/ethnic, and gender or sex identities (Bruhn et al., 2022). This review by Bruhn and colleagues (2020) suggested student age and educational settings had the greatest impact on outcomes as well as the inclusion of goal setting, feedback, and reinforcement—all of which are helpful added tools to strengthen the design of an effective SM intervention.

Adding to the various definitions and typologies that identify an SM intervention, very little research examines the impact of training students in SM, and that is where

TABLE 1.2. Challenges and Study Citations for SM Interventions

Learning and cognitive disability	Studies supporting SM with learning and/or cognitive disabilities
Learning disabilities (e.g., dyslexia, dyscalculia)	McDougall et al. (2017) McDougall et al. (2006) Ozkan & Sonmez (2011)
Mild autism spectrum disorders	Carr et al. (2014) Davis et al. (2016) Lee et al. (2007)
Attention disorders (e.g., ADHD)	Reddy et al. (2018)
Disruptive behavior disorders (e.g., oppositional defiant disorder)	Briesch et al. (2015) Bruhn et al. (2015) Busacca et al. (2015) Maag (2019) Nelson et al. (1991) Sheffield & Waller (2010)

SMARTS is unique. Studies do suggest that the presence of student training has a positive impact on the success of an SM intervention. For example, existing studies suggest that when students are provided with training in SM, they are more likely to have better academic (Greiner & Karoly, 1976; Harris, 1986) and behavioral outcomes (Harris et al., 2005; Ninness et al., 1991). Furthermore, a recent randomized study of SMARTS with fourth- and fifth-grade students and teachers suggested that the training and practice helped to improve students' sense of autonomy and students' ratings of the quality of their relationships with teachers, as well as teachers' reports of students' social competencies (Thompson, 2012, 2014; Thompson, Stinson, et al., 2021).

Nearly all 22 of the prior reviews and studies show SM interventions to be effective; however, none of them use a consistent manner in which students were trained in an SM strategy. Regardless, it is a widely accepted practice to train students in the steps of a practice, give them opportunities to engage in the practice, and then provide feedback and coaching to improve their use of the practice or strategy over time. This is where SMARTS comes in. We have had a unique opportunity to draft a training manual to describe SMARTS and provide explicit instructions for how to best train students in SMARTS. SMARTS does not utilize all 11 self-monitoring practices originally identified by Fantuzzo and others, but does summarize and combine the most effective practices observed across decades of research to effectively train elementary students in the practice of SM.

Whew. Now that we know it works, let's get to the fun part: seeing SMARTS in action.

HOW DOES SMARTS, A SELF-MANAGEMENT INTERVENTION, WORK?

SMARTS has several very specific mechanisms that drive the intervention and explain why and how SMARTS works. As researchers who also happen to be practitioners, we are always asking *how* an intervention works. When we ask that question, we are referring to the *mediators* or *malleable mechanisms* an intervention targets to achieve its outcome. To put it another way, we are asking more specifically about how the intervention activities impart new knowledge or bring together new experiences in a way that activates a sequence of positive downstream changes. Alternatively, the "mechanism" of any intervention (i.e., increased awareness, sense of autonomy, improved relationships, or increased competencies) is the thing that happens in between that explains why

> **What Is It?**
>
> *Mediators:* Also called "malleable mechanisms," mediators are the components that help explain "how" or "why" something downstream happens in time. Think of them as necessary middle steps or objectives toward reaching a larger end goal. For example, flour, sugar, and eggs are the components for a cake, but the correct mixing and baking of these items together are the mediating factors that produce the result: cake!

an intervention works to get us where we ultimately want to go (i.e., healthier outcomes). Ultimately, any effective intervention ought to, at the very least, pass the logical sniff test for which, when enacted, there should be a plausible chain of *if–then* events that drive positive changes for students.

For example, Figure 1.1 shows the SMARTS theory of change that can be understood using an *if–then* series of statements. That is: *If* we implement the SMARTS intervention with a sense of *mattering* (refer to Chapter 6 for a larger discussion of mattering), *then* we will elevate students' sense of autonomy, improve relationships, and impart new social competencies. *If* we can improve those proximal program targets or mediating mechanisms, *then* we will see improvements in social and emotional learning (SEL) and reduce challenging classroom behaviors. *If* we see improved SEL and fewer challenging behaviors, *then* we will observe that teachers have increased instructional time (because they are not addressing challenging behaviors) and that students will increase their time on tasks in the classroom. And finally, *if* we can achieve increases in instructional time and student time on tasks, *then* we will see improved academic outcomes. It is through this *if–then* set of processes that, as change agents working with youth in schools, we can never know where our influence will end!

> **What Is It?**
>
> *Mattering:* When intentional acts communicate to others that an activity you are engaged in is important and valued and that engaging in the activity will make a difference in the lives of yourself and others. See Chapter 6 for more details.

As we look at Figure 1.1., let's talk a bit more about the theory of how SMARTS works. First, SMARTS is guided by the integration of two well-established theories:

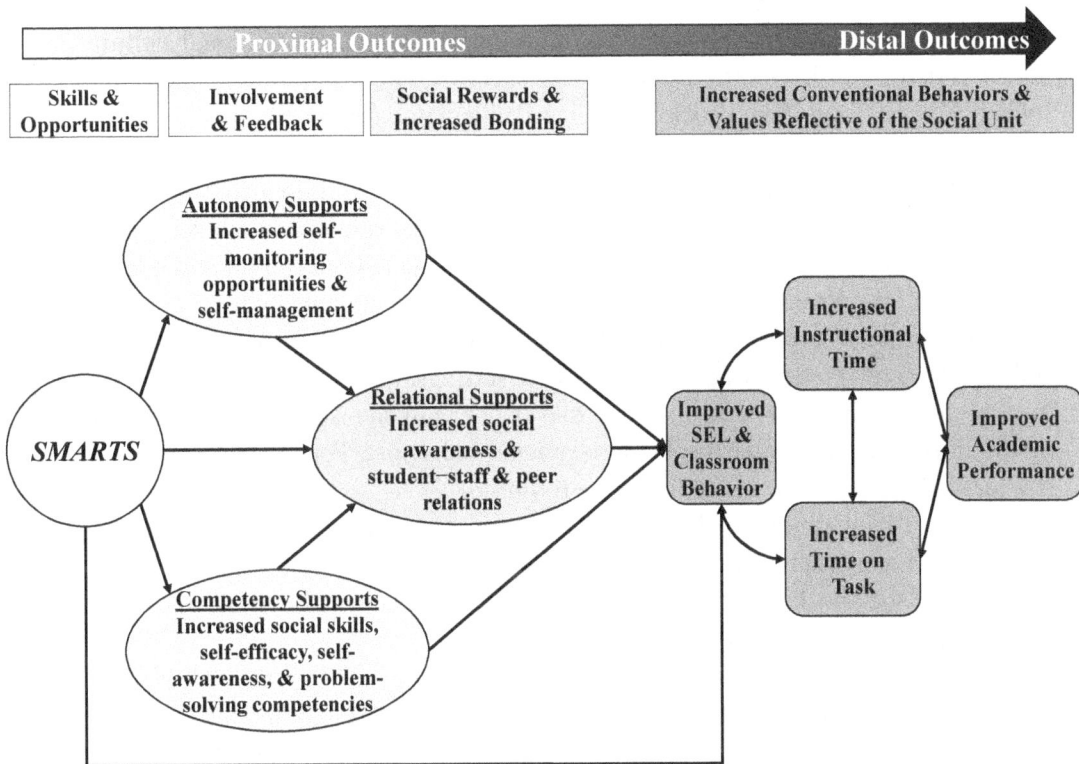

FIGURE 1.1. SMARTS integrated theory of change for SEL, behavioral, and academic performance.

self-determination theory (SDT; Deci & Ryan, 1985) and the social development model (SDM; Hawkins & Weis, 1985). SDT is a person-centered, motivational theory focusing on the intersection of individual needs and contextual demands and supports. SDT argues that the development of self-managed behaviors is enhanced by the degree that autonomy, competency, and relational supports exist in the classroom. SDM theory brings together scientifically supported concepts from social bond, social learning, and differential association theories to describe how we might intervene in the early development of challenging behaviors. SDM argues that as youth develop and age, they engage in activities with social units outside the family. The values associated with those social units shape behaviors in a feedback loop, whereby (1) youth have opportunities to display skills and (2) the skills displayed that align with the values of the social unit are endorsed and rewarded by key representatives of that social unit.

All that is to say, students show up to school with skills learned and developed during their early years from interactions with family at home and peers in their neighborhood—the primary contexts in which we all learn to behave and socially interact. If, upon beginning school, our social problem-solving skill set is accepted by those representatives of schools and schooling (i.e., teachers), then our behaviors, choices, and cultures are reaffirmed, and we have little trouble being successful at achieving the expectations at school. That is, if a student's social norms at home match those embodied and endorsed at school, then those students are highly likely to succeed on day one. The reciprocal process between the display of preferred socialized skills and opportunities to display those skills, accessing formative feedback, and receiving reinforcements for a preferred set of skills encourage us all to adopt and display or repeat behaviors that maximize the attainment of the social approvals and rewards bestowed upon us by teachers and peers at school, which is a positive feedback loop. If, however, we learned problem-solving skills that are not generally accepted in school settings, then we may struggle to engage in expected behaviors (because no one told us) or gain the social acknowledgement of others in school settings for displaying expected behaviors. For those youth, additional support to be successful at school may be required.

Figure 1.1 integrates the key SMARTS concepts taken from SDT (autonomy, competency, and relational supports), representing the temporal framework and procedures of the SDM socialization processes. Combining the concepts from SDT and SDM, the model predicts increasing opportunities and ongoing feedback—underlying proximal supports for autonomy, competency, and relations—and drives changes in SEL, behavior, and school engagement. Given improvements in SEL and behavior and engagement, the model suggests that teachers can provide students with more instruction and that students can display increased on-task behavior—features that improve distal academic achievement. In a nutshell, the SMARTS model fosters positive change in students' behavior, autonomy, and engagement, and therefore, participants are more likely to succeed academically. Let's unpack each of these key mechanisms to better understand the research behind how the intervention works.

> **Why Is It Important?**
>
> The most interesting fact about autonomy support is that it significantly improves students' motivation and performance. When students feel they have control over their own decisions, they are more intrinsically motivated. Students who perceive teachers as autonomy supportive (e.g., teachers who provide choices, encourage self-initiation, validate student perspectives) tend to show greater engagement, effort, creativity, and achievement.

Autonomy Supports in SMARTS

Autonomy refers to a sense of self-agency or self-control (Deci & Ryan, 2004). An autonomous person acts with interest over a task compared to being under threat of coercion, bribery, or punishment. SMARTS imparts skills to increase students' sense of autonomy by training students in self-management and self-monitoring skills, both autonomy-supportive practices that increase involvement, ownership, and motivation to participate in an intervention. If a student wants to do the steps instead of being forced, they are more likely to internalize the skills. Increased participation in any intervention leads to positive improvements. Supporting student autonomy and direct involvement in the intervention also facilitates positive relations with teachers and peers.

The Power of Goal Setting: Here Is the Magic of Self-Management and SMARTS

SMARTS, an SM intervention, structures practices and activities that help students learn to self-monitor, creating a *reactive effect*. A reactive effect is a cognitive principle referring to one's awareness of a goal and observing behavioral change that occurs, regardless of the accuracy of the observations (Nelson & Hayes, 1981). That is, even if our own self-monitoring is not entirely accurate, the fact that we have a goal drives small and positive changes in our behavior. For example, in studies of self-regulated learning (Bandura, 2005; Cleary & Zimmerman, 2004), students who self-monitored their math performance systematically increased awareness of the number of problems they answered correctly. Simply observing and recording one's own performance informs and stimulates neurocognitive reward centers, increasing engagement and enhancing executive control that has a result of improved performance, however large or small (Shapiro et al.,

What Is It?

The *reactivity principle* in goal setting and self-monitoring goals primes the brain's reward system to help you perform better. Here's how it works:

1. Goal setting: First, set a goal—anything from talking in class less often to studying for a test.
2. Monitor progress: Record your progress toward your goal by writing down how often you study or talk in class.
3. Feedback and awareness: Monitor your progress. You become more aware of how well you're doing. This awareness itself makes you more likely to stick to your plan.
4. Reward system activation: When you see that you're making progress, your brain's reward centers get activated. These are the parts of your brain that make you feel good when you achieve something.
5. Positive reinforcement: Each time you notice progress, your brain releases chemicals like dopamine, which make you feel happy and accomplished. This positive feeling encourages you to keep going and to try even harder.
6. Improved performance: Because you enjoy the feeling of progress and achievement, you're more likely to continue putting in the effort. This leads to better performance and helps you reach your goal more effectively.

In essence, by regularly checking how you're doing and seeing your progress, you give yourself little mental "high-fives" that make you feel good and keep you motivated to improve.

2002). This is known as the "reactivity principle," and these effects have been observed in studies examining the self-monitoring of daily caloric intake and the types of foods eaten where weight loss is observed without dietary interventions (Boutelle & Kirschenbaum, 2012; Butryn et al., 2007) and in alcohol and substance abuse studies (Simpson et al., 2005). Although it may appear on the surface that no discernible extrinsic influence or intervention is present during an SM process, the very act of reflecting upon behavior, recording progress, and increasing awareness of one's own progress over time is a metacognitive strategy that appears to passively encourage and lead an individual to alter and improve the targeted behavior in the direction of the goal. *Put simply, goal setting alone can improve behavioral performance in the direction of the stated goal.*

Competency Supports in SMARTS

Competency is the ability to satisfy innate curiosities and efficaciously meet external demands. To satisfy this drive, we select tasks with an optimal level of difficulty so we may experience success; if a task is too difficult or easy, we become overwhelmed or bored. Social and academic demands, developmentally speaking, are the two most important competencies in schooling. SMARTS targets social and academic competencies in two ways. First, SMARTS includes direct instruction in SEL skills, such as problem solving, self-awareness, social awareness, and self-management. These SEL skills are important to both social and academic success and are central to cultivating each student's capacity to reflect upon and record behavioral performance and compare teacher- and self-monitoring data. Second, SMARTS imparts *mindfulness* strategies (e.g., self-calming, body scanning, belly breathing, guided visualization, meditation) as a growing body of literature shows mindfulness practices with high-risk youth are not only feasible but also highly effective at improving attentional control and self-regulatory processes. Third, SMARTS encourages students to see failure as a normal process of learning—a message that encourages students to value persistence and effort on the road to achieving their goals. Specifically, SMARTS structures repeated opportunities for students to practice SEL skills through iterative behavioral self-monitoring.

A key to developing competencies, according to SDM, involves practicing and persisting at tasks and receiving formative feedback either confirming or correcting one's performance. Although existing Tier 2 interventions do provide ongoing feedback, the feedback in these programs represents only teacher perspectives and excludes student perspectives. By contrast, SMARTS explicitly structures a process whereby students develop their own goals, monitor their progress, compare data displaying self and teacher perspectives of that prog-

What Is It?

Mindfulness is a set of practices that assist us in becoming more highly aware of the present moment or paying attention to what is happening right now without making judgments.

ress, and iteratively revise goals comparing those data and are provided ongoing coaching to improve performance. As depicted in Figure 1.1 on page 11, a plethora of research suggests students who display social competencies are also more likely to experience positive relationships with both peers and teachers.

Relational Supports in SMARTS

Relatedness is the need to feel connected to others. Our task as educators is to facilitate opportunities to connect with students. Schools and classrooms where students feel supported, cared for, and experience opportunities to be involved facilitate healthy peer and student–teacher relationships. Relational supports are provided when educators communicate appropriate expectations to students in a warm, engaging, and supportive manner. Strong relationships are a cornerstone to learning or doing anything in schoolwork—particularly when nothing else seems to be helping. That is, when educators encounter a student with a particularly formidable cinder block sitting on their shoulders, the best way to lift this obstacle to learning is to cultivate a positive relationship with that student. Greeting students at the door each day, occasionally sharing lunch with students, and practicing genuine and meaningful interactions with students daily are some of the best ways to do this. We recognize that it can be challenging to foster positive relationships with students who are disruptive and unregulated. The SMARTS curriculum helps create positive bonds between students and adults at school.

SMARTS provides opportunities for school personnel to structure healthy interactions by providing students with access to a trusting person who will provide them with ongoing feedback. Using SMARTS data, school-based support personnel can engage students in a feedback process whereby students compare self and teacher perspectives, identify areas of alignment or discrepancy, and discuss not only differences in these perspectives but also consider behaviors that may have contributed to those differences. SMARTS students can then revise goals before repeating the self- and teacher-monitoring process. Ongoing and formative feedback loops are central to improving performance and assisting students to persist at difficult tasks. SMARTS lessons also directly expose students to the skills needed to assume the perspectives of others. Perspective taking is a necessary SEL skill and is repeatedly practiced in two SMARTS processes: (1) through comparing self- and teacher-performance data and (2) through working with others to identify and resolve problems.

But—and here is the key—for any practice to be effective, we as implementers must make the intervention matter. That is, *mattering*, the present participle of the word *matter*, is the intentional act of making a thing important to affect what happens. We can choose to do this as implementers and be intentional in our efforts to convey the authentic utility of the new skill, when we show students that what they are learning matters. When it matters to students, it will be more likely to be effective for students. If we as educators purposefully infuse mattering into the actions underlying any intervention, students will be more likely to take their involvement seriously.

As such, SMARTS, an autonomy support, SM intervention, has design features that intentionally focus on mattering. Moreover, SMARTS includes strategies designed to address other aspects of motivation and works well when practiced alongside motivational interviewing (MI) during SMARTS training and throughout other areas of implementation.

Motivational Interviewing and SMARTS

For decades, we have had access to behavior-change technologies like SM with strong evidence that they can make a difference in people's lives. We have also known for several decades that behavior-change technologies work only when people use them. Unfortunately, many of these technologies began with the assumption that people would naturally want to use them. As we know, many barriers can undermine the success of even the best behavior-change intervention. Among the most prominent of these barriers is an individual's readiness, willingness, and ability—or their motivation—to use it. In schools, SM intervention success relies not only on students' motivation to engage in training and lessons but also on the motivations of educators, coaches, and other adults who give them access to it.

Fortunately, a companion line of research that emerged over the past 30 years and focuses on motivational enhancement strategies that are best encapsulated by SMARTS dovetails very well with MI practices and incorporates these practices throughout. MI is a person-centered, directive approach grounded in behavioral, motivational, and social psychology. The goal of MI is to increase a person's willingness to change by exploring and resolving their ambivalence to change. MI has been widely applied in many different areas with a great deal of documented success. We have folded MI practices within SMARTS to better facilitate autonomy support, student engagement, and ownership in the SMARTS approach, and to better help you, the facilitator, maintain your role as an educator and encourage students to assume most of the responsibility for improving their own abilities to change their own outcomes. There are several core principles and techniques of MI embedded in SMARTS:

- Opportunities to express empathy
- Alternatives to arguing with students or pressuring them to change
- Skills to detect discrepancies between student behaviors and goals
- Tips to accept and roll through student ambivalence or disinterest in change
- Many ways to promote student autonomy and facilitate student engagement

In addition, if you are in a position of coaching a teacher or counselor who is using SMARTS with students, the same MI principles can apply to your role in helping the facilitator be successful. Just as students may be ambivalent about SMARTS at various points in the lessons, an educator using SMARTS may have their motivation wax and wane over the course of their work. As we will see in later chapters, MI equips coaches with the skills needed to harness an educator's positive motivational intentions and get past periods of ambivalence.

SUMMARY

As a brief summary to the key question of this chapter, we affirm that, yes, SM is effective. SMARTS organizes the most effective and feasible elements of SM as observed and distilled from over 50 years of research studies. It includes these elements in an SM intervention training program that imparts the skills needed to help guide students to successfully identify and define challenges, identify alternative solutions, set goals to implement those alternative practices, monitor performance on those goals, and readjust or select new pathways to promote success. SMARTS also includes self-management or self-regulatory strategies that are lifelong tools that can be used at any point and in any place to assist youth with managing their feelings, thoughts, and behaviors. Finally, SMARTS attends to motivational challenges to ensure students and educators stay focused and engaged in the process.

Looking forward and peeking at the subsequent chapters, we begin by introducing you to Mac D in the next chapter. Mac will be our student, an avatar of our imaginary and typical embodiment of a student, to describe and detail experiences we have observed and encountered while implementing the SMARTS intervention in school settings. We start broadly, with a 30,000-foot view, and talk about how SMARTS fits into a multitiered system of supports (Chapter 3).

We also feel it is important to discuss the theory behind SMARTS (Chapter 4). As with any good theory, it includes guidance for other important practices that have been shown to facilitate successful school experiences for students like Mac. We hope to impart practical strategies to you, the reader, for using motivational interviewing skills (Chapter 5) and other small-group leadership strategies (Chapter 6) to facilitate more impactful interventions with students like Mac (Chapter 5), whether that be a SMARTS group or any other group to assist Mac with learning new skills. This is all important groundwork to cover before we discuss SMARTS specifically. That is, SMARTS Phase I student training is described in detail and begins with lesson plans to guide successful student training (Chapter 7) that are the result of years of research and feedback from students and educators. It is important to train students in the skills needed before providing you with details to set students up for Phase II, student self- and teacher-goal monitoring (Chapter 8). Finally, we discuss important considerations for Phase III, student processing (Chapter 9), to help students have good experiences with you while reviewing their data and comparing it against their teachers' data to help students revise their goals.

Change, particularly behavior change, is a *process* and never a *product*. The reality is that we never arrive at a perfect place, but rather work every day to do the best we can do and to help our students do the same in school and life. The evolution of the SMARTS intervention embodies this process-over-product point of view. As such, the final chapter discusses future directions and advancing applications of SMARTS (Chapter 10). We hope this manual provides you with good tips and strategies to use SMARTS in a meaningful way. Let's get started.

CHAPTER 2

SMARTS Overview

SMARTS is a flexible strategy that can be used as a standalone intervention or as a component in a broader, multi-tiered system of supports (MTSS) for students struggling with a range of challenging behaviors. In this chapter, we:

- Introduce you to our SMARTS student, Mac D; Alex, the school social worker; Teacher Fields; and Rainbow Ridge Elementary.
- Discuss how SMARTS can be used as a stand-alone intervention as well as a component in a schoolwide MTSS.
- Provide an overview of the SMARTS intervention, including the three phases (i.e., Student Training; Student Self- and Teacher Monitoring; Processing Self- and Teacher Data).
- Examine how SMARTS provides students with repeated opportunities to practice the five SM skills previously listed in Chapter 1 (Self-Assessment, Goal Setting, Self-Monitoring, Self-Recording, and Self-Evaluation).
- Explain SMARTS Bucks and Mini-SMARTS Store as a behavior-support option to improve student engagement during Phase I: SMARTS Student Training.
- Provide case examples of implementing SMARTS with several different elementary students.

Before we take a deeper dive into providing an overview of the basics of the SMARTS intervention, let us briefly introduce you to Mac D, our SMARTS student avatar, and Alex, the school social worker at Rainbow Ridge Elementary. Mac is a student scholar in Teacher Fields's classroom at Rainbow Ridge Elementary. Recently, Mac D and Teacher Fields have been working with Alex to learn SM skills using the SMARTS intervention.

MEET MAC D, RAINBOW RIDGE ELEMENTARY, TEACHER FIELDS, AND SOCIAL WORKER ALEX

Meet Mac D, our avatar pal who we will be following, as well as a few other peers who are engaging in SMARTS throughout the rest of this book. Mac D is a unique fifth-grade student in Jamie Fields's class, who brings a mix of challenges and humor to the classroom. Mac has some difficulty with effortful attention, a tendency to be off task, and faces academic hurdles but also finds joy in playfulness and humor. Mac has a group of friends but also encounters typical peer difficulties at school. Known for occasionally challenging authority, Mac's spirited nature adds a dynamic element to the school environment.

Mac D attends Rainbow Ridge Elementary, a vibrant and diverse school nestled in the foothills of Mount Harmony. At Rainbow Ridge, teachers have implemented a MTSS to effectively cater to varied student needs. In the universal tier of interventions at Rainbow Ridge, all students are screened for risk factors each fall and spring semester. The screening data are used to identify areas of concern and select interventions to mitigate those concerns. For example, the data support that all students benefit from daily social skills instruction. The data also identify students at increased levels of risk, and Rainbow Ridge teachers employ differentiated instructional techniques, utilize small-group activities, and rely on curriculum-based assessments to ensure that each student receives the necessary support to succeed. In addition, the data emphasize the use of positive behavior-reinforcement strategies in the classroom and support teacher classroom-management training to prevent and reduce behavior challenges in the classroom.

Despite the success of these universal interventions, Rainbow Ridge Elementary faces challenges in implementing targeted interventions for students like Mac D who require more specialized support. Limited resources, including a shortage of trained staff and counseling services, have hindered the school staff's ability to provide individualized attention to students with complex behavioral or learning needs. Overall, Rainbow Ridge Elementary strives to create a nurturing and enriching environment for all students, even as they navigate the obstacles presented by the implementation of targeted interventions. As a means of helping Mac learn new skills in a manner that aligns with the values of Rainbow Ridge faculty and culture, the school's social worker, Alex, sought to find an intervention that imparts skills for students in goal setting, self-monitoring, and self-regulation skills in a way that supports autonomy.

After a brief literature search of many targeted intervention programs, Alex found SMARTS—or Self-Monitoring And Regulation Training Strategies—a research-based program that emphasizes goal setting and self-monitoring skills in an autonomy-supportive manner. Alex really liked that SMARTS promotes autonomy support and directly involves students in the intervention, and that SMARTS includes self-regulation techniques such as deep breathing, body scanning, and guided mindfulness or relaxation practices. After locating SMARTS and reviewing the evidence of its effectiveness, Alex decided to take the intervention to the school's principal. The first question from the principal was, "Will SMARTS work with the existing MTSS that we are building to support our students?" The answer to that question is, absolutely.

IS SMARTS A STANDALONE INTERVENTION OR PART OF A MULTI-TIERED SYSTEM OF SUPPORTS?

SMARTS can be used as a stand-alone intervention for students struggling with a multitude of behavioral health challenges, and, as we discuss in Chapter 3, SMARTS is also designed to be one element in a continuum of interventions for a MTSS.

To begin, the SMARTS intervention is broken into three distinct phases:

- Phase I: Student Training
- Phase II: Student Self- and Teacher Monitoring
- Phase III: Processing Self- and Teacher Data

As we mentioned in Chapter 1, prior research has listed a SM intervention to have as many as 11 distinct steps. However, our work with SMARTS has found a much simpler framework that consists of five steps, which is a combination of the most effective processes described in Chapter 1. To boil it down, our work with SMARTS and through reviewing the work of other researchers in this area (Briesch & Chafouleas, 2009; Lane et al., 2011; Thompson, 2010, 2012, 2014) has found that the intervention is best defined as students engaging in the basic steps detailed in Table 2.1.

During the self-assessment stage, students identify a challenge they are having in the classroom. Next, students define a goal to reduce the challenge and increase the use of replacement behavior(s) in place of the challenging behavior(s). Once students have a goal, the self-monitoring stage is where students prompt themselves, reflect upon their behaviors, and determine whether the behaviors aligned with their goals. The self-recording stage consists of students documenting their observations (usually on a goal sheet with predefined time intervals). Finally, during the self-evaluation stage, students aggregate their observations across multiple days and compare their performances with their predetermined goals. The self-evaluation stage includes graphing observations, equating current data with prior self- and concurrent teacher observations, and students use the data to formulate a new performance goal with support from a trusted adult. Each phase is described in greater detail in the following sections.

> **SMARTS Fact**
>
> SMARTS can be used as an individual intervention with a single student or used as a group intervention with a small group of students. It can also be integrated into a schoolwide MTSS.

TABLE 2.1. SMARTS Phases and Intervention Elements

SMARTS phases	SMARTS intervention elements	Description
Phase I SMARTS Student Training	1. Self-assessment	A process whereby Alex and Mac D discuss the most challenging experiences that Mac is having in the classroom. The focus is on what Mac can do to reduce challenges and improve the likelihood of achieving an outcome that Mac wants to achieve.
	2. Goal setting	A process whereby Alex and Mac D frame the challenge as an observable and measurable goal that, if achieved, will help Mac experience the success that Mac identified in the self-assessment process.
Phase II SMARTS Student Self- and Teacher Monitoring	3. Self-monitoring	A process whereby Mac reflects upon whether their behavior meets the stated goal during the time frame identified during the goal-setting process.
	4. Self-recording	A process whereby Mac and their teacher, Jamie Fields, record whether the behavioral reflection met the goal over the week by marking *yes*, or whether Mac's choices *sometimes* met the goal during the time frame, or whether Mac's choices did not reflect the goal by selecting *no*.
Phase III SMARTS Processing Self- and Teacher Data	5. Self-evaluation	A process whereby Mac and Alex sit down to review the data, convert the data into percentages, graph the percentages over each of the days of that week, and review whether Mac achieved their goal. Mac and Alex also review Mac's teacher data to see if they agreed and then examine why their responses may have differed.

PHASE I: SMARTS STUDENT TRAINING

Most interesting in our work to understand the landscape of self-monitoring interventions is that our research literature provides very little detail about the best approaches for training students to SM. In a meta-analysis of over 79 independent single-case and group studies of SM interventions, we found 71 of the studies reported training procedures or practices to train students. Furthermore, student training was one of the more important aspects of a successful outcome (Smith et al., 2022), but our review also found very little consistency in how students were trained in SM. A unique feature of the SMARTS intervention is explicit instruction and guided lessons about how to teach and to reinforce necessary skills and concepts for successful SM.

What Is It?

SMARTS Phase I focuses on teaching students to identify challenges they are having at school and alternative strategies or replacement behaviors to help them achieve their goals, and then write goals to reduce their challenging behaviors or increase the use of more acceptable or prosocial behaviors.

During Phase I: SMARTS Student Training, small-group facilitation will occur. Ideally, groups will have three to six students per group; however, SMARTS can be used with only an individual student. That is, if you have a student who adamantly insists on a one-on-one experience, SMARTS can be used this way without the need to make any adjustments. We know that time is precious, and we can often meet targeted youth needs in a group, which has several advantages. First, students learn from each other in a group setting, and second, small groups are an efficient means of teaching skills. Throughout this training phase, school-support personnel teach the 10 scripted SMARTS lessons presented in the following list and provided in full in Chapter 7. Please note: For the purposes of this book, we refer to anyone who is leading small groups or processing with students as a SMARTS facilitator or a group facilitator. In a school setting, this may be a counselor, social worker, school psychologist, or teacher.

The SMARTS curriculum uses a SAFE format (Durlak et al., 2011) to consistently and predictably organize lesson contents. By SAFE, we mean that SMARTS lessons include:

- *Sequencing* of basic concepts that are addressed early, revisited, and even reassembled into more complex strategies in later lessons
- *Active* experiences to encourage learning and engagement
- *Focused* lessons on a topic needed for each student to develop an individualized goal and learn skills for SM
- *Exposure* to concepts in a small-group format with routine iterative follow-up feedback sessions that provide an opportunity to return to those basic concepts

Why Is It Important?

A 2010 meta-analysis of 213 school-based studies of social and behavioral support interventions established that interventions that organized lesson plans for student training using SAFE (Sequenced, Active, Focused, Exposure) were shown to significantly improve students' social and emotional skills, attitudes, behaviors, and academic performances when compared to school-based interventions without SAFE features.

SMARTS lessons also have a predictable structure, which increases students' capacity to know what is next and focus instead on engagement and understanding. In our repeated experience and observations, each lesson takes approximately 40–50 minutes and includes an introduction, an activity, and a reflection. In Table 2.2, we break down each SMARTS lesson, the essential reason it is included, and the basic resources and time commitments that can be expected.

TABLE 2.2. SMARTS Lesson Purpose, Resources, and Time Commitment

Lesson	Purpose	Resources and time commitment
0—Pre-meeting	Provide students time to meet one another and the group facilitator(s) while establishing group expectations and design.	• 20–30 minutes • Chart paper • SMARTS Jar and tokens • Markers • SMARTS folder, one for each student
1—Assessing and defining problems	Assist students with identifying the problems they encounter at school and what behaviors contribute to the problem(s) students self-disclose. After identifying problems, students begin to reflect on their behaviors using motivational interview prompts and brainstorming about replacement behaviors.	• 40–45 minutes • Poster paper and markers • SMARTS folder, one for each student • SMARTS Jar and tokens • Problem Reflection Worksheet (Form 7.1)
2—Generating alternative solutions	Teach students how to think about, create, and monitor goals that follow a SMART formula: Specific, Measurable, Attainable, Relevant, Time-bound.	• 40–45 minutes • Poster paper and markers • SMARTS folder, one for each student • Replacement Behavior Worksheet (Form 7.2) • Examples of Problem Behaviors and Replacement Strategies (Form 7.3) cut into strips • SMARTS Jar and tokens
3—Writing measurable goals to implement the solution	Students learn how to write observable and measurable goals in the contexts of others and themselves. By the end of this lesson, students will have begun constructing their own goal following a SMARTS formula.	• 40–45 minutes • Poster paper and markers • SMARTS folder, one for each student • Practice Goal Monitoring Worksheet (Form 7.4) • Defining a Goal Worksheet (Form 7.5) • Observable Behavior Goal Bank (Form 7.6) • Completed worksheets from Lessons 1 and 2 • Clock • SMARTS Jar and tokens • Computer or pad to watch short video

(continued)

TABLE 2.2. *(continued)*

Lesson	Purpose	Resources and time commitment
4—Observing and recording progress	Students will learn how to revise their goals to be specific, realistic, and measurable. In addition, students will focus on their replacement behavior(s) to meet their goal. Following Lesson 4, students will record their goal progress for three days.	• 40–45 minutes • Poster paper and markers • SMARTS folder, one for each student • Goal Self-Monitoring Worksheet (Form 7.7)—three per student • List of Sample Goals (Form 7.8) • Optional: your own Goal Self-Monitoring Worksheet as an example • Defining a Goal Worksheet (Form 7.5) • SMARTS Jar and tokens
5—Using data and graphs to evaluate progress	In Lesson 5, facilitators will teach students how to graph their goal progress and use graphing techniques to measure their goal progress. This lesson begins to provide students with concrete techniques in self-monitoring.	• 40–45 minutes • Poster paper and markers • SMARTS folder, one for each student • Pencils • Three completed Gold Self-Monitoring Worksheets (Form 7.7) for each student • Self-Monitoring Graph (Form 7.9) • Example Goal Self-Monitoring Worksheet • Example Self-Monitoring Graph • Marble jar and marbles • SMARTS Jar and tokens
6—Taking the perspective of others	Facilitators will work with students to define and understand what perspective is for humans, and what it means to look at a situation through another person's perspective.	• 40–45 minutes • SMARTS folder, one for each student • Completed Teacher Goal Input (Form 7.10) for each student • Copies of Values Cards (Form 7.11) • Paper with either pencils or pens • SMARTS Jar and tokens
7—Reframing mistakes as part of learning	Learning does not exist without making mistakes and experiencing failure. In this lesson, students will learn how to see and use experiences with mistakes and failure as an opportunity to learn how to be proactive rather than reactive.	• 40–45 minutes • Pencils • SMARTS folder, one for each student • Michael Jordan Nike commercial: *http://behindthehustle.com/2011/09/michael-jordan-succeeded-because-he-failed* • Also search for Michael Jordan Nike commercial failure • Michael Jordan's story of failure (Form 7.12) • Reframing Failure/Mistakes as Part of Learning Worksheet (Form 7.13) • SMARTS Jar and tokens

(continued)

TABLE 2.2. *(continued)*

Lesson	Purpose	Resources and time commitment
8—Internal responses to problems	Teach students about physiological responses to internal and external stimuli, and about how these responses impact students' behaviors. Students will learn how to take their own pulse and how to use breathing exercises to reduce their pulse speed.	• 40–45 minutes • Poster paper and markers • SMARTS folder, one for each student • Deep Breathing and Heart Rate Recording Worksheet (Form 7.14) • For the "Houston, we have a problem" clip, use this: *www.youtube.com/watch?v=C3J1AO9z0tA* • Also search for "Houston we have a problem," Apollo 13 (3-minute clip) • SMARTS Jar and tokens
9—External responses to problems	Building on Lesson 8, students will learn about internal responses to external stimuli. To aid in Lesson 9's teaching, students will continue to practice the breathing exercises from the previous lesson and learn how to pair breathing with muscle relaxation techniques.	• 40–45 minutes • Poster paper and markers • SMARTS folder, one for each student • Deep Breathing and Heart Rate Recording Worksheet (Form 7.14) in SMARTS folder • Muscle Relaxation Script (Form 7.15) • Clock/timer • SMARTS Jar and tokens

Phase I with Mac and Alex

During Phase I, Mac meets with Alex and the rest of their SMARTS group. Throughout the first few lessons, Mac starts to note and think about what challenges they face in the classroom with validation and support from Alex and with the rest of the SMARTS group offering feedback. Mac can identify the desire and need to work on their purposeful attention during class and decrease their impulsivity with challenging teachers' authority. With Alex's help, Mac writes and refines a SMART goal to monitor their personal goal, which is to decrease the previously stated behaviors and replace them with new ones learned in the later SMARTS lessons.

PHASE II: SMARTS
STUDENT SELF- AND TEACHER MONITORING

During the monitoring phase, both students and teachers will monitor the individualized goals developed by each student for behavioral performance and goal achievement using the SMARTS forms included in this manual or on the SMARTS web-based app. The

SMARTS app uses pop-up prompts for the students and teacher to rate goal performances within the class period or a set period in the school day. Participating SMARTS students begin each day by responding to three prompts, monitoring (1) how they slept the night before, (2) how they are feeling, and (3) how ready—on a scale of 1 to 10—they are to accomplish their goals. Then, throughout class periods each day, students and teachers select one of three response options (yes, sometimes, or no) corresponding to the

What Is It?

SMARTS Phase II is focused on student self-monitoring while teachers also report on students' goal performances at the same time. Students can use the paper-based self-monitoring sheets included in Chapter 8 of this manual or the SMARTS web-based app.

students' goal performances during the previous class period. Teachers are familiar with recording students' behavior performances, as other selective behavior-support strategies rely on a similar approach (e.g., Check-In/Check-Out). However, unique to SMARTS and not addressed by existing behavioral-support programs, SMARTS students self-monitor their own progress, using the web-based application or physical worksheets to chart and record progress, view teacher perceptions of their progress, use those charts and data to review their performances weekly with student-support personnel (e.g., counselors, school psychologists, social workers) during the processing phase, and compare them to their teachers' perceptions.

Phase II with Mac, Alex, and Jamie

During Phase II, Mac and their teacher, Jamie Fields, have a short meeting to discuss what goal Mac has decided on, and both agree to monitor and record Mac's goal progress individually. Mac begins monitoring their behaviors in the classroom and completing a goal-monitoring sheet. After the first few days, Mac notices they are marking their progress mainly with *no* and *sometimes*. Mac decides to make a small change to their goal after telling Alex and Teacher Fields. Together, the three start noticing progress.

PHASE III: PROCESSING SELF- AND TEACHER DATA

During the processing phase, SMARTS facilitators meet with participating students in a group or individually for approximately 10–15 minutes each week. During this time, they review and discuss the results of the students- and teacher-reported observations collected throughout the week on the SMARTS web-based platform or with the forms included in this manual. Using the percentages and graphs available, SMARTS students compare self- and teacher-observational data. The SMARTS processing forms provide motivational prompts to review the data and guide the conversation (see Chapter 9 for a discussion on processing and associated forms). The prompts help students examine similarities and differences between their performances and their goal progress as marked

What Is It?

SMARTS Phase III is focused on reviewing and comparing student goals with their own performance data and with concurrent teacher data to identify areas of overlap and agreement, as well as areas of discrepancy or differences, and to explore reasons for why there are agreements or differences.

by self- and teacher-monitoring data. Students are asked to reflect on behaviors that may have contributed to possible discrepancies or successes. Using the processing prompts and collected data, students can compare (1) their current goals to (2) their prior goals and self-recorded performance data as well as to concurrent teacher data. During the processing phase, students are encouraged to identify areas where their self-monitoring data and the teacher-monitoring data overlap or agree and connect to what was going right on those days. Alternatively, during the processing phase, students can review areas of difference or discrepancy between their own views of goal performance and those of their teachers and connect to reasons why the data may differ. Using the conversational prompts provided here in the processing documents in this manual, students then work to revise their individual goals. To revise their goals, students may need to add more specific language, revise percentages, or indicate alternative replacement behaviors that may help them to achieve their goals. The students can share their revised goals with the teachers and SMARTS facilitators. These updates should be entered into the SMARTS web-based application or a revised self-monitoring sheet provided in this manual. The SMARTS self-monitoring and processing procedures are repeated iteratively to provide additional opportunities for students to practice, receive feedback, and refine explicitly defined behavioral expectations.

In essence, although SMARTS has three distinct phases, as shown in Figure 2.1, these phases can be overlaid or integrated. By that, we mean to say that Lesson 0 sets the tone for your SMARTS groups, Lessons 1–4 give students the needed skills to begin Phase II's daily self-monitoring and teacher ratings of student goal performances. Subsequent Lessons 5–9 can be covered weekly while Phase II's self- and teacher monitoring occurs and Phase III's weekly processing of the self- and teacher data can occur. Alternatively, a student-support person deploying SMARTS can opt to train students in all lessons before beginning Phases II and III.

Phase III with Mac and Alex

During Phase II, Mac and Alex begin meeting individually once a week to review and discuss Mac's goal-monitoring data, in addition to the data Mac's teacher was tracking. As previously noted, Mac felt they were not reaching their goal and had worked with Alex and Teacher Fields to refine the goal a little. Mac was surprised to discover that there were some days when they did not feel they were making progress on their goal and put *sometimes* when their teacher had noted *yes* that Mac was reaching their goal on that day. This surprised Mac, leading to a discussion with Alex about why Mac and

Phase I: SMARTS Student Training:

•Students meet in a group (or individually) with facilitators one or two times a week.

•Ten lessons are taught using the *SAFE* format (Durlak et al., 2011)

•Lessons 0–3 focus on teaching students to identify problems, develop a SMART formatted goal, and how to refine goals.

•Lessons 4, 5, and 7 focus on how to monitor goal progress and revise goals to meet the student's current needs.

•Lessons 6, 8, and 9 focus on learning and developing awareness of self-regulation and relate these skills to working toward goals.

•Throughout lessons, students are reinforced utilizing the Mini-SMARTS Store and SMARTS Bucks token system.

Lesson 0	Lesson 1	Lesson 2	Lesson 3	Lesson 4	Lesson 5	Lesson 6	Lesson 7	Lesson 8	Lesson 9

Phase II: SMARTS Student Self- and Teacher Monitoring

•Students and teachers will independently complete a daily record of the student's behavioral performance and goal progress with the physical SMARTS form (see Appendix) or through the SMARTS web-based app.

•Students and teachers do not need to discuss their independent daily observations relating to the student's goal. See Phase III.

Phase III: Processing Self- and Teacher Data

•SMARTS Facilitators will meet weekly with *each* student enrolled in SMARTS to review and discuss the results of both the student and teacher's observations throughout the week.

•Facilitators will utilize the SMARTS motivational prompts to facilitate discussion with the student.

•During processing meetings, students will be given the opportunity to discuss what is going well and what may need to be revised with students' goals.

•In addition, these meetings can be used to reinforce and develop problem-solving skills to encourage students to continue monitoring their goals.

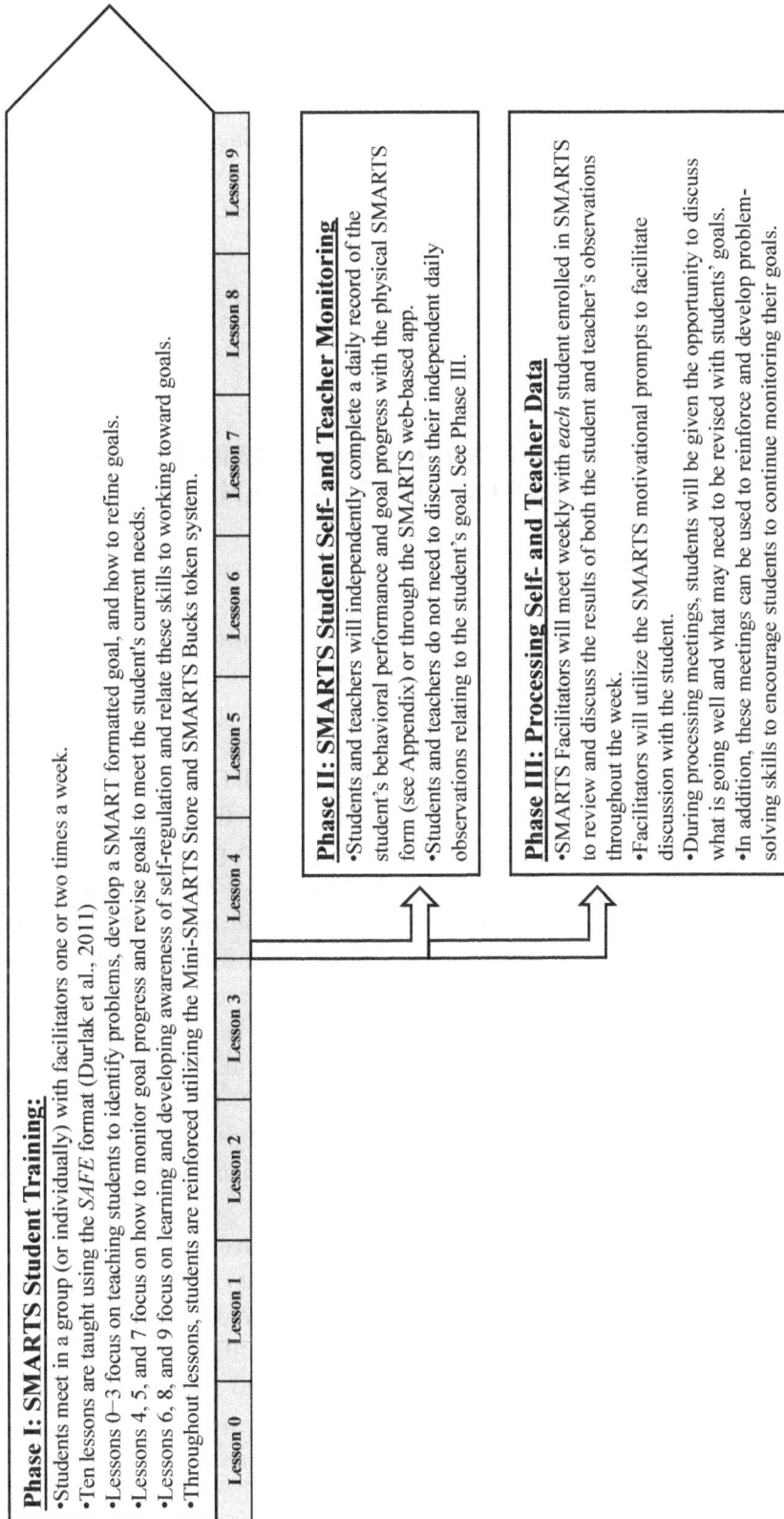

FIGURE 2.1. Three phases of SMARTS.

Teacher Fields may have had different ratings for those days. As the weeks progressed, Mac and Alex noticed that there was usually at least one day each week that Mac and Teacher Fields differed in their ratings. Based on the notes Mac's teacher left for each day and on their processing discussions, Mac began to realize that they had a habit of being hard on themselves and thought Jamie Fields did not like them. This helped Mac and Alex discover that one of the reasons Mac acted out in class was because they assumed Teacher Fields wouldn't like them and wanted some positive attention to compensate for this fear.

SMARTS BUCKS AND THE MINI-SMARTS STORE: A SMARTS SUPPORT PLAN

Because students who are participating in the SMARTS program struggle with choices at times, we recognize that facilitating a small group with three to five challenged students can be challenging. Therefore, the SMARTS intervention dovetails well with an incentive program to promote student success. During each lesson, students have opportunities to earn SMARTS Bucks. Students can spend the SMARTS Bucks in the Mini-SMARTS Store at the end of each session. To receive SMARTS Bucks, the SMARTS group students should display positive participation and expected behaviors. These behaviors can be defined and agreed upon by group members when creating the group rules using the Memorandum of Understanding (MOU) procedures during the first group meeting. When the group facilitator notices students displaying actions that reflect the agreed-upon expectations, students will be provided with SMARTS Bucks. At the end of each lesson, they can use their earned SMARTS Bucks to purchase what is available in the Mini-SMARTS Store or save them for a bigger item later that requires more SMARTS Bucks.

> **What Is It?**
>
> To assist with successful student training and small groups for SMARTS, we suggest implementing a token economy using SMARTS Bucks and the Mini-SMARTS Store. If your school or classroom already has a token economy, then use the system you already have in place.

Students can also work together toward a group incentive. This can be done by tallying the SMARTS Bucks earned individually at the end of each lesson and adding them to a group tally. Together, the group can identify a group goal (e.g., time outside, donut party, game time during group) that can occur once the identified goal amount is earned. It is good practice to ask students what items they wish to have included within the Mini-SMARTS Store. Define some parameters and use free rewards such as iPad time or game time to help keep the incentive program within a reasonable budget. Students can brainstorm individual items and bigger items to save up for, along with possible ideas for group incentives.

SMARTS IMPLEMENTATION CASE STUDIES

Here we provide three SMARTS implementation case examples of students in Mac D's SMARTS group at Rainbow Ridge. Each of Mac's group members (Devin, Remi, and Jasmine) have different challenges, such as challenging behaviors, attentional problems, and internalizing symptoms. Afterward, we work on Mac's SMARTS implementation in their group.

Case Study: Regular Education Student with Challenging Behaviors

Devin is a fifth-grade boy in the gifted program at Rainbow Ridge Elementary. He was referred to participate in the SMARTS groups because of scores on a universal screening measure indicating defiant and challenging externalizing behaviors, along with a low ability for self-regulation. Devin is usually very talkative, outgoing, and often a natural leader with his

> **SMARTS Fact**
>
> The average effect size of using a self-monitoring intervention with elementary students who exhibit challenging behaviors is in the moderate to large range. Bruhn and colleagues (2015) found an average effect size of 0.73 for self-monitoring interventions across different behavioral outcomes.

peers. He is not often challenged by peers, who seem worried to upset him because of a history of outbursts and two fights. Devin is a good student to have on your side in groups or in classroom discussions if he likes or is good at the topic. When he is not invested in the activity, he can be stubborn and refuse to complete the work.

Phase I

During Phase I of the SMARTS intervention, Devin participated in a group to learn the SMARTS curriculum facilitated by Alex. Because of problems with another participating peer, Alex decided to have two smaller groups instead of combining Devin with his opposing peer. This promoted a much smoother group dynamic moving forward. Having a milieu with limited distractions (i.e., other students or educators) helped to keep Devin on track with fewer audience members to challenge authority. Giving Devin helping or leadership opportunities also promoted his buy-in and cooperation. Before group meetings, Alex helped Devin to recognize how his emotions can impact his behaviors. Alex also noted his natural leadership skills and how they can impact others. Alex worked to help Devin to be aware of his feelings, communicate his needs in productive ways, and reduce challenging behaviors during group facilitation.

Community-building efforts are vital for successful group facilitation but can be challenging when working with students with defiant behaviors. Efforts to utilize engaging icebreakers and regular community check-ins that Devin and other students would find interesting occurred throughout the training phase. Alex wanted to make sure Devin was engaged, included, and intrigued by the examples they used and the stories

Alex shared, finding ways to link to basketball and his love for the saxophone and band class. To help define group rules and expectations for the MOU, Alex included Devin and other group members in brainstorming and decision making. Referring to these rules at the beginning of groups and when necessary to help keep Devin and other group members on track was useful. These efforts were vital for students like Devin with challenging behaviors because they felt ownership in the rules and were successfully able to be redirected with reduced negative confrontation.

Prior to beginning each lesson, group facilitators made efforts with Devin to review what would be happening in the group and ways that he could contribute. This helped to partner Devin with the agenda and create mutual efforts. Finding ways to include Devin in activities and acknowledging his strengths helped to keep him more cooperative throughout each group lesson.

Devin was a student who ultimately desired attention and would act out or push authority to gain this response. As the SMARTS facilitator, Alex used this to their benefit and praised Devin regularly in the group environment. He earned praise for working independently, being a respectable group member, and for good ideas and goal progress. Alex used planned ignoring techniques whenever possible to avoid giving attention to any negative attention-seeking behaviors, as long as safety wasn't a concern. Because of Devin's defiant behaviors, he had one incident in which he completed the assignment one-on-one with Alex instead of working with the group, but this was not a repeat behavior. Ideally, to help Devin flourish, Alex aimed to provide at least five positives and moments of praise for every negative remark or correction.

Activities within the SMARTS program can be adjusted to meet students' unique needs. For Devin, it was helpful to make the lessons and activities very interactive to promote strong participation and buy-in. Devin enjoyed using the smartboard in the room, so Alex utilized this tool to promote engagement and keep activities interactive. Alex gave Devin the opportunity for input and choice within the curriculum, including picking different tasks or stories that were of interest to him. Allowing Devin voice and choice, such as tailoring examples to his hobbies and interests, likely helped with his engagement.

The SMARTS program introduces an incentive program that proved useful in group facilitation and in working with Devin. Devin and other group members were consulted about what items would be motivating to work toward within the SMARTS Bucks behavior support plan (BSP). Alex stocked the store with spicy chips, fidget toys, and stylish pens and pencils, along with bigger prizes students could save their SMARTS Bucks for (e.g., board games) to promote motivation. SMARTS Bucks could also be used for nonmonetary rewards (e.g., free time, choice of activity, or one-on-one attention). It was important to praise Devin often and regularly for his participation and good insights. Alex used SMARTS Bucks to reward Devin and other group members for giving positive attention in groups and for efforts toward their identified goals. Students were rewarded individually and as a group, leading to a donut party for Devin and his group members. The SMARTS incentive program was helpful with acknowledging participation and efforts, giving quick feedback, and promoting future positive efforts.

Phase II

During Phase II, Devin and his teacher began monitoring his identified SMARTS goal. Alex checked in with Devin and his teacher to ensure that both monitored Devin's behaviors regularly. In addition, the SMARTS website/app sent automated email reminders to Devin's teacher, as teachers' participation is so important. Devin desired attention, so it was important to focus on the positive things he did. Alex used SMARTS Bucks to reward regular monitoring of his identified goal, hoping it would increase that behavior.

Phase III

During Phase III, Alex began to process with Devin about the monitoring data that was accruing. Alex met with Devin regularly, once a week, during the processing phase. Between group meetings and processing, someone checked on Devin at least two times per week. During the monitoring phase, Alex worked with Devin to become self-aware of his behaviors and how his efforts impact his outcomes. In addition, Alex, in coordination with Devin, looked at how he assessed his behaviors and what factors could promote or detour from a successful day (i.e., sleep, peer issues, preparedness). The processing phase offered a great opportunity to use relational skills to promote Devin's autonomy, motivation, and progress.

Students within the group varied in their processing experiences. Some students exhibited high internalizing behaviors and could be very hard on themselves. Others, like Devin, displayed more externalizing behaviors, blaming others for their difficulties and frustrations. Regardless of the experience, the processing phase provided an opportunity to look at Devin's perceived efforts toward his goal along with what was happening in his various classes. Alex found that Devin was very sensitive to negative feedback and often saw himself as "never good enough." He believed his previous teachers did not like him and, in the beginning, had a difficult time looking at the discrepancy of data on some days and was often less cooperative with the teachers he thought did not like him. Devin's teacher championed for Devin, and the data indicated that Devin seemed willing to give more effort. He was assessed as successful with meeting his goals in class, unlike in previous years when Devin did not feel as connected to his teachers. The data Devin and his teacher provided were great insight into what made Devin shine.

Devin was given praise regularly throughout the processing phase while discussing outcomes openly and respectfully. Alex used specific praise to explicitly share with Devin the ways that he has strengths, strong efforts, and displays leadership. For students who have experienced trauma or mental health issues, the use of praise is fundamental to offset difficult responsive behaviors. In addition, learning this information through the SMARTS intervention, the school gave a more coordinated effort to praise Devin intentionally and regularly in each of his classes.

Case Study: Student with Attentional Challenges

Remi is a fourth grader enrolled in special education at Rainbow Ridge Elementary. He was referred to participate in a SMARTS group because of scores on a universal screening measure indicating academic issues from ADHD behaviors and low ability for self-regulation.

SMARTS Fact

The average effect size of using a self-monitoring intervention with elementary students who exhibit attentional challenges is in the moderate to large range. Reid and colleagues (2005) found an average effect size of 0.83 for self-monitoring interventions used with elementary students with attentional difficulties.

Remi has experienced some significant familial trauma, leading Remi to live with his aunt. He is usually very talkative, and his enthusiasm, coupled with ADHD, often causes him to interrupt others and talk over others. Remi particularly struggles with group-work activities in lessons, as the other children become annoyed when they are interrupted. This leads to some conflicts with Remi's peers as they quickly correct him, which often feels like a form of rejection. Remi becomes extremely upset during disagreements with his peers and has had numerous incidents of verbal altercations and one incident of property destruction.

Phase I

During Phase I of the SMARTS intervention, Remi participated in a group to learn the SMARTS curriculum. Remi is aware that his ADHD symptoms are causing problems for him at school and at home and wants to work on a plan to help curb these impulsive behaviors.

Because of common problems with peers, Remi participated with two fifth graders and only one other fourth grader, instead of combining Remi with peers only from fourth grade who may be a distraction. This promoted a conducive group dynamic that allowed Remi to practice his new SMARTS skills. Because of Remi's peer frustrations, it was extra important to build a strong community within his group. Alex made efforts to utilize engaging ice breakers (i.e., Two Truths and a Lie; Would You Rather?; High/Low/Buffalo) that Alex thought would be engaging to Remi and other group members. Alex also maintained regular community check-ins, which gave Remi designated times that he could talk within the group, promoting successful engagement.

Remi and the rest of the SMARTS group helped to create a MOU to define group rules and expectations. Alex referred to these at the beginning of each group and as needed because of adverse behaviors from Remi or others. These efforts are vital for students like Remi who have attentional challenges because they create a few clear, concise rules that can be referred to regularly. It can be especially beneficial for students with attentional issues to have a visual format of these rules, so printing the MOU to refer to at each meeting may be ideal. This structure provides an opportunity for Remi to participate and talk within the group, while also creating a well-thought-out way to redirect undesirable behaviors as necessary throughout facilitation.

It was important to provide a learning environment that was conducive to Remi's success. An environment with reduced distractions (e.g., other students, open doors or windows) helped keep him on track. Helping Remi to assess his needs and communicate preferences (i.e., individual or group work) in a conducive manner allowed him to focus. Alex reviewed with Remi what would happen in the group before each session. Alex also wrote the agenda in small steps, one activity at a time, to avoid overwhelming or distracting Remi's group participation. This advanced warning helped to ensure the communication of clear expectations and promote smooth transitions between activities.

Activities within the SMARTS program were adjusted to meet students' unique needs. For Remi, it was helpful to have sticky notes with the agenda written as a checklist to create a visual prompt for task completion. For others, having it written on the whiteboard is often helpful. The SMARTS curriculum offered opportunities for Remi to have choices, including picking different activities or story examples that may be of more interest to him. Giving Remi this voice and choice helped to increase his engagement and cooperation.

Alex used SMARTS Bucks to reward Remi, other individual group members, and the group as a whole. Remi's group wanted to use SMARTS Bucks in the Mini-SMARTS Store to "purchase" stocked items (i.e., Cheetos, Starburst candy, Rubik's Cubes, dinosaur pencils, and colorful pens). The group worked toward a goal together to earn group rewards and incentives. This provided a great opportunity for community building when they earned a donut party and some extra time outside for mindfulness activities. Remi and other group members enjoyed the extra time to play games and practice mindfulness skills as an incentive for their hard work and goal progress.

Phase II

During Phase II, Remi and his teacher began monitoring Remi's identified goal. Alex reminded both Remi and his teacher to ensure that both were monitoring Remi's progress regularly. The SMARTS website and app also provided email reminders to Remi's teacher to monitor Remi's goals. This is especially true for students like Remi, who can display significant ADHD symptoms. Remi desired attention and would make big efforts to get attention during the group sessions, and he would often get off track from the agenda. It was important to give Remi attention for things that moved him toward his goals and ultimate success. Alex worked to engage Remi by noticing his strengths and efforts. Alex used SMARTS Bucks to reward the regular monitoring of Remi's identified goal, hoping it would increase those prosocial and focused behaviors.

Phase III

During Phase III, Alex processed with Remi about the monitoring data that accumulated. Between group lessons and processing, Remi had contact at least two to three times per week, with time to process at least once for 10–15 minutes each week. Truthfully, Remi could have benefited from being more consistent with monitoring his goal. Remi was restricted from his iPad and had to use paper forms for a short period of group participation. During this time, Remi lost a couple of the printed forms. A more consistent routine with paper forms, such as keeping them in one spot in the classroom or on a special clipboard, might have helped solve this problem. Ideally, both Remi and his teacher would have documented throughout every day to get a true representation of Remi's overall performance. Alex learned to make time during groups to remind students to monitor, and letting them enter their monitoring data at the beginning of groups was helpful to promote successful monitoring. Alex checked in with Remi regularly to encourage him and to use specific praise. This provided a great opportunity to use relational skills to promote Remi's sense of autonomy, motivation, and progress.

Students within this group varied in their processing experiences. Remi exhibited mostly externalizing behaviors, especially in the group. However, Remi was very hard on himself during one-on-one conversations. Alex processed regularly with Remi, which gave him the opportunity to look at his efforts with goal attainment along with what was happening within the classroom. Alex found that, with Remi, despite not enjoying reading, he received high marks in his writing lessons, probably because of both Remi's strengths in creative writing and his appreciation for how his teacher structured writing time. This information became helpful for school staff, as they utilized Remi's favorite subject in a couple of processing sessions that included his teacher and assisted in creating new opportunities for Remi to practice self-regulation through journaling, writing, and poetry.

Students like Remi, with attentional-challenging behaviors, may especially benefit from individualized attention during the processing phase. Remi received regular opportunities for attention by working toward his identified goals. Processing with Remi included conversations using SMARTS data to show certain times of the day that seemed to be more challenging and how sleep impacted his behaviors. Alex discussed strategies to promote success with the challenges of living with ADHD symptoms and gave attention to the efforts that Remi was making toward his goal and academic successes. Remi and other students benefited from receiving positive attention for their efforts. It was crucial to praise Remi intentionally and frequently throughout each phase, especially the processing phase. This provided a one-on-one environment to discuss data-driven observations, packaged heavily with positivity and praise. Alex praised Remi heavily for participating in and following group norms and expectations, using specific praise to explicitly communicate ways that Remi and other group members displayed strengths, positivity, and robust efforts.

Case Study: Student with Internalizing Symptoms

Jasmine is a fourth-grade girl in the same class as Remi. She was referred to participate in the SMARTS groups because of scores on a universal screening measure indicating academic issues from a lack of classroom academic engagement. In addition, she scored low on her ability for self-regulation, and she often shuts down and avoids difficult topics and situations.

Jasmine seems to lack enthusiasm for her schoolwork and appears to hide from social engagement and strong academic pursuits. Jasmine currently lives with her mom, who has struggled with drug addiction in the past. Jasmine never knew her father but learned of his untimely death 2 years ago. Her grades have dropped since third grade, and she hasn't sought out solutions to make improvements. Jasmine's past and present teachers are concerned about her, describing her as quiet and sad. Her teachers believe Jasmine does not anticipate a bright future. When Jasmine gets upset, she typically cries and is very hard on herself. She often asks to go to the counselor's office, and her emotions overshadow her academic pursuits. Jasmine has a known history of foster care and depressive symptoms, and she recently engaged in her first instance of self-harm.

> **SMARTS Fact**
>
> The average effect size of using a self-monitoring intervention with elementary students who exhibit challenging behaviors is in the moderate range. Pendergast and colleagues (2017) found an average effect size ranging from 0.50 to 0.70 for self-monitoring interventions with students experiencing internalizing symptoms.

Phase I

During Phase I of the SMARTS intervention, Jasmine participated in a group to learn the SMARTS curriculum, identified a possible problem, and developed a goal to promote improvement. Having the group agenda written on the whiteboard each session was helpful to keep Jasmine feeling safe and informed. Alex was intentional in creating a structured, safe, and trustworthy environment and was mindful of her internalizing behaviors. This led to support and encouragement for Jasmine to help keep her on track. To run the group tailored to Jasmine's needs, Alex supported her to assess her own needs and communicate acceptable choices for comfortable engagement. Jasmine got to choose how much she shared with the group and what she shared individually with Alex. Alex did learn that Jasmine was a great reader and quietly had pride in this skill. With no other group member comfortable with reading aloud, Alex worked with this knowledge and asked Jasmine before the lessons if she was feeling up to reading the included

SMARTS stories or examples. Jasmine was praised for her efforts when she did. On days she wasn't feeling up to it, Alex respected her wishes and took on this task instead.

Alex made efforts to use ice breakers that felt safe for Jasmine, often letting other students share before asking Jasmine to share. Alex also typically prepped Jasmine prior to group sessions so she had time to think about what she wanted to share. Alex had regular community check-ins within the group, which created a safe and structured environment for Jasmine to share. The SMARTS group created an MOU to define group rules and expectations, using input from Jasmine and other group members. Alex was intentional to get group goals developed around confidentiality and respect for one another, which this group respected marvelously throughout participation. The MOU rules were referred to at the beginning of each group and as needed throughout facilitation. Alex made efforts to redirect behaviors quietly or privately, when possible, instead of drawing undue attention to Jasmine or other group members. This was especially helpful for Jasmine, who was sensitive to corrections and to what her peers were thinking about her. Alex made effort with Jasmine to review what would happen in the group session prior to it beginning. Alex would often prepare Jasmine for upcoming group activities and give examples of Jasmine's strengths that could be used in those group situations. This helped her to gain confidence. This advanced warning also helped promote smooth transitions between activities.

Activities within the SMARTS program were adjusted to meet the unique needs of students. For Jasmine, it was helpful to let her write down lesson activities and let other participants go before her in discussions. This allowed Jasmine to gradually gain comfort with group participation, offset her associated anxiety, and build her confidence. There are opportunities for these choices within the curriculum. Jasmine had input in various activities and stories that were of more interest to her. She loved the story of Diamond and Amy, as she had similar friendship issues. She also shared with Alex that she liked having these choices and creating feelings of autonomy. Allowing Jasmine and other group members to have this voice and choice likely promoted student engagement.

Alex used SMARTS Bucks to reward Jasmine for participating in groups and for giving attention to her identified goal. SMARTS Bucks were used to reward Jasmine and other group members individually and as a group. Jasmine used SMARTS Bucks in the Mini-SMARTS Store by "purchasing" stocked items, including chips, candy, hair clips, and smiley-face pens. The group worked toward a bigger community goal they identified, including some extra time in the group to talk and listen to music, as well as a donut party, which imparted great opportunity for community building. Using the incentive program tied to the SMARTS program was especially helpful for Jasmine, who often reverted to internalizing behaviors. Jasmine had experienced several difficult struggles in her childhood and was often very hard on herself. She would devalue the positive impact she could have on her world and on others. The SMARTS incentive program allowed an opportunity to reiterate Jasmine's strengths and how others appreciated her participation. Because Jasmine is sensitive to a lot of attention, Alex often waited to go into detail in front of others. Alex would often praise Jasmine individually first and then with the group, per her comfort levels. This allowed Jasmine some control over the narrative others were hearing about her and did not put her as the center of attention, causing her discomfort.

Phase II

During Phase II, Jasmine and her teacher began monitoring Jasmine's identified goal. Alex wanted to ensure that Jasmine and her teacher would monitor regularly. Feedback is especially important for students displaying internalizing behaviors because they can often revert to a strong negativity bias and lack confidence in themselves. Offering Jasmine positive input and encouragement promoted her efficacy and success. It was important to meet regularly with Jasmine during the monitoring phase. Between the group lessons, processing, and additional one-on-one time before group, Jasmine had contact at least two times per week. This provided a great opportunity to build relational skills while promoting her autonomy, motivation, and progress.

Phase III

During Phase III, Alex and Jasmine processed the monitoring data that were accruing. Jasmine exhibited high internalizing behaviors and was very hard on herself. She rarely blamed others for her struggles, and her self-critique often paralyzed her. Students with internalizing behaviors, like Jasmine, may especially benefit from individualized attention during the processing phase to observe strengths and success. Jasmine and Alex sometimes met up to three times per week to get support.

Alex used the processing phase with Jasmine to praise her efforts and to compare her monitoring data with what her teacher reported. Alex found that Jasmine often rated herself lower than her teacher. Jasmine struggled to hear that she had a habit of withdrawing from classroom participation, which hindered her goal attainment. However, she improved in these efforts throughout participation. Information gathered through the processing phase helped to inform Jasmine's teacher about the importance of praise and encouragement with Jasmine. What seemed like a lack of interest was low confidence and self-worth.

Alex gave Jasmine regular positive attention for working toward her identified goal. Jasmine required comfort during some reporting periods when she did not feel things had gone as well as desired. In addition, Alex processed with Jasmine about her internalizing behaviors and had conversations using the data that showcased positive remarks made by her teacher and the extracurricular teachers when Jasmine was engaged in the classroom and about discrepancies when she was a tougher critic on herself than the teachers reported. Alex used specific praise to explicitly communicate with Jasmine about her notable strengths, positivity, and strong efforts. For students like Jasmine who have experienced trauma or mental health issues, the use of praise is fundamental. These check-ins provided a great opportunity to use relational skills to promote autonomy, motivation, and progress. Jasmine showed some great improvement throughout the processing sessions. She adjusted her goal by increasing from 75 to 80% of the time and by adding specific coping skills that she could use to help promote her goal of increased emotional regulation. For Jasmine, the SMARTS intervention had a significant impact. Therefore, it was decided to continue monitoring Jasmine's goal and using the processing sessions through the end of the school year to promote continued success.

SUMMARY

Research suggests that an SM intervention is effective at helping students with externalizing, academic, internalizing, and other types of challenges. The research also shows that SM is helpful for students in lower- and upper-elementary grades and for older students. Although it is impossible to provide case studies for every type of student or scenario that would fit an SM intervention or how we would modify the intervention to fit a student's need, hopefully the few case studies we have provided show how SMARTS works, what steps are essential to making SMARTS work, and how it may need to be altered to fit different students' needs. SMARTS is designed to meet students' individual needs and can be modified to support all students, regardless of their needs.

RECAP OF ACCOMMODATIONS ALEX USED WITH MAC D'S GROUP

- Created a visible agenda for students to see on a whiteboard and on sticky notes.
- Met with some group members for regular check-ins, in addition to processing meetings.
- Kept the group size to only four students and picked group members based on current rapports and relationships among the students. For example, Devin needed to be in a group separate from someone in his class, and Remi was with a group that included only one other fourth grader due to potential peer distractions.

CHAPTER 3

SMARTS as an Intervention in a Multi-Tiered System of Supports

The most important part of what is commonly referred to as a multi-tiered system of supports (MTSS) is the word *system*. An MTSS goes by many names and is essentially a public health model or framework that, over the past three or more decades, has been used in public education settings to an increasing degree. MTSS models can help school personnel structure data-driven approaches to match the academic, behavioral, and social-emotional needs of students with scientifically supported practices or programs previously shown in research studies to improve the areas students are struggling with. SMARTS is an intervention that can be used as a standalone intervention or can be a key component in an MTSS model. As such, in this chapter, we:

- Provide an overview and discussion of schoolwide MTSS models
- Discuss the importance of screening to identify risks in schools
- Provide an example of an MTSS alongside data to inform an MTSS model
- Discuss how SMARTS fits within the MTSS structure as a Tier 2 or Tier 3 support

OVERVIEW OF MULTI-TIERED SYSTEM OF SUPPORTS

There are many MTSS or public health models designed for school contexts, including *Whole School, Whole Community, Whole Child Model* (Centers for Disease Control and Prevention, 2014); *The Comprehensive School Health Program: Exploring an Expanded*

Concept (Allensworth & Kolbe, 1987); *Health at School: A Hidden Health Care System Emerges from the Shadows* (Lear, 2007); *A Framework for School Health Programs in the 21st Century* (Kolbe, 2005); and *Safe Schools/Health Students* (Substance Abuse and Mental Health Services Administration, 2016), to name only a few. As shown in Table 3.1, the three most common MTSS or public health tiered-response models deployed in school settings are positive behavioral interventions and supports (PBIS; Sugai & Simonsen, 2012); response to intervention (RTI; Fuchs & Fuchs, 2006); and MTSS (Sugai & Horner, 2009). For simplicity here, we will call these various iterations an "MTSS model." MTSS models match varying levels of student risk with a continuum of evidence-based prevention and intervention strategies to mitigate or reduce those risks. Though terminology varies across disciplines (e.g., education, social work, school psychology), most MTSS models consist of three tiers of intervention.

Common Language

An MTSS is similar in structure and design to the PBIS model or the RTI model. The concepts embedded in these models were developed in public health and medicine, and many of these practices date back to the 1950s and even earlier.

MTSS Fact

Tier 1 strategies include screening, basic safety and security, common schoolwide expectations, and having a multidisciplinary team to review data and identify risks among other strategies. Once data are collected, for any risk factors that data suggest are adversely affecting more than 20% of students, school-based teams should consider selecting a schoolwide evidence-based strategy to buffer or improve the conditions around the selected risk factors.

Tier 1 (primary or universal) strategies are delivered to all students in a school or a classroom. Tier 1 strategies can include schoolwide or common expectations for all students, social-emotional-behavioral curriculum taught in all classrooms, a schoolwide focus on all teachers providing relevant and rigorous classroom instruction, and training and support for all teachers in classroom-management practices to reduce challenging behaviors and improve task instructional time. If a school-based team identifies they are most concerned that screening data reveal less than 20% of a school's students are struggling with organization and concentration—which is a precursor to later academic risk and, if left unaddressed, can result in emotional problems for some youth—then it is most efficacious to identify an evidence-based program that can be taught to all students in the school to help everyone learn skills for organization and better focus. Simply put, Tier 1 strategies are preventative practices and programs that are provided to all students and have been scientifically proven to lower the overall risk for all students in the school.

MTSS Fact

Effectively implementing Tier 1 strategies reduces risks overall and lessens the number of students requiring Tier 2 interventions, which are more intensive. For students in need of additional Tier 2 supports, be sure that data are identified and collected that will help a school-based team to determine the success of the Tier 2 supports.

TABLE 3.1. Comparison of Most Common Tiered Models Applied in School Settings

Features	PBIS	RTI	MTSS
Focus	Focus on student behavior and creating positive school environments through use of evidence-based interventions.	Focus on identifying and supporting students with learning and academic difficulties with early and systematic learning supports.	Focus on an integrated, comprehensive framework that addresses both the academic and behavioral needs of students.
Levels of support	• *Universal:* Focus on behavioral needs of all students. • *Secondary:* Focus on the needs of 10–15% of students at risk for challenging behaviors. • *Tertiary:* Focus on tailored support for 1–5% of students who present challenging behaviors.	• *Tier 1:* High-quality classroom instruction • *Tier 2:* Targeted support for students not making progress (e.g., small reading or math groups) • *Tier 3:* Intensive and individualized intervention for students struggling despite Tier 1 and Tier 2 supports	• *Tier 1:* Universal instruction support addressing both academic and behavioral needs • *Tier 2:* Targeted support for students at risk of not meeting academic or behavioral expectations • *Tier 3:* Intensive, individualized support for students with significant academic or behavioral needs
Key features	• Emphasizes prevention strategies • Relies on data to drive decisions • Evidence-based strategies • Involves teachers, students, and parents	• Focus on academic achievement and early identification of learning problems • Regular monitoring of student progress and responsiveness to academic interventions • Data-driven decision making to adjust intensity and nature of interventions • emphasis on evidence-based instructional strategies • Involves teachers and students	• Holistic integration of academic and behavioral supports • Reliance on data, evidence-based practice, and continuous monitoring • Collaborative team problem solving • Focus on prevention, early intervention, and systematic support

Note. PBIS, positive behavioral interventions and supports; RTI, response to intervention; MTSS, multi-tiered system of supports.

Tier 2 (secondary or selective) strategies are provided to small groups of students who have been identified through the screening data as experiencing similar or common concerns. Often, Tier 2 or selective prevention efforts are delivered in small groups. For example, students who are shown to display poor letter identification in first grade—a concern predictive of later reading problems by third grade—can be placed in a small group to receive direct instruction in letter identification. If a school-based team, upon reviewing schoolwide data, notice that 20% or fewer of a school's students are experiencing a concern, then a Tier 2 intervention using direct instruction, which has shown to improve letter identification, is the most efficient practice to impart the needed skills to the students who require it the most.

Tier 3 (tertiary or indicated) strategies are evidence-based interventions (i.e., practices and programs) for children identified at risk or as having significant academic or social, emotional, or behavioral needs. It is at the tertiary level that "prevention" effectively becomes "intervention" (Cicchetti & Cohen, 2006), though tertiary intervention services do indeed prevent further decline or worsening of the identified risks. Tier 3 services in schools are holistic, intensive to apply and support, individualized to meet the students' specific needs, and may involve special education identification and an individualized education plan (IEP).

MTSS Fact

Tier 3 students should have access to all Tier 1 and Tier 2 supports as well as data for each practice to help determine the success of the package of supports. Be sure that all interventions at each level are being delivered as designed by the school-based team before adding new interventions or moving students to a new tier of intervention intensity.

THE IMPORTANCE OF SCREENING FOR SOCIAL, EMOTIONAL, BEHAVIORAL, AND ACADEMIC RISK

Screening Fact

Data commonly collected in school settings, such as disciplinary data, counts of attendance, suspensions, grades, and achievement test scores, are NOT screening data. Screening data are indicative of current and early indicators of oncoming academic problems and later social, emotional, and behavioral challenges.

As MTSS models utilize screening data to better understand the population or schoolwide risk factors predictive of poor social, emotional, behavioral, and academic outcomes, there is no shortage of packaged screening systems widely available for schools to purchase. For example, the *Social Skills Improvement System* (Gresham & Elliott, 1993), the *Behavior Assessment System for Children* (Kamphaus & Reynolds, 2007), and the *Elementary School Success Profile* (Bowen, 2006) are three commercially available student-screening systems. Each of these screening systems focuses on different risks or protective factors, and each has strengths and weaknesses. Each utilizes behavior rating scales to assess multiple domains of social-emotional and behavioral functioning (e.g., internalizing and externalizing problems, social problems) and the contextual risk factors intensifying or contributing to these conditions. Another more recently developed and cost-effective newcomer to the cadre of school-based screening tools is the *Early Identification System* (EIS; Huang et al., 2019).

The Early Identification System

The EIS has been developed by researchers and educators at the Missouri Prevention Science Institute (MPSI) and is the base of the MTSS prevention model developed by MPSI faculty for the United States Department of Education's National Center for Rural School Mental Health (*https://ruralsmh.com*). The EIS system screens K–12 students for risk factors across seven key domains predictive of later social, emotional, and behavioral problems (e.g., attention and academic issues, peer relationship problems, externalizing behaviors, internalizing behaviors, emotional dysregulation, school disengagement, bullying behaviors). The EIS system can be used to screen all students, and once all students respond, the EIS system coalesces all the student data into several easy-to-read reports. These reports can assist school personnel with quickly identifying areas of risk, groups of students who have similar risks, and individual students at the greatest levels of risk. These reports assist school-based teams with identifying areas of concern in the data. Furthermore, the EIS reports are directly linked to a publicly free intervention hub (*https://ruralsmh.com/intervention-hub*) that provides resources and information on evidence-based practices organized by Tiers 1, 2, and 3 and that are separated by elementary, middle, and high school's student developmental groupings.

What Is Not Screening

It should be clearly stated that relying solely on existing types of school and student data is not "screening." For example, many schools rely on existing forms of data (e.g., office discipline referral counts, attendance, grades, subsidized lunch participation, achievement scores, suspensions) to identify and select students who are at risk of academic or behavior problems and to drive decisions about interventions or resource allocation to address those risk factors. To this point, the National Center on Response to Intervention presents over 50 screening tools to measure present academic performance (*https://charts.intensiveintervention.org/ascreening*), and the Technical Assistance Center for PBIS states that office disciplinary referrals, attendance, and academic performance data can be used to identify students who are at risk and in need of supports. Though

MTSS Fact

A properly designed and effective MTSS model is a schoolwide affair and should involve all people in the school community, such as students, teachers, student-support professionals, administrators, and parents.

these data are excellent indicators of student- and school-level progress monitoring for how students are doing, *these existing indicators are not screening data.* That is, these data do not assess early signs of oncoming social, emotional, behavioral, and academic problems, but they do provide information about the size or magnitude (i.e., intensity and frequency) of an existing problem that a student may be experiencing. To properly develop an MTSS model, educators must select and use early social-, emotional-, and behavioral-screening tools that will identify student levels and contextual risk factors underlying the development of later problems (Thompson et al., 2020).

When it comes to school-based screening for social, emotional, behavioral, and academic well-being, schools in the United States must do more. For example, in 2005 about 2% of the United States' public schools practiced regular screenings for social-, emotional-, behavioral-, and academic-related concerns (Romer & McIntosh, 2005). Five years later, a 2010 survey revealed screening practices in the United States' schools increased to 12.6% of schools (Bruhn et al., 2014), and a later study in 2015 suggested only 15.5% of schools were screening students for known risk factors (Siceloff et al., 2017). These estimates, if extrapolated, predict that about 25% of schools should be engaging in mental health screenings by 2025. When contrasted against the backdrop of the rate of increasing incidence and prevalence of diagnosable mental health conditions in youth across the United States, all schools should be actively screening all students for social, emotional, behavioral, and academic concerns.

The activities of screening and identifying schoolwide, small-group, and individual student risk factors; selecting evidence-based interventions and practices that map onto those risk factors; and ensuring that those interventions are implemented at Tiers 1, 2, and 3 are necessary but not sufficient actions to properly develop an effective MTSS model. Other key elements to an effective MTSS model are necessary. For example, it is important to monitor the progress of every intervention by relying on data. Ongoing progress-monitoring data are needed to track students' progress to determine the effectiveness of interventions. If a student is not responding, then we need to alter or increase the intensity of the exposure to the intervention(s). Data-based decision making not only ensures that interventions are implemented as intended but also ensures that interventions are adjusted and modified as needed based on a student's response.

An MTSS model also emphasizes collaboration among all involved to achieve success. Generally, schoolwide teams should consist of a broad representation of faculty, students, and administration and use schoolwide screening data to drive universal programming. Likewise, more targeted, and specific student-support teams should utilize schoolwide and assessment data to determine a package of interventions for students identified with specific risks and who are eligible for Tier 2 support services in a school. Finally, a more specific team would be required for a youth being served at Tier 3—generally, professionals, family, and community program specialists might contribute to an individualized plan like wraparound or even a special education referral and development of an IEP or 504 plan that details the supports that students need. In short, properly developed MTSS models are the result of school professionals' teamwork to use data to identify risks, select a range of interventions to address areas of concern, set up data-tracking systems to examine whether those interventions are effective, and, as a team, regularly include procedures to review data as well as steps to intensify efforts where the data show that efforts are not helping students improve.

Figure 3.1 displays an MTSS model overview. On the left side of Figure 3.1 are suggested data types that need to be considered in the development of an MTSS model. On the right side of the figure are suggested interventions and practices commonly used in schools—more information on these tools can be found in the National Center for Rural School Mental Health website under the intervention hub link (*https://ruralsmh.com/ intervention-hub*). The data needed to inform the model begins with screening all students in a school building—these data are used by the school-based team to select a Tier 1 intervention, such as posting common schoolwide expectations, teaching those expectations, training all teachers in evidence-based classroom management strategies such as using the Classroom Check-Up (Reinke et al., 2011), teaching students skills using any of the widely used and effective social-emotional curricula (e.g., Second Step [Committee for Children, 2002], PATHS [Kusche & Greeneberg, 1994]), and using other strategies in all classrooms, such as PAX, previously known as the Good Behavior Game (Embry, 2002).

Once Tier 1 strategies are in place and the data suggest that those practices are routine in classrooms and that all students are being exposed to those efforts, the school-based team may then develop Tier 2 supports. Tier 2 supports are generally focused on fewer students, but they are more intensive to implement and require more staff effort and time. What is important to note is that Tier 2 students also have everyday access to the Tier 1 strategies. To save effort and time, Tier 2 strategies should include or consider data-collection tools and methods alongside the strategies. For example, using SMARTS as a Tier 2 strategy produces student self-monitoring data as well as teacher-monitoring data. These data are a natural by-product of the intervention itself and can be used to gauge whether the SMARTS student is progressing toward their intended goal. Other types of data that are helpful with targeted or Tier 2 strategies include data collected as a function of running a school, such as Office Disciplinary Referrals (ODRs), grades, attendance, Functional Behavior Assessment observational data, Check-In/Check-Out (CICO) teacher-monitoring data, or other routinely collected information. Regardless of Tier 1 and Tier 2 strategies being in place, some students will always need more assistance.

For students in need of Tier 3 strategies, we should consider evidence-based approaches as well as the data we need to assess the success of those efforts. Examples of Tier 3 strategies include access to all Tier 1 strategies and collected data, access to available Tier 2 strategies and collected data, and access to Tier 3 strategies. Just as with

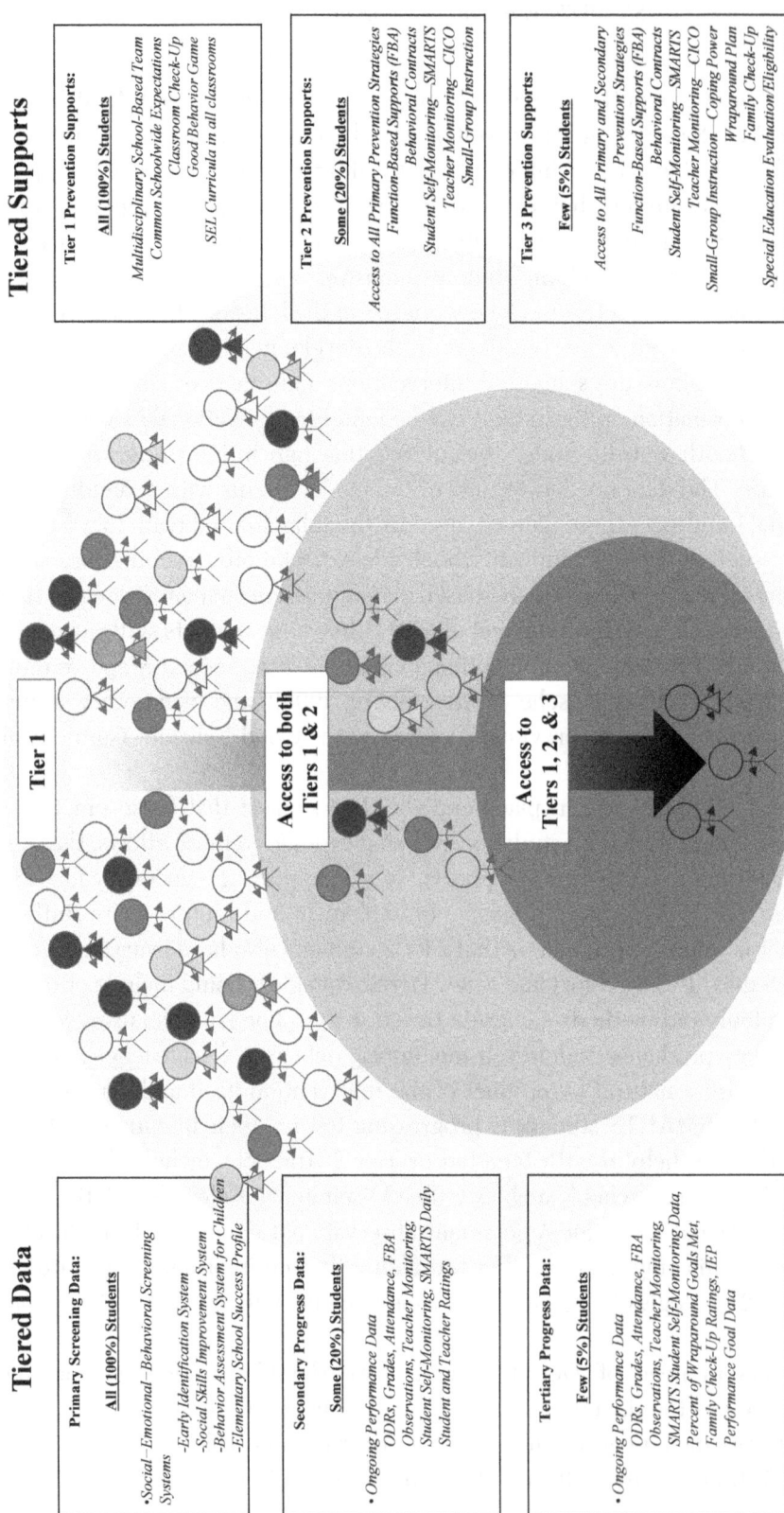

Tiered Supports

Tier 1 Prevention Supports:

<u>All (100%) Students</u>

Multidisciplinary School-Based Team
Common Schoolwide Expectations
Classroom Check-Up
Good Behavior Game
SEL Curricula in all classrooms

Tier 2 Prevention Supports:

<u>Some (20%) Students</u>

Access to All Primary Prevention Strategies
Function-Based Supports (FBA)
Behavioral Contracts
Student Self-Monitoring—SMARTS
Teacher Monitoring—CICO
Small-Group Instruction

Tier 3 Prevention Supports:

<u>Few (5%) Students</u>

Access to All Primary and Secondary
Prevention Strategies
Function-Based Supports (FBA)
Behavioral Contracts
Student Self-Monitoring—SMARTS
Teacher Monitoring—CICO
Small-Group Instruction—Coping Power
Wraparound Plan
Family Check-Up
Special Education Evaluation/Eligibility

Tier 1

Access to both
Tiers 1 & 2

Access to
Tiers 1, 2, & 3

Tiered Data

Primary Screening Data:

<u>All (100%) Students</u>

•*Social–Emotional–Behavioral Screening Systems*
-*Early Identification System*
-*Social Skills Improvement System*
-*Behavior Assessment System for Children*
-*Elementary School Success Profile*

Secondary Progress Data:

<u>Some (20%) Students</u>

• *Ongoing Performance Data*
ODRs, Grades, Attendance, FBA Observations, Teacher Monitoring, Student Self-Monitoring, SMARTS Daily Student and Teacher Ratings

Tertiary Progress Data:

<u>Few (5%) Students</u>

• *Ongoing Performance Data*
ODRs, Grades, Attendance, FBA Observations, Teacher Monitoring, SMARTS Student Self-Monitoring Data, Percent of Wraparound Goals Met, Family Check-Up Ratings, IEP Performance Goal Data

FIGURE 3.1. MTSS model with supports and data.

Tiers 1 and 2, we must align Tier 3 efforts and interventions with data that will be used to determine the success of those Tier 3 strategies. Examples of Tier 3 strategies include wraparound or using the Family Check-Up to support individual students and connect with their families in a comprehensive support plan as well as more individualized supports offered through special education identification and services if a child is found to be eligible for such services. In short, as the risk for any student increases, so does that student's access and exposure to supports that target the specific risks of that student, and data are collected alongside each effort to gauge the success of the intervention package.

SMARTS AS A TIER 2 INTERVENTION IN A MULTI-TIERED SYSTEM OF SUPPORTS

Tier 2 interventions are designed to provide targeted supports to smaller groups of students who may be experiencing similar risks and require additional assistance beyond what is provided through universal or Tier 1 approaches. SMARTS is considered a Tier 2 strategy for many reasons. There are many traits to a Tier 2 intervention, but the most common traits are listed here, followed by the specific reasons that SMARTS is a Tier 2 approach:

1. *Targeted and individualized.* Tier 2 strategies target a specific need or skill set that an individual student is struggling with.
   - SMARTS targets a specific set of skills and offers strategies to students to enhance their goal setting, self-monitoring, and self-regulation skills. In addition, SMARTS students may individualize their goals to meet their needs, including varying the frequency of the self-monitoring checks to match the frequency and intensity of some challenging behaviors.
2. *Small-group setting.* Tier 2 strategies are offered in a small-group setting with youth who have similar needs.
   - SMARTS is designed to train students in specific skills in small groups.
3. *Evidence-based.* There are existing scientific studies of the practice communicating its effectiveness as a Tier 2 strategy.
   - SMARTS has evidence from both single-subject and randomized-group studies that shows it to be effective at improving students' behaviors and students' sense of autonomy. Self-monitoring as a strategy alone has over 50 years of independent research and hundreds of studies to support it as an effective behavior practice.
4. *Progress monitoring.* Tier 2 interventions produce data collected at regular intervals to determine the effectiveness of the practice and to drive decision making about adjusting, continuing, or dispelling with practice. Progress monitoring

should also help gauge fidelity or whether students are adequately exposed to the intervention.

- SMARTS produces, as an element of the intervention, daily student ratings of confidence, readiness, and competencies to follow their goals as well as daily teacher and student ratings of goal performances. SMARTS also has built-in checklists to indicate students' readiness (see Figure 3.2) and lesson plan worksheets and daily ratings to gauge student exposure or implementation fidelity.

5. *Increased intensity and exposure.* Tier 2 interventions are more intensive and may require groups or contact with students multiple times per week.

- SMARTS is intensive, more so than some Tier 2 interventions such as CICO and less than others such as Check and Connect (Christenson et al., 2008). In general, student training in SMARTS has been studied under real-world conditions where students were exposed to at least two 45-minute lessons per week for Phase I, Phase II's self- and teacher-monitoring of goals each day, and Phase III's processing sessions occurring at least once per week.

6. *Collaborative.* The implementation of Tier 2 supports requires collaboration among students, teachers, and other school-support personnel and may also involve parents or others.

- SMARTS is designed to remove or share the implementation burden with teachers while still structuring teacher input into the process. Student-support personnel should train and manage a SMARTS student plan with input on goals and daily performance from teachers. SMARTS also requires students to be directly involved. Parents may be included in the SMARTS support plan by sending daily progress notes home or by sharing access to student performances each day or each week, depending upon the need.

7. *Flexible and responsive.* Tier 2 interventions are designed to be flexible and responsive to the changing needs of students, based on ongoing progress-monitoring data.

- SMARTS can support students' needs as those needs shift. Just because a student starts with a SMARTS plan to address one area or concern does not mean that it cannot be adjusted to support a new concern, should it arise.

8. *Integrated with Tiers 1 and 2.* We first make certain that Tier 2 students are getting access to Tier 1's universal practices and programs, that these practices and programs fit well with Tier 2, and that they complement Tier 1 strategies and act as a bridge to Tier 3 strategies if needed.

- SMARTS has been studied in many schools with existing Tier 1 and Tier 3 strategies and has been shown to integrate and complement both levels well. SMARTS focuses on self-management and self-regulation, frequent goals of many social-emotional skill programs and also the focus of other Tier 1 strategies. As a tool in a package of supports for youth requiring a coordinated behav-

Step 1: Assess schoolwide practices and readiness for SMARTS	Score
1. We have 3–5 positive schoolwide expectations visible to all students in the school.	Y=1/ N=0
2. We regularly teach how to comply with the 3–5 school expectations.	Y=1/ N=0
3. We have a schoolwide positive behavior support team.	Y=1/ N=0
4. Behavior support team monitors student compliance of 3–5 expectations.	Y=1/ N=0
5. Behavior support team uses data to identify students (15%) needing targeted supports.	Y=1/ N=0
6. Targeted behavior support is a priority for our school staff.	Y=1/ N=0
7. Eighty percent of teachers in our school support the use of SMARTS as a targeted intervention.	Y=1/ N=0
8. My administrator supports using SMARTS as a targeted behavior support strategy.	Y=1/ N=0
Score: *SMARTS Ready (7–8), SMARTS Near Ready (5–6), SMARTS Not Ready (0–4)*	**Sum:**

Step 2: 20% of students needing additional supports are identified and prioritized using schoolwide data. Students are referred, consent is gathered, and student support staff organize SMARTS groups.

Step 3: Phase I—SMARTS Student Training begins—recommend meeting SMARTS groups 2x/week.

Step 4: Phase II—SMARTS Self-Monitoring. Following Lesson #5, all SMARTS students will have a goal to begin daily self-monitoring. Teachers also must rate student performance during these times.

Step 5: Phase III—SMARTS Processing. After 5 days of teacher and self-monitoring, students meet in groups to graph and review data, revise goal if needed, and then steps 4 & 5 are repeated iteratively.

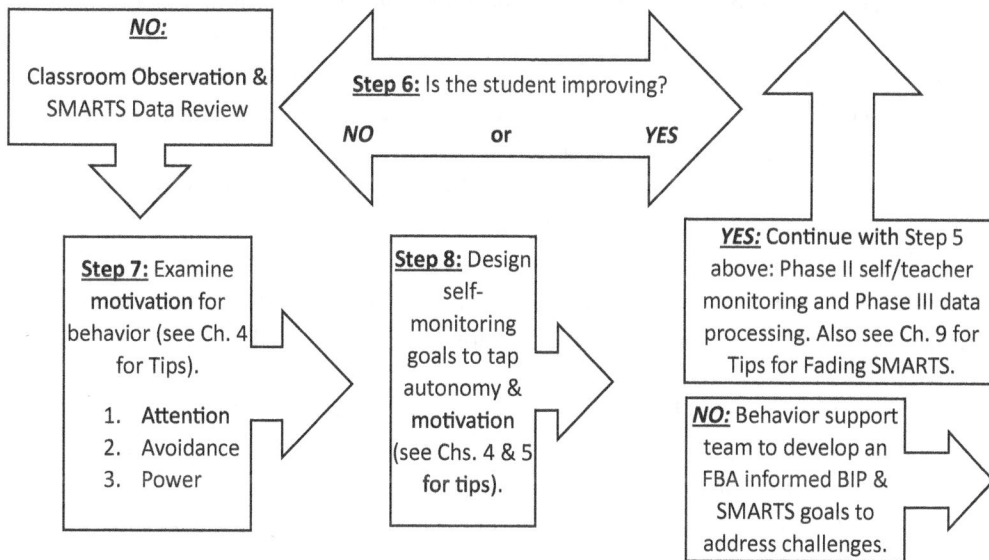

_NO:_
Classroom Observation & SMARTS Data Review

Step 6: Is the student improving?
NO or **YES**

Step 7: Examine motivation for behavior (see Ch. 4 for Tips).
1. Attention
2. Avoidance
3. Power

Step 8: Design self-monitoring goals to tap autonomy & motivation (see Chs. 4 & 5 for tips).

YES: Continue with Step 5 above: Phase II self/teacher monitoring and Phase III data processing. Also see Ch. 9 for Tips for Fading SMARTS.

_NO:_ Behavior support team to develop an FBA informed BIP & SMARTS goals to address challenges.

FIGURE 3.2. SMARTS School Readiness Checklist and process.

ior plan including Tier 3 supports, SMARTS can be used to help focus a student on the areas they want to improve and can, for example, be integrated with an IEP's social-emotional goal or reflect the goals set forth in an individualized behavior intervention plan (BIP).

SMARTS AS AN ELEMENT OF INDIVIDUALIZED EDUCATION PLANS AND BEHAVIOR INTERVENTION PLANS

The Individuals with Disabilities Education Act (IDEA) of 2004 is a federal law that outlines the rights of students with educational disabilities in a way that ensures those students receive a free and appropriate public education in the least restrictive environment. Although IDEA does not explicitly outline specific requirements for individual student-behavior support plans, it does provide guidelines for developing IEP goals that address specific student needs. Further, SMARTS goals can (and should!) reflect the intent and purpose defined by social-emotional or behavioral goals set forth in a student's IEP. Some key IDEA provisions relevant to designing effective behavior support goals include the requirement of schools to conduct a functional behavioral assessment (FBA).

Although an effective FBA is beyond the scope of this book, it is enough to say an FBA is a systematic process of gathering data to understand the purpose or function of a student's maladaptive behavior. IDEA requires schools to conduct an FBA when a student's behavior may be interfering with their own learning or with the learning of others. The data from an FBA can be used to help design a suitable goal for a student's IEP. Similarly, this goal could also be a suitable SMARTS goal for a student to self-monitor and for a teacher to report on as well. The data collected from students' self-monitoring and teachers' monitoring of goal performances can be used to gauge and report progress on students' IEPs for those goals, which is a requirement of IDEA to report progress not only annually but also to produce evidence before any other adjustments to the students' IEP are made.

Unlike IEP goals to address areas of concern for student performance, which are required elements of the IEP, BIPs are considered addendums to the IEPs and are not created for every child or for every student with an IEP or a 504 plan. However, a BIP may be a helpful guide if a child does present behaviors at school that interfere with learning. The student's team should decide whether the child would benefit from a BIP— hopefully in an autonomy-supportive way by appropriately including the child in the decision-making process. For example, a student who may have impulsivity off-task or difficulty with work completion in the classroom may have an IEP goal that sounds like the following example:

Remi will demonstrate on-task behavior in the general education classroom for 75% of the instructional periods for Math and English by the semester's end with the use of an appropriate fidget toy and one adult reminder.

Remi's behaviors may interfere with his learning because when redirected, maybe Remi has a dysregulated and explosive response. As such, Remi's IEP team decides—with Remi's input—that he will benefit from having a BIP. In this event, Remi's team will ensure that an FBA is relevant and up-to-date and will design a BIP to address these challenging behaviors by:

> **SMART or Not?**
>
> A SMART goal has key criteria that are important to achieving the goal. Examine Remi's goal and see if you can identify each element in the goal statement that meets the SMART criteria.

- Defining the target behavior
- Providing an FBA-driven description of why the behavior occurs
- Suggesting positive strategies to encourage Remi to use replacement behaviors or making modifications to the environment to prevent the occurrence of Remi's maladaptive behaviors

In this case, Remi's BIP might look something like:

1. Define target behavior: Remi displays outbursts when redirected to be on-task.
2. FBA description of behavior: Remi wants to avoid math/language assignment work.
3. Positive strategies:
   a. Provide Remi with a skip card for one assignment for every two completed assignments to be used at Remi's discretion.
   b. Provide Remi with a shorter assignment.
   c. Allow Remi to complete the assignment verbally.

As with the IEP goal, Remi and his teacher can just as easily monitor their observances of this BIP goal using the SMARTS framework. In essence, any IEP goal, whether directed at learning or self-regulation or behavior support, can be translated into the SMARTS self-monitoring framework so long as the goal is written correctly and includes the basic elements of a SMARTS goal. In the case that Remi does indeed need support around self-awareness, coping, goal setting, self-monitoring, self-management, or self-reflection, Remi's IEP SMARTS goal might read something like the following:

- *Increase self-awareness:* By the end of the school year, Remi will demonstrate improved self-awareness by accurately identifying and verbalizing his emotions and triggers in at least 80% of observed instances as documented by SMARTS self- and teacher-goal monitoring.

- *Develop coping strategies:* By the end of the school year, Remi will develop and utilize at least three effective coping strategies to manage stress or frustration, as evidenced by self- and teacher-monitoring data reported through the SMARTS intervention.
- *Enhance goal setting:* By the end of the academic year, Remi will improve goal-setting skills by setting specific, measurable, achievable, relevant, and time-bound (SMART) goals in at least 90% of identified areas for improvement in self-regulation during social skills training and as reflected by teacher- and self-reported data collected through the SMARTS intervention.
- *Improve self-monitoring accuracy:* By the end of the semester, Remi will demonstrate improved self-monitoring by accurately tracking and recording instances of emotional reactivity on the daily SMARTS self-monitoring log, showing at least 50% agreement with teacher monitoring through the SMARTS intervention.
- *Improve self-reflection:* By summer, Remi will engage in weekly self-reflection exercises as evidenced by journaling or self-assessment surveys and in each reflection demonstrate his ability to identify patterns, strengths, and areas of growth related to self-regulation skills in at least 80% of the reflections.

Solid effort, and keep up the hard work, Remi!

SUMMARY

We hope you can see how SMARTS can be used to support students with special needs, those who require IEPs, those like Remi who agreed with their teams to have a BIP, and regular education students who can also use support around self-management and self-regulation. To be sure, SMARTS grew out of a special education setting, has been tested with students who have special education needs as well as general education students, and mirrors what we want for all students to learn—the power of setting relevant goals to help them achieve the things they want in life!

In this chapter, we spoke about the basics of a well-designed MTSS model. Although this is not intended to be a complete guide on implementing an MTSS model, the description of the key elements and strategies flow from our experiences supporting schools to fully implement MTSS models. Every school is different; students from school to school have different needs rooted in complex communities. As such, to build a well-designed MTSS model, the following considerations must be made:

- Schools must rely on primary data collected from students and teachers to help school professionals target areas of concern.
- For any risk factor that more than 20% of a school is experiencing, select an evidence-based, schoolwide approach to addressing those risks.
- Tier 1 universal strategies will reduce risks for all, but some students will still

need targeted (Tier 2 or Tier 3) supports that are more intensive and resource demanding.

In the next chapter, we introduce the concept of autonomy support as a primary SMARTS program target. Promoting student autonomy—or encouraging students to feel and perceive that they have choice, input, and options at their disposal—is an essential mechanism to ensuring that students feel SMARTS matters, making students feel autonomy supported, and ensuring that SMARTS matters are the key to making these practices effective in other areas of their lives.

CHAPTER 4

SMARTS

Tapping the Power of Autonomy Support

Autonomy support is a crucial element in SMARTS because an autonomy-supportive and trusted adult at school can foster engagement and intrinsic motivation in an unmotivated, untrusting, and challenging student. SMARTS embodies autonomy support as well as the spirit of motivational interviewing—two powerful tools that, when used with care, can impact students positively. As adults in schools, we aim to encourage our students to be engaged, hardworking, and persistent in the pursuit of goals. But not all students are innately motivated by schooling. To move a student who has been historically difficult to engage, often the first instinct we have as adults is to tighten the rules or freedoms around that student to persuade them to select different choices. However, a good body of motivational research suggests a punishment orientation toward motivation is not a helpful strategy to motivate most students.

In this chapter, we hope to instill in you the spirit of motivational interviewing and autonomy support. Addressing challenging students at school using autonomy support and motivational strategies does two positive things. First, it puts the responsibility and guided decision making about a student's choices and behavior where it belongs—with the student. And second, approaching challenging-to-teach students through an autonomy-supportive lens frees you, the trusted adult, from feeling like you need to directly motivate your student. Simply put, motivational interviewing strategies and being autonomy supportive shifts the responsibility to the student, creates a noncontrolling context, and encourages self-motivation and engagement—things we all need to feel psychologically and socially healthy. In this chapter, we:

- Clearly define autonomy support as a key concept of self-determination theory
- Unpack difficult details of why autonomy support is crucial in school
- Present a framework to identify students on a motivational continuum
- Present a range of practical autonomy-support strategies to move students along that continuum from feeling unmotivated and unengaged to externally and internally motivated and engaged

PREDICTORS OF SCHOOL SUCCESS

Decades of research reveals a consistent and strong consensus on the social conditions that contribute to student and school success. These conditions include high expectations and individualized standards of academic performance and conduct for students, relevant and engaging curriculum, safe and supportive classrooms and school culture, and quality relationships between students and between students and teachers. In schools where such conditions exist, we are likely to see students socially and academically engaged and connected to the concept of school and achieving at higher levels than in schools without these conditions.

The Greatest Predictor

Teacher–student relationships are important not only for socializing youth but are the greatest predictor of students' academic success.

It is simple enough for the average person outside of the education profession to understand the need for engaging and relevant curriculum and high expectations for performance and student conduct; to most folks, that is the point of schooling. However, is it necessary to have quality relations between students and their teachers and a supportive classroom and school culture to foster academic success? Decades of research suggest that quality and trusting relations and a supportive school context, not the materials or teaching methods, might be the most important and predictive factors of academic success. Indeed, when we stand back and think of it, the primary mission of schooling in the United States is not academic achievement or preparing young people to participate in a democracy or the workforce. Rather, the overarching purpose of our public education system is to successfully socialize our youth in ways that facilitate personal development, self-management, and well-being, and to encourage civic engagement and responsibility toward others. Yes, an important function of schooling is also centered on teaching reading, math, writing, and to essentially equip humans with the skills needed to successfully participate in the workforce and in society at large. Others will say that we need an educated public to safeguard and maintain the systems of our democratic republic. However, as a baseline, without teaching tolerance, social skills,

The Purpose of School

The primary purpose of school is to successfully socialize our youth. Academic skills are secondary to assisting students to learn about healthy socialization skills.

the importance of integration, and moral and ethical development—all socialization factors—academic skill development will never occur in school settings or matter once a student leaves school. As such, the reality is that healthy socialization is of paramount importance in schooling, and academic skill development is a secondary goal. If we as educational professionals can better promote a context where students can successfully learn socialization skills, then students are more likely to experience academic and intellectual development.

All this to say that positive, supportive, and caring student–teacher relationships are possibly the most important objective of schooling. Students need to feel that teachers are aware and involved with them, and that the adults at their schools care about how they feel and about how they are doing inside and outside of school. If students are struggling, they need a trusted adult to turn to at school. Students need to feel that they are involved at school and that they can make decisions affecting their educational journeys as well. And though students want to be involved and make decisions, as young people, they also need and will benefit from structure and knowing that the adults at school apply fair and consistent expectations and consequences to guide them in their decision making. While the purpose of education is continually evolving to meet the shifting needs of youth, families, and communities, study after study consistently shows that in settings where students feel valued and safe, where they have positive relationships with their peers and with their teachers, these relationships contribute to students' academic successes, emotional well-being, motivations, social skills and development, and an overall sense of belonging and purpose. As such, our job in schools is to cultivate this fertile environment where students can thrive. Autonomy support is a big part of actualizing this responsibility of ours to foster healthy relations with our students, particularly with youth who are historically difficult to serve. Indeed, those who are sometimes the most difficult to care for are the ones who need it the most.

> **The Impact of Positive Student–Teacher Relationships**
>
> In addition to academic outcomes, positive teacher–student relationships are linked with emotional and mental health outcomes as well.

AUTONOMY: WHAT IS IT AND WHY IS IT IMPORTANT?

Autonomy is a key concept in self-determination theory (SDT), which is a social-psychological theory that explores the underpinnings of human interactions and the contextual supports needed to facilitate the development of internally motivated and healthy people. SDT focuses on three essential needs: *autonomy*, *competence*, and *relatedness*. SDT theorizes that these three elements are essential and interrelated to facilitating intrinsic motivation and achieving optimal performance at a task.

Autonomy refers to the capacity to make choices, to act on one's values and beliefs, and to take responsibility for those actions. Autonomy is central to personal growth and development. When we have the freedom to make choices that reflect our values and interests, then we are better able to experience a sense of empowerment and we are more likely to engage in a task with a feeling of enjoyment and innate satisfaction. That is, when we can exercise decision making in the execution of a task, we experience increased intrinsic motivation for doing the task as well as greater self-confidence, self-efficacy, and a stronger sense of identity. The key elements of autonomy as a concept are presented in Table 4.1 alongside a description of each element and some details about how these features of autonomy are operationalized in the activities of the SMARTS intervention.

> **Autonomy**
>
> Autonomy, as it relates to self-determination theory (SDT), is the capacity to make informed, uncoerced decisions about one's own actions and goals. It signifies self-governance and the ability to act in accordance with one's own values and interests.

Competence relates to the need to feel effective and capable at what we do. It includes acquiring new knowledge and practicing new tasks amid supportive contexts, developing and mastering those tasks into skills over time, and experiencing a sense of progress and accomplishment when engaging in tasks that are challenging yet attainable. Competence, in educational terms, is developed by exercising what Vygotsky referred to

TABLE 4.1. Key Elements of Autonomy, Description, and SMARTS Features

Key element of autonomy	Description	SMARTS features
Self-determination	Independence and sense of personal agency in choices	• Students set their own SMARTS goals • Students self-monitor goal progress • Students determine their goal success • Students alter goals and verify success
Informed decision making	Access to relevant information and the ability to understand and make decisions	• Students collect their own progress data • Students compare their own data to that of teachers • Students use data to inform goal refinements • Students use data to analyze trends
Moral and ethical attributes	Respect for others as moral beings with an emphasis on informed consent and personal choice	• SMARTS lessons strengthen perspective-taking skills • Reviewing teachers' data provides objective perspective on students' behaviors • Self-monitoring encourages voluntary behavior change
Psychological and social aspects	Intrinsic motivation, empowerment, and belief in one's own abilities	• SMARTS lessons strengthen strategies for self-regulation • Self-monitoring enhances self-efficacy • Self-monitoring encourages intrinsic motivation

as the "zone of proximal development," where new knowledge presses learners to practice tasks and exercise judgments that nudge them gently out of their comfort zones along with the appropriate scaffolding and supportive guidance needed to be successful at a new task. When students experience competence at tasks in a classroom or at school, they feel capable and effective in their actions, which builds, adds to, and compounds their motivation for learning. By fulfilling the need for competence in our students, they are more likely to experience enhanced motivation and well-being at school-related tasks. Table 4.2 displays the key elements of competency alongside a definition of each element and some details about how these features are operationalized in the activities of the SMARTS intervention.

Competency

Competence, as it relates to SDT, refers to an individual's need to feel effective in interacting with their environment and to attain valued outcomes within it. It is one of the three basic psychological needs identified by SDT, alongside autonomy and relatedness, which are essential for fostering intrinsic motivation, psychological growth, and well-being.

TABLE 4.2. Key Elements of Competency, Descriptions of Each Element, and SMARTS Features

Key element of competency	Description	SMARTS features
Efficacy and mastery	Feeling capable and effective in one's actions, having a sense of mastery	• Students track their own progress • Data will show mastery over time
Positive feedback and support	Receiving encouragement and positive reinforcement from the context	• Feedback is essential and integrated into the SMARTS process • Successes are reinforced by the data and discrepancies are clues to success
Repeated opportunities to incorporate feedback and practice	Accepts that mistakes are part of learning new skills and that students need repeated practice opportunities to develop expertise at a task	• Daily SMARTS self-monitoring will repeatedly remind students of goal direction • Weekly SMARTS data-processing and review meetings will provide students with repeated practice at mastering the skills of self-reflection.
Optimal challenges and intrinsic motivation	Engaging in tasks that are neither too complex nor too easy, tasks that are directed at a person's own interests	• SMARTS will be challenging for students with demanding goals • SMARTS focuses on goals that students themselves select

Relatedness

Relatedness, as it relates to SDT, is about feeling cared for and understood by others and having a sense of mutual respect and support. When individuals feel that their relationships are authentic and nurturing, they are more likely to be motivated, engaged, and satisfied in various aspects of their lives.

Relatedness involves our common and collective need for social engagement, belonging, and meaningful connections with others. It involves feeling understood, supported, and cared for by others. It relates to a sense of belongingness in social groups and contributes to the development of our identity. Meeting new challenges amid supportive peers and teachers within a caring context allows individuals to test newly acquired skills without fear of judgment, appraisal, or rejection if they get them wrong. Furthermore, supportive contexts and people in those spaces encourage taking risks and trying new tasks with the expectation that making mistakes is not only expected and normative but also seen as a clue to success rather than a dead-end road that stops at failure. Table 4.3 displays the key elements of competency alongside a definition of each element and some information about how these features are operationalized in SMARTS activities.

TABLE 4.3. Key Elements of Relatedness, Descriptions of Each Element, and SMARTS Features

Key element of relatedness	Description	SMARTS relatedness features
Connection	Feeling of being emotionally close and linked to others in school	• SMARTS students track, reflect, and compare self- and teacher data, noting differences and similarities in perspectives and expectations • SMARTS lessons are designed for groups of students to work together and create connection
Belonging	Sense of being accepted and integrated into the school community	• SMARTS students reviewing teachers' feedback provides a sense of integration, mattering, and belonging • SMARTS lessons have active learning components for students to work together
Support	Perception of receiving help, encouragement, and understanding from others at school	• Daily SMARTS self-monitoring and comparing self- to teachers' perspectives will extend understanding of school expectations and support for appropriate behavior at school
Mutual respect	Experiencing reciprocal respect and valuing of one's own thoughts and feelings	• SMARTS processing prompts placing value on students' responses to teachers' feedback

SELF-DETERMINATION THEORY: GETTING PHILOSOPHICAL WITH ONE-UP AND ONE-DOWN

SDT states that when the context and the people perceived as being in control of those contexts facilitate activities in a manner that supports these three innate needs (i.e., autonomy, competency, and relatedness), learners are more likely to experience intrinsic motivation, well-being, and optimal performance at the tasks required in the context. By contrast, when these needs are ignored, individuals will likely experience reduced motivation to engage in the tasks required in the context and are more likely to experience negative emotions and diminished well-being.

SDT distinguishes between intrinsic and extrinsic forms of motivation. Intrinsic motivation to engage in work and complete a task stems from internally experienced factors such as personal interest and joy from engaging in a task. Extrinsic motivation arises when a person engages in a task for external factors or reasons such as working to obtain rewards or to avoid punishment or shame. The key for us as educators is to engage in practices that foster and facilitate a student's capacity to exercise autonomy, provide supportive instruction that scaffolds student competencies toward learning new skills, and do it in a way that maintains and reflects the importance of student and teacher relationships.

> **The Key to Motivating Students**
>
> The key for us as educators is to engage in practices that foster and facilitate students' capacity to exercise autonomy, provide supportive instruction that helps those students' competencies at learning new skills, and do it in a way that reflects the importance of student and teacher relationships.

SMARTS, as an autonomy-supportive intervention, includes key autonomy-support activities that stimulate feelings of perceived autonomy in students, moving those students from feeling unmotivated to feeling invested and motivated when used properly.

One-Up and One-Down

Schooling, as it is presently organized in the United States, inadvertently creates a power imbalance where the students are in school to learn, and the teachers are there to teach. These roles are very specific, and SDT suggests that these roles generate what is referred to as a "one-up, one-down" power dynamic. SDT argues that this one-up and one-down power dynamic is inescapable. It is everywhere and embedded in all human interactions. At its basic element, whenever any two people find themselves in any given situation, there will inevitably be a power imbalance—however slight or great—where one of those two people has more knowledge and contextual experience about the task at hand, and thus is perceived by the other to have more control and authority.

Take any two random people, no matter how seemingly equally intelligent and skilled—two loving life partners, two incredible athletes, two colleagues or students

Self-Determination Theory

SDT argues that the "one-up" and "one-down" power imbalance dynamic is inescapable in all human interactions, that we will all be in the one-down position at some point and at a disadvantage, and it is incumbent upon the person in the one-up position to recognize their power and close the imbalance.

in the same school—and place them in any random context, and one will ultimately possess more prior experience, expertise, or awareness of the setting or the required task than the other. This power dynamic can change if the context, players, or task changes. Thus, the one-up and one-down power dynamic is an essential and underlying dynamic of all the social human interactions we experience every day. This inevitable pattern can influence the satisfaction of the person in the one-down position if the person in the one-up position utilizes the advantage in an oppressive manner. Put simply, depending upon the dyad make-up, context, and external demands, any of us can find ourselves in the one-up position just as often as we can find ourselves in the one-down position. It is a fixture of being a human.

The upside is this: When the person in the one-up position is aware of their positionality, sees they have an advantage in this inevitable power dynamic, and accepts that they have a responsibility and duty to reduce that imbalance as a cost of that advantage, then they can empower their one-down partner. The one-up person can use their own expertise to promote the autonomy and competence and improve their relatedness to the other by fostering their sense of enablement and sharing the accoutrements, ideas, knowledge, and any other aides that will assist the person in the one-down position to be more successful in the context or the task at hand. In the end, because we all find ourselves in the one-down position as often as the one-up position, there is an innate logical rationale or good reason to recognize and balance out this one-up and one-down experience of being human. That is, because we all will inevitably be in the one-down position as often as we will be in the one-up position during our lifetimes, there is every reason to acknowledge and work to reduce the discrepancy between ourselves and our compatriots when we are in the one-up position so that we may expect the same when the roles are inevitably reversed. We are then free to engage in supporting the growth of our one-down partners when we are in the one-up position. Failure to do so will result in an imbalance in this dynamic and will likely harm our sense of autonomy, competency, and relations—and ultimately our well-being—when we find ourselves in the one-down position.

It is important to recognize at this time that for a school full of young people who have developing brains and are not known to think through consequences, teachers, administrators, and student-support personnel must certainly adopt a position of authority. However, it is in the best interest of both the adults and the students to also moderate this inevitable one-up position by not abusing that authority, by promoting the decision making and autonomy of students, by providing them with instructional support and feedback about tasks they need to competently achieve, and by providing this instruction in a safe and judgment-free manner indicative of healthy relationships and social exchanges. Failure to do so consistently will result in students feeling disconnected and unmotivated, and their learning and interactions in the context will suffer.

The one-up and one-down position clearly exists in educational settings, but years of research show there are many ways to counter this social interactional dynamic and decrease the distance between the one-up teacher and the student who is in the one-down position. By recognizing and addressing power imbalances, we are already on our way to fostering the autonomy, enriching the competence, and improving the relationships between our students and us. By recognizing that this imbalance exists and by taking small actions to reduce its presence, we can improve the decreased motivation, diminished well-being, and sense of disempowerment that many students feel in their relation to schooling. Indeed, when we begin to factor into our calculations and reflect on what people in a one-down position feel by considering the concepts of intersectionality that are based on socially constructed concepts such as sex, gender, skin color, and other human features that create false yet very real hierarchies, we begin to address our own positionality and use our one-up position to reduce the perceived gap. Whether the gap is perceived or not, it is real, and it impacts motivation and ability to self-regulate and is connected to how students behave and treat others while at school.

Figure 4.1 includes the key concepts of two theories. The first theory, SDT, is present in the top of Figure 4.1 and describes three processes on a continuum: the primary locus of control (not self-determined to self-determined), motivational styles (amotivated or not motivated to extrinsically motivated, to intrinsically motivated), and associated regulatory styles (dysregulated, external, introjected, identified, integrated, and self-regulated). The second theory present in the center of Figure 4.1 integrates key processes embedded within the social development model (SDM; Hawkins et al., 2008). The SDM is a theory that explains how socialization processes leverage social bonds and environmental influences to shape individual behaviors. Both the SDT and the SDM have confirmed these concepts predict and drive behavior and motivation and provide us with a lens to better understand how we can support an unmotivated and challenging student with adopting a position of feeling motivated and of valuing school-related tasks.

At the far left of the continuum in Figure 4.1 is a non-self-determined locus of control marked by students who experience amotivation and whose behaviors reflect a style of *dysregulation*. These students are difficult to motivate, are uncompliant, do not trust teachers or other adults in schools, suffer from peer problems, and their academic and social skills often suffer as well. If, as a response to the challenges the students present, the students' teachers usurp their

Amotivated Student

Amotivation is associated with a locus of non-self-determined control and dysregulation styles, leading to displaying disorganized or antisocial behaviors. In response, it is common that authority figures install tighter rules or parameters around the students to elicit compliance. Doing so, however, smothers the contextual supports needed to move students to the right of the continuum toward more internally motivated behaviors.

Autonomy Support, Motivation, Self-Regulation, & Social Support Processes

Locus of Control	Not Self-Determined					Self-Determined
Motivational Styles	Amotivation	Extrinsic Motivation				Intrinsic Motivation
Regulatory Styles	Dysregulation	External Regulation	Introjected Regulation	Identified Regulation	Integrated Regulation	Self-Regulation
Social Development Processes	Disorganized & Antisocial Behavior	Involvement with Skills & Opportunities	Rewards & Commitment to Activities & Setting	Belief & Association	Attachment & Bonding	Social Bond & Conventional Behavior
(+)"One-Up" Orientation: 1. Control vs. Autonomy 2. Isolated vs. Related 3. Inability vs. Competence	Punishment Indifferent Unresponsive	Coercion Conflicted Indifference	Bribery Civil Contrary	Convincing Cordial Demanding	Negotiation Friendly Interested	Compromise Connected Attentive
(−)"One-Down" Perception: 1. Control vs. Autonomy 2. Isolated vs. Related 3. Inability vs. Competence	Disruptive Untrusting Inept	Challenging Apprehensive Low Ability	Yielding Suspicious Limited Ability	Compliant Guarded Able	Agreeable Believing Competent	Autonomous Bonded Skillful

FIGURE 4.1. SDT-SDM model.

autonomy and tighten the rules and controls to elicit compliance, these students likely will not to move to the right side of the continuum where they may be more invested in school and display fewer disorganized and antisocial behaviors.

To the far right of Figure 4.1, intrinsic motivation aligns with *self-regulation* and reflects a student who is self-determined. Self-determined students have strong social development bonds with school, are skilled at school-related tasks, and are highly autonomous people. Educators who compromise with students, are attentive to students' individualized competency needs, and are emotionally available and socially connected to their students are intentionally cultivating a classroom where those students can feel internally motivated and successful. These students are more likely to try new tasks, embrace failures as a clue to success, and are supportive of others while they do the same. Intrinsically motivated students engage in conventional behaviors valued by and reflective of the school as a social institution (i.e., hard work, equity, responsibility, respect) because they genuinely value those expectations for themselves personally and for others.

In the center of Figure 4.1 is extrinsic motivation with four corresponding, subregulatory states. The most control-oriented and first regulatory state of extrinsic motivation is described as *external regulation*. Externally regulated students possess limited ability, are socially hesitant and apprehensive, and often pose resistance or challenge the demands or expectations at school. Students who are surrounded by one-up teachers who leverage their positions in a manner that is coercive and conflictual, and who lack investments in the development of healthy relationships, are more likely to be bounded as externally regulated people who, despite being involved at school, will comply only with reservation and great difficulty. The next extrinsically regulated state is called *introjected regulation*, which is marked by students with a yielding, suspicious, and limited ability to pursue and achieve external demands. These students are managed rather than being taught to manage themselves. In these environments, one-up adults may use bribery as leverage to get students to behave and to accomplish tasks amid civil, yet contrary, social interactions and low levels of competency supports. Stated differently, students in introjected states are best described as reliant on contingencies and ego-oriented desires to appear competent with the goal of maintaining their own self-esteem and worth.

> **Intrinsically Motivated Student**
>
> Intrinsic motivation is correlated with the self-determined side of the locus of control and self-motivation. Students at this end of the continuum are more self-regulated and tend to have stronger social bonds with peers and teachers at school. They are also more likely to try new tasks and embrace failure as a part of learning.

The next extrinsically regulated state is slightly more autonomous and is referred to as *identified regulation*. Identified regulation is denoted by compliance, collaboration, a conscious awareness, and appreciation that achieving an expectation is recognized as personally important. Teachers who are good at convincing students to comply in a cordial, yet demanding, manner may facilitate this state in their students. Identified students begin to believe that there is benefit from abiding by what is expected at school but have not yet fully adopted the values of schooling as a means to meet their goals. Finally, the most autonomous, yet still externally motivated, regulatory state is referred to as *integrated regulation*, whereby a student has absorbed or is acculturated to the expectations at school. A student who is experiencing integrated regulation has assimilated to school, has bought into the expectations at school to advance their own goals, and recognizes that effort to meet those expectations as reflecting their own values. These students are agreeable, believe and trust in relationships with others at school, and are competent students at achieving school tasks. The social development process sees these students as feeling attached to the institution of the school and beginning to feel bonded to their teachers as agents of that institution.

The idea of explicitly breaking down the different levels of connection and engagement is to gain a better understanding of how student behaviors are malleable and reflective of the social dynamics around them. This understanding helps those who directly work with challenging students to reframe their thinking. The truth is, our most common reaction to students who enter school and present behaviors and attitudes that align with the left side of the continuum is generally not correct. In other words, when students are perceived by educational professionals as being "difficult" or disruptive, the most common response by adults in the school is to reduce that student's degrees of freedom, choice, and autonomy. We crack down. We put parameters around the student attached to controlling expectations and contingencies, and the student needs to comply to get out from under the controls. However, these reactions are not only counterintuitive, they are counterproductive. Indeed, this is exactly what Figure 4.1 suggests: When encountering a youth who is disruptive, we must engage in practices that are the opposite of our initial response. Instead of tightening their freedoms, we need to identify where they are at and work with them to learn the needed skills, provide them with autonomy support, and invest effort into cultivating a stronger relationship. As the old saying goes, those who are the most difficult to love need it the most, and those who need it the most will not feel love by being controlled. SMARTS structures specific activities that do just this, by helping students identify areas they want to improve, supporting their decisions, and helping them achieve the competencies and knowledge needed to obtain those goals. We will help those students experience success and be better aligned or bonded to the values of schooling and the teachers and peers who extoll those values.

Now that we understand the theories, it is time to explore the realities of the school day. How does this theory apply to the daily challenges of disruptive students? How can we show love to a student who is testing every boundary? How do we get a student from one side of the diagram in Figure 4.1 to the other? We can move students toward being self-determined, self-regulated, and intrinsically motivated by adopting and engaging in everyday autonomy-support practices with intentionality toward students, such as relying on SMARTS and other autonomy-support strategies. Let's unpack autonomy support, what it is, why it is important, and list everyday actions we can take to promote student autonomy.

HOW SMARTS OPERATIONALIZES AUTONOMY SUPPORT

Every detail of SMARTS is aimed at helping educators use words, actions, instructional strategies, and student support to optimize and take advantage of autonomy-support strategies to move a student from the left side of Figure 4.1 to the right side, where they are more internally motivated. SMARTS intentionally creates activities and the contextual scaffolding to assist students with learning to self-monitor in a supportive environment. SMARTS cannot make you a supportive adult, but when the student-training lessons and activities of SMARTS are utilized in an autonomy-supportive manner, students are more directly involved in independent learning, exercising independent thinking, and taking responsibility for their own outcomes. SMARTS autonomy-support practices believe that you as an educator can see a student bring their own expertise into the classroom; it acknowledges that your role as a teacher is not to be the "sage on the stage," but rather "a guide on the side" by facilitating experiences that acknowledge students' need to be at the helm of their own ships with your steady and supportive guidance at the ready.

SMARTS research has shown that autonomy support in education settings is linked to numerous positive student outcomes, including increased intrinsic motivation and engagement, improved academic performance, greater self-regulation and healthy behaviors, and improved self-care. Supporting the autonomy of students during the school day and with school-related tasks will not only provide the necessary ingredients to foster increased competency in those tasks, but engaging in autonomy support will also lay the cornerstone necessary for improving relationships with students. The key elements in SMARTS are summarized in Table 4.4. However, these practices can also be woven into any activity throughout the school day, and the more they are used, the more students will gravitate toward you as a supportive and trusted adult at school.

Remember, autonomy-support practices are not limited to the examples. There are many other approaches too vast to name. It is important to question our own orientations to our students, discuss these practices with others, and explore and try new autonomy-support practices. Not all of them will work, and that is OK. But start by acting as a self-determined educator willing to try something new. Start by asking your students (which is autonomy supportive!) what they need, keep a list of practices available, and try one each day. If it does not work, reflect on what went wrong and try again. Remember, mistakes are road signs along the highway to success, and they become opportunities for helpers to foster autonomy and renewed motivation.

As we discuss in much more detail in the next chapter, motivational interviewing is a conversational style that can help educators develop autonomy-supportive relationships with students to stimulate their motivation. MI builds off basic listening skills to

TABLE 4.4. Everyday Autonomy Support Practices

Autonomy support	Definition	Example
Provide choices	Offer meaningful choices embedded in the learning process.	Jamie offers Mac the option of sharing a summary of their free-reading book orally with the class or writing a half page that only Jamie will read.
Support relevant learning	Engage students in the process of understanding "why" they are learning about certain materials.	Alex chats with Mac during group about what Mac wants to work on for their goal. Mac asks Alex why it's important that Mac doesn't talk to their classmates while Jamie is teaching.
		Alex asks Mac, "How do you feel when someone talks while you are talking?"
		Mac thinks for a minute and responds, "Not very good. I don't like it when I can't finish my story."
		Alex looks at Mac and says, "Do you think your teachers also feel that way?"
		Mac's eyes get wide as they respond, "Oh, when I talk with Devin during our math lesson, I'm talking over our teacher. I understand now."
Encourage active participation	Support autonomy through encouraging student collaboration and participation through discussions, asking questions, and sharing their thoughts and ideas.	When Alex first meets with Mac and their SMARTS group, Alex pulls out a blank poster board for the students to see. Alex then addresses the students by saying, "I want to hear from all of you about what rules and expectations you think are important for our group to follow when we meet. Are there any suggestions?"
		At a later lesson, Alex asks group members to participate.
Recognize student expertise	Regardless of age, everyone is an expert in their own lives and at many things. Taking time to ask questions and gain insight into students' expertise can assist them in building their autonomy *and* the teacher–student relationship.	During a writing lesson, Jamie asks the class to write about something they believe they are really good at. During this lesson, Jamie sees Mac frown and goes over to Mac's desk to inquire about Mac's frown.
		JAMIE: Mac, you had a frown on your face when I was explaining the assignment. Is there some way I can help and support you?
		MAC: I'm not really good at anything.
		JAMIE: That sounds like a rough thought to have. What are some things you enjoy doing?
		MAC: Well, I like playing checkers, swimming, and playing with my friends.
		JAMIE: You know, Mac, I actually don't know how to swim. I grew up in a big city and never had the chance to learn.
		MAC: Really? I bet I could teach you!

(continued)

TABLE 4.4. *(continued)*

Autonomy support	Definition	Example
Recognize student expertise *(continued)*		JAMIE: I bet you could. Maybe you could use this writing assignment to talk about some tips I would need to be able to learn to swim. MAC: For sure! I can write it like I am your teacher!
Recognize your own unfinishedness as a learner	Even being in an authority-figure role with knowledge and expertise, it can be easy to not want to make mistakes or not know the answer. However, acknowledging our own limitations and times when we don't know the answers allows us to be humble. In addition, these moments allow students to know that even adults are still learning new things and may not always know the answers.	During math class, Remi and Jasmine share a look of confusion. Their teacher, Andy Smith, notices the students' shared look and asks the two if they have any questions about the material. JASMINE: *(Bites her lip)* REMI: We both are confused because 12 divided by 3 is 4. ANDY: That is true. REMI: So, if 12 divided by 3 is 4, then wouldn't 120 divided by 3 be 40? Andy looks at the board and shakes his head before laughing. "Remi, you are so right. I forgot to add the zero after the 4. Good catch! Sometimes even teachers made little mistakes, and I am so grateful to have smart students like you all who will help me correct them!" Both Remi and Jasmine smile at each other.
Nurture self-regulation	Providing guidance and support to students while they analyze problems, set goals and objectives, monitor goal progress, and reflect on learning.	During a later SMARTS lesson, Alex introduces Mac, Remi, Jasmine, and Devin to the concept of paced breathing. After the group completes the lesson and practices paced breathing, Remi raises his hand and shares that his mom taught him this skill before, and he used the skill while also journaling when dysregulated. Alex notices Jasmine smile, and during their processing meeting a day later, Jasmine shares that she used paced breathing earlier that morning when she was feeling anxious during math.
Provide supportive feedback	Providing constructive and supportive feedback involves a combination of the following elements: being timely and concrete (specific and clear), emphasizing effort and process, balancing praise and constructive criticism, being descriptive, and offering guidance moving forward.	Alex and Mac meet to process through Mac's goal-monitoring progress. Mac looks at the ground and admits that he has not completed his own goal-monitoring sheet for the last 3 days as he pulls out his one completed monitoring form for the week. Mac says he is "stupid" for forgetting. Alex takes a minute before telling Mac, "Developing new habits take time, Mac. It is understandable that you are having a hard time remembering to complete this form each day. Although I am a little sad you forgot the last few days, I do not believe for one minute that you are stupid. Look at the way you filled out this worksheet. You wrote in

(continued)

TABLE 4.4. *(continued)*

Autonomy support	Definition	Example
Provide supportive feedback *(continued)*		a lot of detail, and I can see that you completed each part of the worksheet."
		Mac looks up and says, "Really?"
		Alex nods and smiles: "Yes, and I wonder, if you wrote a reminder on a sticky note to complete these worksheets at the end of the day, would that help?"
		Mac smiles. "I can try that! I can draw a pencil and checkmark on it. That way my classmates don't know, and I will have a reminder."
		Alex says, "That sounds like a good idea, Mac!"
Facilitate positive relationships	Foster and demonstrate a supportive and open classroom environment by demonstrating characteristics of warmth, empathy, humor, and how to reframe mistakes as a part of learning.	During their last processing meeting, Jasmine looks at Alex and says, "Thank you for letting me take my time to talk and warm up to the group. Remi and I never talked or played together at recess, but since we joined SMARTS, we talk all the time! I am actually going to his house this weekend to play games! And Mac and Devin say hi to me in the halls. I have never really had friends at school, so this is exciting and new. Even when I made a mistake in our last group, no one laughed and everyone was supportive. Devin even shared that he has made the same mistake and told me how he corrected it *after* group!" She then looks really seriously at Alex. "Will I still be able to talk to you about things at school after today?"
		Alex smiles at Jasmine. "Of course, Jasmine! Just because SMARTS ended doesn't mean my office is closed to you. You can come to me when you need to."
		Jasmine smiles back. "Good, because you are safe."

include strategies for drawing out of the other why that they want things to be different (their desires, reasons, and needs) and the skills they have to make it happen. MI refers to these statements of desire, need, reasons, and skills as change talk. On the other hand, statements indicating why a person can't or won't change are called sustain talk. One of the key skills in learning MI is to be able to hear change talk and sustain talk in real time during conversations. The idea is quite simple: The more you draw out and encourage change talk and reduce sustain talk, the more likely it becomes that the person will decide to alter their behavior.

In the following example, we highlight an exchange between our school social worker, Alex, and our student, Mac D, in which Alex strategically uses basic MI skills to help move Mac in a new direction. Mac is struggling a bit with completing math assignments. We note the MI strategy behind each statement by Alex and any instances of change talk that they evoke in Mac.

> ALEX: Hey, Mac, how's it going today? I noticed you've been having a tough time getting motivated to complete your math assignments lately. What's been going on? (*Open-ended question*)
>
> MAC: I don't know. Math just feels really hard, and I don't see the point in doing it. (*Sustain talk*)
>
> ALEX: I hear you; math can be challenging sometimes. It's OK to feel that way. (*Affirmations*) What are some reasons you think that we all have to learn math? (*Open-ended question*)
>
> MAC: I mean, you gotta learn basic math to deal with money and change and stuff. (*Change talk*)
>
> ALEX: Great point. (*Affirmation*) I'm just curious. What, if any, downsides are there to you not doing your math work? (*Open-ended question to elicit reasons for change*)
>
> MAC: Well, my grade sucks and my parents get on my case. You know, just hassles. (*Change talk*)
>
> ALEX: So, lots of annoyances to not doing math. (*Reflection*) What about the flip side? What upsides, besides fewer annoyances, are there to doing it can you think of? (*Open-ended question to elicit reasons for change*)
>
> MAC: I mean, it would be nice not have to worry about my grade. (*Change talk*) It would be nice if it came easier to me. (*Change talk*)
>
> ALEX: How would that be helpful? (*Open-ended question to elicit change talk*)
>
> MAC: You know, it feels good to learn stuff and be good at it. (*Change talk*) I was good in math when we did, like, adding and subtracting, (*Change talk, Ability*) but when we got to division, man, I just couldn't get it. Well, I get it, but I'm just slow. (*Sustain talk*)
>
> ALEX: It'd be nice to get to a point where division came as easy to you as those earlier skills. (*Reflection of change talk*)
>
> MAC: For sure. (*Change talk*) But I don't know how that will happen. (*Sustain talk*)
>
> ALEX: You would like to get faster at division, but you would need some help to get there. (*Reflecting change talk and reframing "not know how" as "need some help"; in MI, this is called "agreement with a twist"*)
>
> MAC: Yeah, I mean, I don't just need someone to tell me to do it; I already have that. I would need someone to, like, help me figure out a better way to do it. (*Change talk*)

ALEX: That makes a lot of sense. (*Affirmation*) It's totally your choice, (*Autonomy support*) but I'm wondering if you would be open to me helping you with that. (*Open-ended question*)

Note a few things about this interaction. First, it is a very different interaction than many students typically encounter at school with adults, especially around topics they are struggling with. Commonly, an adult would have simply told Mac what to do (e.g., do your work), given him advice, or told him the bad things that would happen if he didn't improve (e.g., you are going to get a bad grade). These typical interactions with adults at school usually have the opposite effect from their intent; that is, they draw out of the student reasons they can't or won't change.

In contrast, notice how Alex never gave Mac an explicit command during this exchange. Instead, Alex used basic MI listening skills that are captured by the acronym OARS (i.e., <u>O</u>pen-ended questions, <u>A</u>ffirming responses, <u>R</u>eflections, <u>S</u>ummaries). In particular, notice how Alex strategically used open-ended questions to draw out of Mac his own reasons for wanting to change (i.e., change talk). Note also that change talk doesn't only have to be positive reasons for wanting things to be different. Change talk includes statements about why the person is unhappy with the status quo (e.g., parents get on my case).

It is also important to note that even in a productive conversation like this, sustain talk still occurred. It's natural during a typical conversation for both change talk and sustain talk to happen. This just indicates the common place most of us are in when we contemplate a change: ambivalence. The key is that Alex keeps the momentum in favor of change talk through strategic reflections and questions. For instance, when Mac agreed that it would be good to become better at division but followed with sustain talk (e.g., "I don't know how that will happen"), Alex focused on the agreement and reframed Mac's lack of plan as needing help. This in turn drew out more change talk from Mac. Even in the final statement where Alex offered to help, they preceded it with a responsibility statement by noting it was Mac's choice if they wanted to do it. The entire conversation was a form of autonomy support, where Alex communicated that it was Mac's ideas, beliefs, and preferences that were the most important considerations in whether they would commit to changing their behavior.

SUMMARY

Intrinsic motivation is closely linked to the self-determined aspect of the locus of control, indicating that individuals driven by internal rewards and enjoyment are more likely to feel in control of their actions. Students who exhibit intrinsic motivation are often self-motivated, meaning they are driven by their own interests and values rather than by external factors. These individuals tend to employ self-regulation strategies, demonstrating the ability to manage their behaviors, thoughts, and emotions to achieve goals. In addition, students with intrinsic motivation tend to have strong social development bonds, forming positive relationships with others who support their growth and development. They are more inclined to take on new tasks, challenges, and experiences, viewing failure as a natural part of the learning process rather than a setback. From this chapter, and as you use SMARTS to support and promote autonomy for your students, we hope that you stretch yourself and your view of your role as an educator. Specifically, we hope you:

- Understand the correlation between intrinsic motivation and the self-determined side of the locus of control and see how these features are woven throughout SMARTS.
- Recognize the characteristics of self-motivated individuals and how they differ from externally motivated individuals, and how we can use SMARTS to encourage the development of self-motivated behaviors.
- Learned about self-regulation strategies and how they contribute to goal achievement.
- Explore the importance of strong social development bonds in supporting intrinsic motivation and see how SMARTS can assist you to develop stronger bonds with your students.

The following chapter builds on autonomy support in a very natural way by discussing how MI dovetails, compliments, and promotes the autonomy of your students as well.

CHAPTER 5

Motivational Interviewing and SMARTS

While self-monitoring training helps youth develop success-related behaviors, youth will only benefit from these skills if they engage in SMARTS activities. Thus, in addition to promoting autonomy, self-awareness, and self-regulation through self-monitoring tools, SMARTS systematically incorporates motivational enhancement strategies throughout the process. In each chapter, we provide examples of these motivational strategies. In this specific chapter on MI and SMARTS, we provide more in-depth coverage of the skills needed as a mentor or coach to be effective motivators.

As mentioned in Chapter 1, MI serves as the foundation of effective motivational engagement strategies. MI is a well-established intervention in virtually any situation where compliance or ambivalence is a concern; that is, in nearly every area of human behavior change. In this chapter, we delve into the theory of MI and its essential skills. Please note that our goal here is not to prepare you to be fluent and proficient in MI. That would require extensive training and ongoing supervision. Here, our goal is to make you aware of the guiding principles or big ideas of MI and its core skills. You do not need to be an expert in MI to do SMARTS well. But it is helpful to have the frame of reference that MI provides and understand some simple strategies to help you manage the inevitable situations of student or teacher ambivalence about change.

BACKGROUND AND RATIONALE

SMARTS Research

In one of our studies on SMARTS (Thompson et al., 2020), we were interested in capturing the daily changes students experienced in their motivation levels related to their progress in the program. As noted in Chapter 1, SMARTS tends to work comparably well for students across a range of settings and student characteristics. However, in this study, we found a small subset of youth for whom feedback led to reduced motivation over time. In turn, we found that these youth were more susceptible to reporting future depression than youth who did not experience these downturns in motivation. These findings suggest that although SMARTS, on average, is helpful to most youth who experience it, some youth may need additional attention to motivation levers to fully benefit from it. We believe the findings from this study highlight that the way in which teacher feedback is delivered can be improved to help maximize the benefit for all students and reduce the likelihood that any student will experience a drop in motivation after receiving negative or constructive feedback. It is important to note here that the principles of motivation enhancement strategies to accomplish this goal are well established and apply equally well to youth who are initially motivated and to those for whom their motivations start low or wane over time.

SMARTS Research

Although, on average, SMARTS is helpful to most youth who experience it, some may need additional attention to motivation levers to fully benefit from it.

FRAMES

William R. Miller developed one of the most influential approaches to understanding and leveraging motivation in clinical support contexts. In the 1980s, Miller was dissatisfied with the current state of interventions for people with substance abuse issues. Many interventions at that time focused on shaming clients or directly confronting them about their substance abuse problems. Miller was convinced that these approaches were more harmful than helpful and rooted in misunderstandings about motivation. Some common misconceptions that led to these types of approaches included beliefs that individuals who abuse substances needed to hit rock bottom before deciding to change and that they needed to be directly challenged and confronted with the harm they were doing. Essentially, they needed to be educated, shamed, and told what to do. Miller took a different approach. Trained originally as a client-centered Rogerian, Miller knew the power of being a supportive listener who communicated nonjudgement, acceptance, and empathy for clients to help foster change.

Miller was also a scientist. Thus, as the foundation of his work, he reviewed existing literature at the time to identify the critical ingredients of brief interventions. He summarized these six ingredients with the acronym FRAMES: Feedback, Responsibility, Advice, Menu of options, Empathy, and Support self-efficacy.

First, effective brief interventions provide *feedback* to the recipients. Miller noted that studies found that not all feedback was the same. To be motivational, feedback needs to be personalized or tailored to the individual. As we have written about in prior chapters, SMARTS provides students with personalized feedback about their behaviors, thus aligning well with this MI ingredient.

Second, Miller wrote about the importance of *responsibility*, that is, the explicit communication that the decision to change one's behavior is ultimately the choice and responsibility of the individual. Consistent with this critical ingredient of brief interventions, SMARTS supports student choice and autonomy throughout the training sessions and process.

Advice is the third ingredient in Miller's FRAMES acronym. This refers to evidence that effective brief interventions often include direct advice to participants. Advice is most effective when the individual requests it or when the helper asks permission to give it. In addition, it is helpful to couple advice with a responsibility statement, acknowledging that it is ultimately up to the individual whether or not they follow the advice. In SMARTS, advice is used sparingly, but, consistent with FRAMES, it can be given with permission.

Miller also found that providing individuals with a *menu of options* allowed for an additional motivational lever. When individuals are given a choice about how they can best change their behaviors, this further supports their autonomy and increases their motivation to change. As you learned in Chapter 4, SMARTS incorporates choices and options throughout the process for students to support their autonomy.

Empathy is a fifth key ingredient for supporting motivation. This refers to efforts by the helper to show that they understand the emotional experiences of the individual. Empathy is best conveyed with effective listener skills where the helper accurately reflects to the individual what they hear them saying. Most impactful is when the helper offers accurate reflections about what the person is feeling. Effective SMARTS Facilitators are skilled listeners who use reflections, summaries, and affirmations to demonstrate empathy.

Support self-efficacy is the final ingredient that Miller identified in effective brief interventions. This refers to communicating the belief that the individual can and will be successful in accomplishing their goals and building their sense of belief in their own skills and power to influence the outcomes they want to achieve. SMARTS Facilitators use many strategies to instill beliefs in students' that they can be successful in accomplishing their goals and mastering challenging situations.

MOTIVATIONAL INTERVIEWING

Over many years, in collaboration with his colleague Stephen Rollnick, Miller coalesced these pillars of effective brief interventions into a comprehensive theory and approach to helping people change. They called their approach MI, most recently summarized in the fourth edition of their classic book *Motivational Interviewing: Helping People Change and Grow* (Miller & Rollnick, 2013, 2023). MI is arguably the most influential and effective approach to supporting motivation to change. It is a conversation about change that includes a focus on ambivalence, autonomy, and benevolence. A central premise of their approach was that telling people that they need to change was counterproductive and nearly always had the opposite effect. Instead, they argued that helpers needed to help draw a person's own reasons for changing out of them.

> **Motivational Interviewing**
>
> A central premise of their approach was that telling people that they need to change is counterproductive and nearly always has the opposite effect.

MI Spirit and Change Talk

Two key components of MI are referred to as *MI Spirit* and *change talk*. MI Spirit is the foundation for effectively fostering change. This includes the interpersonal qualities a helper conveys that make others feel trust and connectedness with them. Essential to the MI Spirit is acceptance, empathy, and benevolence. Throughout any social interaction helping another change, displaying these aspects of MI Spirit increases the likelihood that the support you are offering will be perceived as helpful and that the subsequent strategies you offer will lead to real change. As such, the MI Spirit is a necessary but insufficient ingredient to MI.

The second key ingredient to MI is change talk. Change talk refers to the language of change. These are the words that one communicates to indicate one is ready, able, and willing to change. In MI, the more a person uses change talk, the more likely they are to enact change. Five types of change talk include desire, ability, reasons, needs, and commitment, which can be summarized by the acronym DARN-C.

> **MI Spirit and Change Talk**
>
> The more a person uses change talk, the more likely they are to enact change.

Desire refers to expressions of a preference for change. Key words that signal a desire statement include "I want . . . ," "I wish . . . ," and "I would prefer. . . ." Desire statements are general and do not specify reasons for changing, just a want. Some examples you might hear from SMARTS students indicating they have a desire to change are:

"I want to stop getting in trouble at school."
"I wish I were better at walking away from trouble."
"I'd like to have more friends."

Ability, or optimism about change, refers to statements that indicate the person has the skills needed to make the change and the belief that they will be successful in making the change. Examples include "I can . . . ," "I could . . . ," and "I have. . . ." Some examples of ability statements you might hear when working with SMARTS students include:

"I think I'm getting the hang of this."
"I stayed out of trouble all week."
"I know I can do this homework assignment because I'm good at staying calm."

Statements that indicate personal successes using SMARTS are also gateways to ability statements.

> "You should have seen me! I just used mindfulness skills instead of punching him or going off."

You might reflect this statement by focusing on how the student is likely feeling about their success: "You are really happy about how you handled that problem." You might also ask an evocative question to empower the student and build invitation statements about autonomy and self-efficacy. "How did you do that?" is an excellent question to ask when inviting a student to elaborate their successes. This question gets them to think deeper about the specific steps they took to be successful, and it centers their success in their actions and decisions and not in the program or the coach.

<u>Reasons</u> for change are statements expressing the specific rationale for or benefits of change. Some examples include: "I would be stronger if I did this"; "My life would be better if I did this"; and "I don't like how my current decisions make me feel." Some reasons we have heard SMARTS students say include:

> **MI Spirit and Change Talk**
>
> "How did you do that?" is an excellent question to ask when inviting a student to elaborate their successes.

> "I think it will be helpful for me to use this breathing technique when I am upset in class or when I get upset during soccer."
> "I can see using this again because it made my day go better."
> "This skill would also be helpful for me to use at home."
> "I think I could use several of these skills when upset in the future. I really like the deep breathing technique and several mindfulness skills to help with that."

<u>Needs</u> are statements indicating an urgency, requirement, or obligation to change and a dissatisfaction with how things are going. Stem words indicating a need statement include "I ought to . . . ," "I should . . . ," and "I've got to. . . ." Some examples of needs we have heard in SMARTS groups are:

> "I need to get better grades."
> "I should stop getting on my teachers' nerves."
> "If things don't change soon, I'm worried what will happen."

Finally, *commitment* statements are those that indicate a willingness or intention to change. This is the most important and powerful type of change talk because it is the strongest predictor that someone will follow through on their intentions and change their behavior. Commitment statements include "I will . . . ," "I promise . . . ," and "I'm going to make this happen."

"I'm definitely going to do the homework tonight."
"I will get my teacher to notice how much progress I made today."
"I promise I will remember to keep track of my behavior tomorrow."

Commitment falls under a broader category of change talk referred to as mobilizing. Mobilizing refers to statements that a person makes, indicating intention or actual steps they have or that they plan to take to change their behavior. Thus, commitment, action ("I plan to do the homework"), and taking steps ("I practiced meditation every day last week") are referred to as CAT language, and DARN-CAT spells the full acronym of change talk.

> **MI Spirit and Change Talk**
>
> Commitment language is the most important and powerful type of change talk, as it is the strongest predictor that someone will follow through on their intentions and change their behavior.

Some other indicators we have noted in our group sessions that suggest students are embracing SMARTS include their use of _we_ and _us_ language. Statements like the ones below can be affirmed or reflected and elaborated.

"We practiced that skill last time and made some improvement."
"When is the next time we are meeting?"
"What do you want us to do for the next group?"

It is also a helpful sign when students indicate that they want to share the skills with others. Again, these types of statements can be affirmed and reflected.

"I think my friend could use this . . . I am going to tell them about it."
"I am going to tell my little sister about this. She is bad and this will help her."

Sustain Talk

One of the key skills in learning basic MI is getting comfortable with hearing expressions of change talk and distinguishing them from sustain talk. Sustain talk consists of statements indicating that the person is not ready, is unwilling, or is unable to change. Examples of sustain talk include:

"I'm not going to do this."
"I don't want to do this."
"I don't need to do this."
"I can't do this."
"This is not helpful."

When you learn to identify change amid a conversation, it becomes your guide for how to respond. When you hear change talk, you learn to invite more of it. One way to do this is to ask the person to elaborate the change talk by saying, "Tell me more about that." For example:

STUDENT: I really want to get better at setting good goals.

SMARTS FACILITATOR: That makes good sense to me. Tell me more about that.

> **MI Spirit and Change Talk**
>
> Sustain talk consists of statements indicating that a person is not ready, is unwilling, or is unable to change.

In this example, the SMARTS Facilitator first affirms the student's response and then invites them to say more about their desire for better grades. These are two MI skills that we describe in more detail in the following example. For now, just notice that this type of response from the facilitator will evoke more change talk from the student. In this case, the student will most likely respond with more statements about their desire to change.

As an alternative, the facilitator could ask an evocative question to keep the change talk going. For example:

STUDENT: I really want to get better at setting good goals.

SMARTS FACILITATOR: How would it be helpful to you to get better at setting goals?

Here, the facilitator asks a question that encourages the student to reflect more deeply about their desire. The student's response will most likely be an elaboration of change talk. The student will likely provide one or more ways that their life would be better if they set goals well. In turn, their response might lead to specific reasons that they want to change.

As another alternative, the facilitator could simply reflect the change talk back to the student. For example:

STUDENT: I really want to get better at setting good goals.

SMARTS FACILITATOR: It is important to you to become a better goal setter.

With this response, the facilitator uses a basic listening skill, reflective listening, to convey empathy and also to invite the student to talk about why being good at setting goals is important to them. Their response will most likely include more change talk and, again, possibly also include reasons for wanting to change their behavior.

Similarly, sustain talk can become a barometer for how well you are doing MI and can also provide direction for how to respond. In general, over the course of a conversation or group meeting, you hope to hear increasing levels of change talk and decreasing levels of sustain talk. You prioritize change talk by reflecting it and asking the student to elaborate it through statements and questions. You minimize sustain talk by redirecting or reframing it. In truth, reducing sustain talk can be challenging when you are first learning MI because you cannot simply ignore it. To be genuine and to demonstrate empathy, you need to show that you hear and understand a student's ambivalence or concerns about changing. So, sometimes you will reflect sustain talk. For these reasons, in this brief chapter on MI, we emphasize responses to avoid when responding to sustain talk.

Miller and Rollnick (2023) described the righting reflex as a common ineffective response to sustain talk. This is the tendency to respond to statements about not wanting or needing to change by arguing against it. That is, sustain talk can draw out helper responses to counter it. These are ineffective responses because, when we as helpers argue against a person's reasons for not wanting to change, it evokes

> **MI Spirit and Change Talk**
>
> Over the course of a conversation or group meeting, you hope to hear increasing levels of change talk and decreasing levels of sustain talk.

more sustain talk from them. Some examples of unhelpful responses that SMARTS Facilitators might be drawn into when hearing sustain talk include education, advice giving, or scare tactics. Education is when we provide information in hopes of swaying a person to change their position or commitment to change. For instance, if a student said they did not want to participate in the groups any longer, an education response might be, "Did you know research shows that students who participate in SMARTS do better than those who do not?" While this is true and intended to be helpful, it is unlikely this response will promote the student's motivation to engage in SMARTS. In fact, it will most likely lead to more sustain talk in which the student then provides reasons why the research does not apply to them and further reasons why SMARTS will not work for them.

Another unhelpful response to sustain talk is advice giving. This may sound contradictory given that we previously said advice giving can be a helpful brief intervention. As noted, however, giving advice is most likely to be helpful when it is offered with permission and when used sparingly. When given in response to sustain talk, however, it will likely be met with further sustain talk. Consider a student who has not been consistently tracking their behavior. Consider if the facilitator responds with direct advice like, "You know, it's important that you keep track of your behavior several times a day. I recommend that you set an alarm on your watch to remind yourself to do it." Again, though this is well intentioned, it is very likely that the student will reply with reasons why it is not important or why that solu-

> **MI Spirit and Change Talk**
>
> When we as helpers argue against a person's reasons for not wanting to change, it evokes more sustain talk from them.

tion will not work. This is because of the righting reflex. When someone expresses one side of an argument (in this case, for changing), it invites the other to "right" the ship by expressing the other side of the argument (not changing). For these reasons, when you hear sustain talk, avoid your automatic response to it. Avoid being drawn into an argument or into giving advice or direction. If in doubt, when you hear sustain talk, pause and do nothing. A very simple response is to reflect it, to convey empathy, and then to shift the focus by starting a new topic.

One final response to sustain talk that we highlight here because it is common and particularly damaging is the use of scare tactics or power. Sometimes adults get frustrated by student sustain talk, and it can draw out authoritative responses. We may have the urge to tell students they have to do it or to provide responses about the dire consequences students will face if they do not improve their behavior (e.g., get suspended or held back a grade). Like the previous responses, scare tactics and power messages will draw out more sustain talk, and worse, will likely undermine your relationship with students. These responses are highly inconsistent with the MI Spirit and will increase the likelihood that a student will not be responsive to other MI skills.

SPECIFIC MI SKILLS

OARS

As alluded to previously, MI uses basic listening skills as the core for establishing the MI Spirit. Miller and Rollnick (2023) summarized the four essential elements of listening with the acronym OARS.

Open-Ended Questions

These are questions that cannot be answered in a single word (yes or no). They are contrasted with closed questions that can be answered with a single word. Open-ended questions are helpful for drawing out thoughts and experiences and for clarifying any points of confusion. As indicated in each of the prior examples, they are also an essential tool for evoking change talk. Questions should be asked sparingly and followed by one or more of each of the following responses every time they are asked. In general, try to provide two or three reflections before asking another question.

Affirmations

Affirmations are statements or nonverbal behaviors that communicate acceptance and acknowledgment. To be helpful these statements or actions need to be genuine. In addition, they are more likely to be well received if they are specific.

Reflections

Reflections are single statements (not questions) that repeat what someone has communicated. There are two types of reflections: simple and complex. Simple reflections and paraphrasing are very similar, if not identical, to directly communicating what another has said. For instance, if someone said, "I don't understand this," a simple reflection would be, "This is hard to understand." Complex reflections state what you hear or understand a person to be communicating, even though they have not explicitly communicated it. In particular, complex reflections communicate unstated feelings to the client that you infer based on their statements and nonverbal behaviors. For example, a student might come to your group session and say, "I didn't do my homework." Noting their dejected appearance, you might respond, "You are really disappointed that you didn't get to your homework."

Summaries

Summaries are similar to reflections in that they are statements, but they are longer and attempt to bring together a lot of information that has been shared during the conversation. Typically, they are one to three sentences that summarize part of a conversation. One goal of summaries is to check in to be sure you are understanding all the key ideas that the student or group has expressed and seek their input on any areas you have missed. Summaries can also serve as useful transition points during a meeting to communicate what you have discussed so far and then prepare the student(s) for the next topic. A final purpose of effective summaries is to highlight a theme you have heard expressed by the student or group.

Evocative Questions

OARS emphasize the importance of open-ended questions as basic listening skills in MI. Here, we highlight them as one of the primary tools for evoking change talk. In each of the examples previously described, we should notice how evocative questions can be used to draw out more change talk. We show

> **Evocative Questions**
>
> Evocative questions are one of the primary tools for evoking change talk.

how particular questions are effective for evoking each of the specific types of change talk defined by DARN-C. The goal is not to get you to memorize a bunch of questions for each type of change talk, but simply to provide you with examples of effective evocative questions. Note that the answer to all these questions will be a change talk.

Desire for Change

"Tell me about things you want to be different."
"What do you want to be different or better?"
"What do you think will happen if you don't make a change?"

Ability/Optimism about Change

"What makes you think that if you decide to make a change, you could do it?"
"What encourages you to feel like you can change if you want to?"
"What do you think would work for you if you decided to change?"
"What would make you feel even more confident that you could make a change?"
"When else in your life have you made a big change like this? How did you do it?"
"What personal strengths do you have that will help you succeed?"

Reasons for Change

"How would you like things to be different?"
"What would be some good things about changing?"
"What would the advantages of making this change be?"

Need for Change

"What makes you think that you may need to make a change?"
"In what ways has this been a problem for you?"
"What makes you feel like you should do something different?"
"What worries you about how things are going?"
"In what ways does this concern you?"
"What do you think will happen if you don't make a change?"

Commitment/Intention to Change

"If you could easily make any changes, what would you do?"
"Never mind the 'how' for right now; what do you want to have happen?"
"How important is this to you? How much do you want to do this?"
"What would you be willing to try?"
"What are you going to do? What's the next step?"

Rulers

Rulers offer a structured way to evoke change talk along with personal reflection, questions, and reflective listening. Common rulers focus on two key aspects of motivation: how important change is to the person and how confident they are that they can make the change. Whenever a student sets a goal or makes a commitment to engage in a new behavior, it can be helpful to ask these questions.

The importance ruler takes the following form: "How important is it for you to make this change on a scale from 0 to 10, where 0 means not important at all and 10 means extremely important?" After the person selects a number (X), the SMARTS Facilitator replies, "Why are you at X and not $X-1$?" For clarity, let's say the person replies, "Five."

The facilitator would say, "Why are you at a 5 and not a 4?" In fact, the facilitator can ask any number lower than the one selected by the person, all the way down to 0. For instance, "Why are you a 5 and not a 0?" The key is to ask about a lower number, not a higher number. Lower numbers will invite the person to talk about reasons that change is important (i.e., change talk). A higher number, on the other hand, will invite the person to talk about reasons for not changing (i.e., sustain talk).

It can be helpful to ask a follow-up question to explore how to grow the student's sense of importance. For example, you might ask, "What would it take for it go from a 5 to a 6?" Here, the response will be examples of what the student could picture happening where the goal would become even more important. Note the different language structure here that allows you to ask for a higher number (i.e., "what would it take") to avoid evoking sustain talk occurs if you asked about a higher number with the first question. Also, it is important to follow each student's response to your queries with a reflection and perhaps a summary.

We often follow importance-ruler questions with confidence questions. These take the same form: "On a scale from 0 to 10, how confident are you that you can make this change, where 1 is not confident at all and 10 is extremely confident?" The same follow-up questions apply to the confidence question as well. Importance and confidence tap different aspects of motivation, and these questions allow you to pinpoint where motivation may be stronger or weaker. For instance, someone who responds that they are at a 9 on the importance ruler but a 3 on the confidence ruler is someone who is very motivated to change, but they lack the confidence to be successful. In turn, this helps you plan supports to help the person be successful. In this case, strategies helping to foster a sense of self-efficacy would be important.

MI-Consistent versus MI-Inconsistent Responses

Much research has shown that a basic distinction can be made in terms of consultant responses to client utterances, whether they are MI consistent or inconsistent. MI-consistent responses include using OARS and avoiding confrontation or directive responses. MI-inconsistent responses include the opposite. When we use MI-consistent responses, clients are more likely to move in the direction of change; the opposite happens when our responses are MI inconsistent. This is important as you attempt to develop your MI skills. It means that you do not need to do MI perfectly to be successful; instead, focus on increasing your MI-consistent responses and reducing inconsistent ones.

> **Rulers**
>
> Importance and confidence tap different aspects of motivation, and these questions allow you to pinpoint where motivation may be stronger or weaker.

SMARTS AND MI

We end this chapter by focusing on some common challenging situations where MI skills might be helpful.

Responding to Challenging Student Behaviors

Disinterest/Disengagement

Students may demonstrate disinterest in the program or disengagement in its content in various ways. For instance, students may not show up to meetings, may show up late, or may require the facilitator to send an adult to get them. You may also hear any number of sustain talk statements indicating disinterest or disengagement.

> "This is dumb! This isn't going to help anything!"
> "I don't have anything I want to change about my behaviors!"
> "You go ahead and keep talking [through the lesson]; I can multitask."
> "We should just spend the day playing chess."

It can be helpful to have a direct conversation with the student about missing SMARTS activities or sbeing late. The meeting should be in a private space, and you can let the student know in advance what you hope to talk about. For instance, you might say, "I wanted to touch base to see how SMARTS is going for you." At the start, you might begin with some open-ended questions about how the student feels about SMARTS, how it's going, what they like about it, and what they would change. This can help you pinpoint the student's areas of disinterest and also convey your concern and empathy.

You might provide direct, personalized feedback about their explicit behaviors followed by an open-ended question: "You have missed the past three SMART sessions. What has gotten in the way?" Early in the conversation, it can be helpful to communicate responsibility. For instance, you could say, "I can't make you come to meetings. It is totally your choice." You might also provide or co-develop a menu for addressing the issue. "If we came up with a few options that might be helpful for you, then you can decide which one(s) work best for you." If the student agrees, invite them to contribute ideas to the menu and ask permission to add items of your own. For instance, you might propose the following: "As one example, I could send you a reminder each day before the meeting. Or you might make a public commitment or create a contract to attend the meetings."

Rulers can also be very effective tools at facilitating these conversations and drawing out student engagement and motivation. You might ask, "How important is it for you to attend the next meeting?" and use the follow-up questions described previously. Here, the follow-up prompt about what could make it more important can be especially valuable in identifying ways to increase the student's engagement. Remember, it is important to follow up this question with the confidence ruler, as it may be an issue that the student is disengaged because they lack the confidence and skills to fully engage in SMARTS.

Defeated/Hopelessness/Doubting Autonomy

Another type of challenging behavior we have encountered includes communicating a sense of defeat or doubt about their own self-efficacy or about the autonomy. Some examples of language we have heard that express these concerns are:

"It doesn't matter if I make my goal."
"Even if I tried, I would not have any control over that goal."
"I just don't see my teacher letting me take that break when upset in class."
"I am not sure anyone would even notice if I tried."
"Who will even care if I try?"
"I'm trying; they don't notice."
"I don't always have the opportunity to complete my goal during class."

All these statements provide an opportunity for a reflective listening response to build the relationship with the student and demonstrate empathy. Thus, a reflective response is nearly always a good first option, especially if you can accurately capture their feelings (complex reflection). For example, you might reply, "That's frustrating to feel like your efforts won't make a difference." Other more advanced MI responses attempt to evoke change talk from these sustain statements. For instance, an amplified reflection is a type of reflection that exaggerates the student's response in hopes that the student will respond with a less extreme version. To be effective, amplified reflections need to be stated in a matter-of-fact, genuine way without any hint of sarcasm. In response to a student comment like, "Even if I tried, I would not have any control over that goal," you might say, "You have zero influence over whether or not you can achieve goal." The purpose of such a statement would be to get the student to talk about what aspects of control they do have, even if they are minor. There are several other more advanced MI skills for responding to sustain talk that are beyond the scope of this chapter. To learn MI in more depth, we encourage you to seek more detailed sources like Miller and Rollnick (2023) or an MI book focused on school applications by Herman and colleagues (2020).

Aside from MI responses to the statements, it may be helpful to ask some open-ended questions to better understand the concerns. Some of the statements about goals may indicate the student has not set a realistic goal and may need to revisit the goal itself. In fact, the student may have experienced barriers to controlling certain aspects of the school environment that make the goal difficult to accomplish. Focusing the conversation on what behaviors the student has control over can help recenter and reenergize them.

In addition, many of these defeated or doubting statements suggest a lack of confidence, which is, as we have noted, a key component of motivation. Thus, their expression may signal that the student needs stronger self-efficacy supports. The confidence ruler question can help center these conversations. In particular, asking what would make your confidence go from X to $X + 1$ can elicit ideas from the student about what supports they need from you or others that can build their confidence. This leads to the companion set of comments below that indicate low self-efficacy.

Low Self-Efficacy

Students may make the following types of statements:

> "I suck at this/I can never do this/I will never get better at this."
> "I just don't think I am very good at this."
> "When I am upset, nothing will calm me down! I just am not sure this will be helpful."

These are all sustain statements of low self-efficacy for achieving the desired outcome of being able to successfully self-monitor their behavior. Recall that building self-efficacy is a key goal of MI and a critical ingredient of effective brief interventions. Simply telling the student they can do it or to stick with it is a common response but unlikely to be effective on its own. In fact, these types of responses run the risk of evoking even more sustain talk ("No, I'm just hopeless at this"). Instead, use some of the strategies we reviewed earlier for responding to sustain talk. A simple strategy is to try a complex reflection. This involves guessing at the feeling behind the statement and expressing it in a statement. "It's disappointing that you are not seeing the progress you expect." Another strategy is to reframe the statement to highlight the positives about the student. MI refers to this as agreeing with a twist. "I'm impressed at how strong you are to persevere, even when it is frustrating." When stuck, it can be helpful to simply shift the focus. "Can you tell me about a time when you did this well?"

> **Low Self-Efficacy**
>
> Simply telling the student they can do it or to stick with it is a common response but is unlikely to be effective on its own. In fact, these types of responses run the risk of evoking even more sustain talk.

Embarrassment/Stigma

One other area of concern we have observed from some SMARTS students is feeling embarrassed or worried about stigma related to participating in it. We have tried to circumvent this in the curriculum by emphasizing that participation is a sign of strength and by normalizing help-seeking as a common and valued behavior. In addition, asking evocative questions to engage the students in this type of adaptive thinking to change their beliefs about participation can be helpful. These types of conversations can also be helpful to do in a group so that some students who may struggle to answer questions can get ideas from others who may more easily answer them.

"What are some reasons being part of SMARTS shows you are strong?"

"What are some other areas that some students need and get more support for at school (like math, reading, writing, sports, public speaking)?"

"What makes you proud about being part of SMARTS?"

"What would you say to your friend who was in SMARTS if someone told him only troubled kids are in it?"

Coaching Teachers to Be MI Consistent

Teachers like to teach, so we should not be surprised to see them using instruction and information giving as a preferred strategy when a student is noncompliant or disengaged. Some examples include giving students advice, telling them why it is important for them to participate, demanding that they participate, and giving them information about how they will benefit. Recall that in MI these types of responses are likely to evoke sustain talk, that is, the opposite of what the teacher intends.

To help teachers unlearn these typical or automatic responses, it can be helpful to provide them with information about MI and a rationale for why it works. As a subsequent step, helping them to identify change talk and distinguish it from sustain talk can also be beneficial.

Keep in mind that teachers may vary in their own motivation levels for participating in SMARTS or delivering it with fidelity. Thus, as you coach them, it is important that you also use MI. This not only elicits their motivation but also serves as a model for them in how to engage in MI when working with students. This may include providing teachers with personalized feedback about what they are doing well in SMARTS and what they might improve.

Recall that earlier we mentioned students who may get discouraged about their feedback. Here, it is helpful to prepare teachers to anticipate these types of students and prepare them to deliver alternate responses. You might provide them with a script of useful open-ended questions to ask in these situations. "How is this going for you?" or "How are you feeling about this feedback?" The script might include some example simple reflections when they observe a student appearing disheartened, such as "You seem discouraged." These pivotal points can also benefit from providing students with genuine affirmations, such as "I want you to know that I'm proud of you.

> **Coaching Teachers to Be MI Consistent**
>
> Keep in mind that teachers may vary in their own motivation levels for participating in SMARTS or delivering data with fidelity.

It's common for everyone to have ups and downs when learning new things. The key is to track it over time and see trends going up." You might encourage the teacher to offer words of encouragement and offers of support: "What other ways can I help you learn these skills?"

In addition, in other chapters, we have built in strategies that can help inoculate students against these tendencies to be discouraged by negative feedback. For instance, as part of the reflection exercises in the lessons, we ask students first to reflect on what they would tell a friend who received negative feedback to help them feel less discouraged. Later, we focus these types of reflection questions on themselves by asking what they can say to themselves when they feel discouraged by negative feedback.

SUMMARY

In this chapter, we described motivational interviewing and its role in SMARTS. MI provides a guide for the interpersonal skills and strategies that SMARTS leaders can use to build and sustain rapport with students (and teachers), evoke their motivation, and manage challenges when their motivation wanes. In particular, OARS describes a set of listening skills that allow a leader to accomplish goals. In addition, learning to identify change and sustain talk are critical skills for becoming fluent in MI. When SMARTS leaders develop these skills, it allows them to stay attuned to the moment-to-moment changes that naturally occur during conversations and to provide responses that encourage change talk to continue and that diminish the likelihood of subsequent sustain talk. Perhaps most fundamental, MI Spirit is the core of effective MI in that it ensures that the SMARTS leaders are focused on establishing and sustaining a caring and empathetic relationship with students. Without it, the other strategies of MI will likely be ineffective. With MI as our foundation, in the next chapter we describe key tips for success in leading SMARTS groups.

PART II

IMPLEMENTING SMARTS

CHAPTER 6

Tips on Preparing for and Implementing SMARTS

School-based, small-group interventions are invaluable as a means of supporting youth who struggle with similar concepts, challenges, or issues. There is no better way to impart advanced knowledge or provide extra time and space to practice skills than in a small group where students can benefit not only from direct instruction but also interactions with each other. After all, if not everyone in a class, grade, or school needs the skills being offered, then a small group of students who can benefit from the topic are provided with increased time and individualized support from a caring adult through a small-group format. Also, as pointed out in Chapter 3, small groups are generally used for students in need of targeted Tier 2 or Tier 3 supports, which are an essential component of a well-developed multi-tiered system of supports (MTSS) in a school setting. Because SMARTS is a targeted intervention for youth with challenging behaviors, we want to spend a bit of time sharing with you what we have learned about effective practices for setting up and delivering group interventions in schools.

Schools are busy places with various challenges and happenings. There are limited human and financial resources to provide adequate social behavioral-support personnel, and most school-based student-support personnel lack the appropriate time to engage in the evidence-based practice process where they collect needs-assessment or screening data, use that data to identify areas of concern, and pair those concerns with evidence-based approaches previously shown to alleviate those concerns. Even if they did, manualized interventions are not always studied under the conditions and populations that might reflect the students and community of your school, and they often lack practical information on adaptations to implement the program with different students or settings. In this chapter, we discuss:

- Getting buy-in from your colleagues and other issues a student-support person in a school might need to consider before adopting SMARTS as a stand-alone intervention or as an element in their MTSS model
- Some common concerns and strategies for overcoming those concerns when implementing small-group interventions in school settings for students who present challenging behaviors
- Approaches for selecting students appropriate to participate in the SMARTS intervention
- Other evidence-based and scientifically supported practices for running small groups that will optimize student participation, group cohesion, and maximize the effect of SMARTS as a targeted behavior support program

GETTING BUY-IN FOR SMARTS

Before deciding to adopt any intervention—SMARTS or other approaches—it is very important to consider several factors and lay some groundwork for success. Not all interventions are the same, and no single intervention approach will address the needs of all students. However, the better school personnel can select an evidence-based approach, use that approach as often as possible with as many students who need those supports, and work to individualize those approaches to meet students' needs, the more likely students will be to experience success. Simply put, doing one or two things well will most often beat doing many things halfway. But this view of offering only one or two behavior-support programs must be balanced with the reality that different students require different supports. In this way, we find ourselves implementing various interventions and practices, depending on what students need.

SMARTS is an evidence-based program with several studies indicating improvement in youth behavior, feelings of autonomy and motivation, and improvements in student and teacher relations (Thompson, 2014; Thompson & Webber, 2010). SMARTS allows for individualization for students in how goals are written, how often students report on their goal progress, and also draws in student interest and input during training. SMARTS is more intensive than Check-In/Check-Out and thus can be considered alongside other commonly used interventions at the Tier 1, Tier 2, or Tier 3 levels of an MTSS. All this is to say that SMARTS and the practice of self-monitoring are highly effective and adaptable to the needs of students and settings. However, before integrating the SMARTS program and practices within a school building, it is good to build buy-in and input from others in the school and to speak with parents as well. Sample letters and forms you can use to promote buy-in for SMARTS are listed in Table 6.1.

TABLE 6.1. Getting Buy-In for SMARTS

Forms	Who receives/completes	Distribute	Collect (completed)	File
SMARTS Summary for Principals, Teachers, and Caregivers (Form 6.1)	Principals, teachers, caregivers	☐		
SMARTS Caregiver Letter (Form 6.2)	Caregivers	☐		
SMARTS Caregiver Consent Form (Form 6.3)	Caregivers	☐	☐	☐
SMARTS Student Assent Form (Form 6.4)	Students	☐	☐	☐
SMARTS Teacher Nomination Form (Form 6.5)	Teacher	☐	☐	☐

Note. Reproducible versions of each form are available at the end of this chapter and on the book's companion website.

Start with Principals and Teachers First

As a start, we suggest discussing the purpose, the general logistics, and the evidence of the effectiveness of the SMARTS intervention with your building administrator. It is important to involve your building and district leaders early in the process. Our experience has certainly shown that if a program or practice is not supported by building and district leaders, then that practice is viewed as less valued than other initiatives, is not implemented as intended and designed, and will therefore be less effective.

Indeed, the opposite can happen; a half-supported intervention can not only take up time and energy but might prove to be harmful for students. In prior studies of SMARTS, data have shown that in buildings where principals do not provide support for implementing SMARTS, teachers fail to contribute ratings to daily student-goal-directed behavior. The result in these cases was that students in the intervention appeared to fair worse and to display more disruptive behaviors when they saw that teachers did not contribute to daily SMARTS-goal performance ratings. So, it is key to gather principal input and request their support before investing time and resources.

After securing preliminary support from your building administrator, speak with the teachers who will be expected to do daily goal monitoring. SMARTS is designed to lessen the teacher workload burden for a Tier 2 intervention by relying on student-

Making SMARTS Work

Research shows that a principal's support for any school-based initiative, practice, or program is associated with successful implementation and sustainability of tiered interventions, leading to increased academic achievement and behavioral outcomes for students.

support personnel to train students and carry out much of the work. Nonetheless, teachers need to be consulted on the work required of them and briefed on the benefits of their classroom environments participating in SMARTS. Teacher buy-in is essential to making SMARTS work. Again, our data show that when teachers fail to engage in goal-reporting procedures for SMARTS students and then students go to review their own goals and see teachers who have not

> **Making SMARTS Work**
>
> Studies have shown that when teachers refuse to fully implement evidence-based targeted support-intervention practices in schools, it may negatively impact students' academic, emotional, and behavioral performances.

contributed daily ratings, then the SMARTS intervention loses its meaning. In these situations, data suggest that, absent teacher input, SMARTS students can experience what is known as an iatrogenic effect, or a worsening of the condition that the intervention is intended to alleviate. And if teachers do not participate, students get the sense that it does not matter, and they may even get the message that teachers who do not participate also do not care about them.

In the opposite direction, our data show that when teachers consistently contribute to daily ratings for SMARTS students, those students are likely to have better outcomes.

> **Making SMARTS Work**
>
> SMARTS was designed to lessen teacher implementation burden and structure collaboration between students, student-support personnel, and teachers. Teacher input and burden for SMARTS is the same as teacher input and burden for implementing Check-In/Check-Out.

The important part is this: The adults in the building make things matter in school through words and actions. The concept of "mattering" was mentioned in Chapter 1 as the intentional act of adding meaning and importance to an act. If you are going to select a targeted intervention to implement and teach students skills in self-monitoring and self-regulation, then all the stakeholders need to agree that this will be done well. Students need adults in their lives to make meaning and sense of the things they are asked to do, whether it is completing math homework, participating in P.E./gym class, or monitoring a behavioral goal that they are struggling with at school.

When you approach administrators and teachers, be prepared with some information from this manual so you are ready to hold informational discussions and answer questions. Here are some helpful topics to discuss in addition to a sample SMARTS-program summary found in Form 6.1:

1. Prepare for considerations before meeting with administrators and teachers about SMARTS.
   a. Consider how many students you feel you can support on a SMARTS behavior-support plan. First and foremost, consider the number of SMARTS group sessions that, with four to six students in each group, it is feasible to run in balance with your other duties, current caseload, and time needed to prep

and prepare for running SMARTS groups. With these two numbers, you can communicate the percentage of your time and effort that you need to dedicate to implementing SMARTS as well as the number of students you will support using the SMARTS program.

b. Consider how you can use existing data to identify appropriate students or simply request that teachers prioritize and nominate students who may benefit from participating in a self-monitoring and self-regulation training program.

2. Prepare for what administrators and teachers need to know about SMARTS.

a. Explain that the purpose of SMARTS is to train students in self-monitoring and self-regulation skills that will lead to better behavior and academic outcomes.

b. Explain the evidence underlying SMARTS. In Form 6.1, there is a short summary of the effects of SMARTS from prior single-subject and randomized studies to assist with a summary.

c. Discuss the need to select meeting times for the SMARTS groups. Gather input from principals and teachers to consider the best times to pull students from classes or from other school activities to participate in Phase I's training and Phase III's data-processing meetings. Phase I's training sessions consist of a short SMARTS pre-meeting and nine SMARTS skills lessons, which are a bit longer than the pre-meeting. Phase III's data-processing meetings are quicker but still need to occur once per week while the students and teachers report on student-goal performances the rest of the week.

d. Explain the process of implementing SMARTS. Form 6.1 contains a summary template of core activities and process for SMARTS to assist you with summarizing this for teachers and administrators.

3. Prepare for what parents may need to know about SMARTS.

a. Discuss the need to seek parent consent for their child to participate in SMARTS. SMARTS is a targeted behavior-support program, which means some students will be appropriate and others will not get access. In such cases, your school or district likely has policies in place for targeted behavior-support participation. Review your school's policy about obtaining parental consent in these cases.

b. Request active consent and explain that consent can be rejected by parents at any time. This book includes a suggested letter for parents/caregivers (Form 6.2) that explains the purpose and intent of SMARTS, the process, and why their child was selected to participate in SMARTS. You may use this letter or one your school or district has approved for students in need of targeted supports. This letter should be distributed in tandem with the caregiver consent form (Form 6.3) referenced in its final paragraph.

4. Prepare for what students may want to know about SMARTS.

Discuss the need to request assent from students to participate in SMARTS. It is an ethical and autonomy-supportive practice to seek student assent to participate in any targeted intervention. Assent is different from consent. Assent denotes agreement to participate provided by someone not of the age to provide legally valid consent. Consent is a process by which a guardian, who is legally able to provide consent after they are provided with information about the process of the intervention, signs a consent form indicating their willingness to permit their child under the age of 18 to participate. In Form 6.4, you will find a suggested assent script to read to students selected to participate in SMARTS. Seeking assent is an autonomy-supportive practice and in line with the spirit of both MI and SMARTS.

> **Making SMARTS Work**
>
> Be sure to actively request parent consent for implementing a targeted intervention with your students, as well as request assent from your students to participate in SMARTS; assent denotes agreement to participate from someone not of legal age to provide consent. Seeking assent is a good way to show your support for student autonomy. Example consent and assent letters can be found at the end of this chapter.

SELECTING STUDENTS FOR SMARTS

When selecting students to participate in a SMARTS group, start by using existing data to identify which students might be appropriate. If your school uses a universal social-, emotional-, or behavioral-screening tool such as the Early Identification System (EIS) teacher checklist or some other tool, then use those data to identify which students are at risk for externalizing or for self-regulation problems. This information would be helpful with selecting SMARTS students. If your school does not use a social, emotional, or behavioral health-screening system, then relying on teacher nomination is the next best way. See Form 6.5 for a usable teacher nomination. It is recommended that each teacher nominate students for a SMARTS group who are the most challenging in their classroom.

> **Making SMARTS Work**
>
> If your school uses a schoolwide or universal social-, emotional-, and behavioral-screening system that identifies students who are at high levels of risk for externalizing or self-regulation challenges to participate in SMARTS, it will be useful to use those systems that are already in place to determine if students will benefit from SMARTS. A teacher nomination list can also be found at the end of this chapter.

Once students have been selected for SMARTS—and before you send parental/caregiver consent forms home with students to participate—you may want to check in with each student who has been identified by their teacher. Table 6.2 includes several common student questions we have encountered when implementing SMARTS, followed by suggested responses.

TABLE 6.2. Common Student Questions When Selected for SMARTS Group Participation

Why was I chosen for the SMARTS group? All teachers in our school were asked to identify students who they thought could benefit from small groups. The SMARTS group will help you with setting goals that are important to you and that will help you be successful at school. SMARTS groups will also have some fun activities and tips about how to better achieve the goals you want to focus on. But before you can participate, we want to know if you want to participate, and we want to ask your caregivers if it is OK with them too.

What will happen in the SMARTS groups? There are 10 group sessions that we will go through together. Each group lesson focuses on an aspect of setting a goal and monitoring your progress for your goal. There are also skills to help you learn life skill strategies for self-regulation or self-management, skills that are important to all of us. Each lesson has a fun activity. When we are done with the 10 group sessions, you will have a goal that you have written down, and both you and your teacher will monitor your goal each week. Then we will meet to review your progress and compare your progress self-ratings to those of your teacher.

Do I have to attend the SMARTS groups? If you want to attend and your caregivers say it is OK, then we would like for you to participate. It is up to you. The groups are fun, and past students liked participating in the activities and learning new skills—but again, it is up to you. We hope you will try it out to see how it goes.

Will others (my teachers, friends, parents) know what I say in SMARTS groups? We have a rule that what you say in our SMARTS group will stay in our SMARTS group. We will have a lot of time to talk about problems, goals, and how we manage stress in our lives. I am sure that some group members will share stories you might already know, and some information could be new. We want all group members to feel safe and to share what they want. Since you will be with other students, you will want them to respect your privacy, so we must agree to respect their privacy too. Before we start the group, we will discuss the SMARTS group pledge to not share any information outside of the group, and I, too, promise not to share any information that you share in the group with anyone else, unless you say you want to hurt yourself or someone else during our group meeting. That is the only time I will have to tell someone about what was said in the group—to make sure everyone is safe. Does that sound all right?

PREVENTING RISK OF PEER CONTAGION AND IATROGENIC EFFECTS IN SMALL GROUPS

Preparedness, organization, and a skilled group leader are essential elements to running effective groups. Considerable evidence exists to support the notion that putting youth with challenging behaviors in unorganized and poorly managed group settings can—and does—result in what is referred to as *peer contagion* or *deviancy training* that can have iatrogenic or unintended negative effects (Dishion et al., 1999). That is, putting youth with challenging behaviors in the same group or setting together, absent organized and planned activity led by a competent practitioner, can cause adverse and unintended negative consequences. These consequences are particularly salient where you have youth experienced in delinquent and challenging behaviors and other youth who are referred to as late starters (Patterson et al., 2000) because they do not initiate deviant behaviors until later in life. When placed in group settings without adequate organization and supervision, studies have shown that late-starter youth can learn and be reinforced by displays of deviant and negative behavior from other more experienced group members, such that the intent of the intervention to improve behavior is not realized and instead may be unintentionally harmful. However, there are several known buffers that, if intentionally addressed, eliminate the concern for deviancy training and its iatrogenic effects.

Although there are other studies that contradict the actual power and influence of peer contagion (Gifford-Smith et al., 2005), the very risk of it is enough to cause concern and take action to prevent it. Also, as the SMARTS group facilitator, you have a vested interest in making sure the group runs smoothly. As research suggests, there are a constellation of evidence-based practice suggestions that, if followed, significantly reduce the power and impact or likelihood of peer contagion. Furthermore, many of these practices are reflected in the structure of SMARTS lessons and overall intent of SMARTS as an intervention. Here is a list of research-based, overall best practices to keep in mind as you plan and facilitate your SMARTS group lessons.

Before you meet with your group:

1. *Prepare a SMARTS folder for each student.* Once you have selected students for your groups whom you feel will get along and participate in a group together, make a folder for each student. Maintain those folders for students until the end of the group. In each folder, you can keep the SMARTS lesson checklist (see Chapter 7), any student worksheets that are completed for each SMARTS lesson, a copy of the signed SMARTS Constitution (Form 6.6), and any other SMARTS group–related documents. In addition, preparing your materials ahead of your groups will be helpful to having an organized start. See Table 6.3 for a checklist of items that you will want to have set up before you begin engaging students.

2. *Predetermine SMARTS group seating arrangements.* Before groups begin, reflect on students' social dynamics (which are always changing), engagement, and social behaviors from your prior groups with these students, and predetermine the seating arrangements. To facilitate this expectation, simply place the SMARTS group folders on the chairs or in the locations where you want students to sit and instruct them to sit where their folders are placed.

3. *Encourage timely attendance for groups.* As a part of the SMARTS group contract, encourage students to commit to attending all of the group sessions. There are several good reasons for this. First, SMARTS lessons build upon each other such that early lessons include prerequisite skills for later lessons. For example, the second SMARTS lesson focuses on skills for identifying a problem—which is sometimes the hardest part of

TABLE 6.3. Shopping List Items for SMARTS Groups

Item(s)	Have	Need
Binders for facilitators	☐	☐
Folders (with pockets) for *each* student	☐	☐
Writing utensils for facilitators and students	☐	☐
Markers	☐	☐
Chart/poster board (whiteboard can be a substitute)	☐	☐
SMARTS Jar and tokens (or punch cards)	☐	☐
Items/prizes to fill Mini-SMARTS Store	☐	☐
Full sets of worksheets for each student (extra copies are recommended for facilitators to keep on hand)	☐	☐
Facilitator lesson guides (Lessons 0–9)	☐	☐
Notepad for facilitators	☐	☐

solving the problem! If students miss this lesson, then they will not be prepared to engage in the third lesson, where we identify alternative solutions to the problem, or the fourth lesson, where students write SMART goals to implement a solution. Making attendance part of a group goal and including it in the SMARTS group contract will use the power of social expectations to encourage students to be present and to be on time.

SMARTS lesson plans include several elements that have been shown to improve instructional quality and to maximize student engagement and participation. However, a good deal of research indicates that there are many student factors and instructional practices that can improve engagement and learning for students and can also improve the success of SMARTS.

1. Studies show that younger students are more attentive to adult direction and developmentally less influenced by peers. Although this is not always the case, in general, the earlier we can start to work with students in small groups, the better positioned we are to encourage and experience positive outcomes.

2. Studies show that modeling is an effective instructional practice. Modeling is the process of learning by watching others. To learn through modeling, students should first watch you mimic the steps of a skill. This provides a visual example of what is expected

and frees students to try what is demonstrated. Each lesson has modeling built into it, but as a general strategy, it can be helpful throughout your SMARTS lessons.

3. Studies show that telling students why we are talking about a particular topic helps them see the relevance of what they are learning. SMARTS lessons start with the objectives, and, using examples, this explicit instruction helps students connect with why each of the objectives are important to them in an accessible way. Telling students why they are talking about a particular topic helps them see the relevance of the material and increases the mattering.

4. Studies show that relying on intervention agents with a master's level education and with adequate training increases the likelihood that challenging behaviors are effectively curtailed. Therefore, it is best practice to have your SMARTS group facilitator be a trained and experienced counselor or school-based practitioner.

5. Relying on school-based practitioners who already possess a relationship with the students positioned in a small group has several advantages. Take time to talk with students' teachers to find strategies that are successful with each student.
   a. Teachers know the students well and can more effectively organize groups to prevent or avoid arranging group members that have preexisting peer conflicts or prior peer problems. In the case that they are not able to effectively divide the students into separate groups, school-based practitioners can address these concerns in other ways beforehand by meeting with students, setting goals and boundaries, and directly addressing and planning to avoid peer conflicts.
   b. Teachers know the students well and can more effectively redirect inappropriate behavior.

6. Have a consistent format and structure. All SMARTS lessons follow the same format and structure each time. Utilizing a highly structured approach to guiding small groups and members' time together, SMARTS lesson plans are highly structured and follow basic best practices when instructing students. These elements of SMARTS lessons include:
   a. Detailed lists of materials needed for each lesson.
   b. A clear list of achievable objectives.
   c. Early lessons building single skills into more complex skills.
   d. Basic instructional practices in modeling preceding student practice of skills.
   e. Nonexamples and exemplary examples being built into lessons.
   f. Opportunities for students to practice skills.
   g. Active components to maintain student engagement.
   h. Each lesson ending with processing questions to encourage student reflection; along with the structured lesson, it helps to meet in a consistent location at a consistent time to maintain the feelings of structure and predictability.

7. At the first meeting, establish clear expectations and guidelines for interactions. Discuss the importance of confidentiality and set clear and fair consequences beforehand with your groups. The Pre-Meet Lesson 0 for SMARTS structures this conversation, seeks student input into the expectations, seeks agreement between students in the group about the group expectations (see Form 6.6 for the SMARTS group contract), and utilizes a group social-reward system such as the SMARTS Jar (see the following explanation) as a tool to encourage whole-group student participation and behavioral harmony during your groups.

There are also other best-practice and evidence-based approaches to managing groups: being prepared before each group, planning for students to use the bathroom, tending to the room or space that the group will meet in, and having basic needs addressed, such as safety, water, snacks, and other group supports, will help facilitate successful groups. Particular attention should be given to how students are arranged in a group such that students with deep-seated emotional or social conflicts should not, obviously, be placed in a group together. Here are other ideas to keep in mind as you start to meet with your groups:

1. ***Create an emotionally safe environment.*** Students will take appropriate risks and excel in emotionally safe contexts. Be certain to directly address name-calling, put-downs, and sarcasm in a calm and direct manner. There is no secret formula for creating an emotionally safe environment, but it starts with the group leader recognizing behavior that is not kind or contributing to safety, directly and calmly identifying what it is, and politely asking that it stop immediately.

2. ***Create a SMARTS Constitution.*** "We, the SMARTS students, in order to form a more perfect SMARTS group, establish justice, ensure domestic tranquility, provide harmony, promote general well-being, and secure the SMARTS practices for ourselves and our prosperity, do ordain and establish this SMARTS Constitution for the SMARTS group. . . ." OK, maybe we took that too far. Regardless, the idea is to generate input from your students in a creative and fun way, to develop a document that lists how SMARTS students expect their groups to run that they will all sign. In Form 6.6, you will find an example SMARTS Constitution that you can copy. It even has an amendment process added to it in case your group discovers the need to add a rule by a two-thirds, veto-proof majority!

3. ***Keep lesson introductions short.*** As soon as students get into the room and sit, get started right away. A brief greeting is OK, but do not pause. Do not linger on the introduction or purpose too much. Move directly into the main subject and get to the activities of the lesson. Be light and fun, but get down to business. Your leadership in this fashion will help students also get down to business.

4. ***Establish an "antigravity" command.*** This can be included in your SMARTS group contract and can be any word or term the group agrees upon. This means you physically freeze, your eyeballs don't move, you can't speak, and students should hold their breath! Then, whenever you or anyone in the group uses the predetermined and agreed-upon command, all group members agree to freeze and go into suspended animation in whatever physical position they are in. Practice this a few times occasionally to be sure students are paying attention and to reinforce the meaning of the antigravity command.

5. ***Keep any feedback short and to the point.*** Each SMARTS lesson plan ends with suggested processing questions for student groups. However, always direct your questions in a manner that challenges your students to explain the most important features of what happened during the group. That is, focus on *what* happened, *why* it happened, and *what* it means considering the lesson topic. It is also good to point out what worked well and what could work better next time. Avoid long lectures on the benefits and finer points underlying the lesson, as these could be counterproductive and cause students to lose attention and the meaning of the activity. As the facilitator, you have dual roles in the feedback process. The first role is to decide how the discussion will take place. Make sure students are finished with the activity and are ready to hear what you and others say. Your second role is that of question generator. There are suggested processing questions at the end of each lesson, but these are only suggestions. By observing students, you may wish to include other questions. Stress the following as you process with students:

  a. There are no right or wrong answers. Be cautious of overly praising a student for providing an "excellent" answer, as it cues students to think there are right answers.

  b. Use standard follow-up comments such as "thanks for sharing" or a good-ol' "OK."

  c. Allow silence once you ask a question. Students may not always jump to answer, so allowing a space for them to choose to answer is a good strategy. You can also use an alternative. Ask yes-or-no questions. Have students each raise their hand in unison if they feel the response is a *yes*, use thumbs-up or thumbs-down, or hand in slips of paper with their answers written on them.

6. ***Reinforce the need for students to share opinions.*** Through discussions, reinforce students who share thoughtful opinions, thank them for sharing, and encourage the valuing of those opinions. It is also important to identify an opinion of your own, encourage students to do the same, and ask others if it is OK if they share their opinions too.

7. ***Use persistent persuasion and permission.*** At times, you, the facilitator, will have to restate requests while maintaining control of your tone, posture, and eye contact until a student agrees to follow through. There are two crucial elements to persistent persuasion. First, kindly refuse to relent until there is a resolution to the request. Second, do not escalate a power struggle or deepen the demand. If you feel you need an off-ramp

in case a student does want to escalate a situation, then make the conscious choice to give the student permission to refuse. Do this by saying, "I can see that you are not in a place where you want to _____ right at this moment. Let me give you a minute, and I will come back to you." When you return to the issue, it might be best to negotiate with the student by asking what it is that you can do for them in that moment or simply ask what they need to move forward. Negotiation is an excellent skill and should be celebrated. This is not to say that you should give away the store, so to speak, but to choose battles carefully and listen to your students' requests and see what it is they need. Once established, the likelihood increases that the strategy will work in the future.

STRATEGIES FOR MANAGING OVERLY CHALLENGING STUDENTS

As a SMARTS group leader, you can put in place all of the suggestions we discussed, have students sign a SMARTS-group contract expressing all expectations, rely on your best-practice skills and tremendous patience, and remind students in a kind tone about the structure and ground rules of the group. Predictably, there will still be one student who will need additional guidance, or days where all of your SMARTS students are just not following the game plan. This should be expected; it is also certain to happen. The best crystal ball cannot tell you exactly when it will occur or how it will look, but as a group leader and professional who knows their students best, you should be certain there will be students and days when everyone is doing their best, but one or more group members will violate the SMARTS-group contract. It helps to have a few preplanned strategies to try in the moment:

1. *Use proximity and movement.* Use your best prediction to consider who is in the group, who might experience some challenges in paying attention, who might be a bit chattier than others, or who is the most provocative and unregulated. Then, when determining seating for SMARTS group members, place who you predict to be the most challenging student right next to you. Alternatively, if you prefer not to sit, use movement to your advantage during your group session. That is, when you see group members getting off task or derailing the goal of your lesson for that group, move near those students. If appropriate and you know your students well enough, a light touch on the shoulder or upper arm will communicate that you are present and will draw attention to the moment—but do not always assume that a light touch will be appreciated by all students. Always be prepared to have students stand, stretch, and switch seating if you need to maintain focus.

2. *Use co-regulation with dysregulated students.* Co-regulation refers to the process of providing external support to help a dysregulated child modulate their hyper-arousal. If a student is having a hard time maintaining, approach that situation calmly

and help them sort out the issue while demonstrating co-regulation or the capacity to help them regulate modeling behaviors with these strategies in mind:

   a. Stay calm and regulate yourself.
   b. Create a safe and a predictable environment.
   c. Validate their emotions—show empathy for how they are feeling.
   d. Use calming strategies—breathing, counting to 10, or using a sensory object.
   e. Offer choices and support or promote the student's autonomy.

   3. *Use behavioral propulsion.* Behavioral propulsion is a strategy used to increase compliance and cooperation by setting up a series of easy tasks or requests, followed by a more challenging one. In behavioral propulsion—or behavioral momentum, as it is sometimes called—there are two types of behaviors: low-probability behaviors and high-probability behaviors. Low-probability behaviors are requests for acts that students may resist or that they are less likely to comply with. High-probability behaviors are requests for acts that students see as more desirable and are more likely to comply with. Knowing your students and noting the differences between things they are likely to comply with and things they may resist will be a good first step. When you experience resistance, behavioral momentum starts with:

   a. The "two or three before me" rule, by applying two or three high-probability requests, acknowledging effort and thanking them for following through, and then immediately following up with a low-probability request
   b. Following compliance of the low-probability request with appreciative and positive recognition
   c. Keeping the momentum going by minimizing delays or interruptions for the next task and gradually increasing the difficulty over time

It is suggested to keep a log of high-probability requests. Treat these requests as tasks that can be completed by the student to help you, easy tasks that need to be accomplished, and ones that will be very much appreciated.

   4. *Ignore the ignorable.* Ignoring negative behavior and comments can be an effective strategy for discouraging and extinguishing unwanted behaviors. It always helps to recognize the intentions of the behaviors; by understanding the motive or function, you can better determine when and how to ignore them and redirect your attention to appropriate behaviors/comments in a way that feeds the reason behind why the student engages in those negative behaviors. You can ignore certain behaviors by redirecting attention to the next item on the lesson plan, recognizing another student who is presenting desirable behaviors, and by setting up or using nonverbal cues for repetitive negative behaviors that keep appearing.

   5. *Praise expected behavior.* Praising positive behavior in students is an effective way to motivate and reinforce desirable actions. When praising students, be genuine and

specific about what exactly you are praising. Instead of a general "good job," be specific in your feedback and identify what exactly you liked about the display, such as, "I really appreciate the way you helped your SMARTS groupmate with graphing their data from last week. Your patience and willingness are incredible. Nice work." Other tips for providing positive feedback include:

a. Provide feedback near the behavioral occurrence.
b. Use nonverbal cues such as a thumbs-up. Some students do not like to be praised verbally in public and may prefer this more low-key approach.
c. Use a nickname if the student is OK with it. Using a nickname or other personalized approaches tailors your feedback. If you are not sure if a student will appreciate a nickname, just ask if it is OK. Simply asking can communicate great respect for the student.
d. Be consistent and fair. Do your best to use praise with all your group members to avoid even the perception of favoritism.
e. Focus on efforts, not outcomes. This type of feedback and praise appreciates hard work and recognizes that it is just as important to do your best and try your hardest as it is to get a thing correct or right.

6. ***Directly address significant or repeated violations of group expectations.*** Confronting inappropriate behavior is important for maintaining a respectful and healthy SMARTS group setting. Repeated violations of the rules, or one violation that is so egregious that everyone sees and notices it for what it is, must be addressed. To address the behavior and still maintain the relationship that you are working hard to build with that student, here are some helpful guidelines:

a. Address the behavior right away.
b. Remain calm and check your body language.
c. Be specific and objective—that is, address the behavior.
d. Use an "I" statement to express your concern.
e. Refer to the SMARTS-group contract about how the behavior violates that agreement.
f. Seek their perspective and listen actively; agree to discuss in more detail after the group.
g. Set clear expectations about professional behavior.
h. Offer guidance and support for how the student can get what they want another way.

7. ***Establish a time-out.*** In cases where a student is repeatedly disrupting the goals of the rest of the group, it might be time for a time-out. To be most successful, establish and discuss the time-out before having to use it as a strategy. Establish clear guidelines for when and how the time-out will be implemented. Preselect an appropriate time-out location. Develop a duration for the time-out beforehand. Lay out the process for stu-

dents and be sure to discuss or debrief the situation with the student after a time-out is completed. Be sure to use a time-out with consistency and fairness and always regulate yourself when implementing a time-out so as not to escalate the situation. We all need a time-out, and as educators we should treat a time-out as an educational tool for teaching and never use it for punitive purposes.

8. *Roll with resistance.* SMARTS, being a self-management and self-regulation training strategy that seeks to increase internal motivation in students to make changes that benefit them in school, fits well with the concepts embedded in MI as detailed in Chapter 5. MI is an evidence-based approach that focuses on facilitating a conversation that seeks to resolve ambiguity toward positive behavior change. MI connects many conversational practices that are aimed at enhancing internal motivation as well, and one of these practices is specific to working with students who may be particularly challenging. This key MI principle is known as "rolling with resistance." Rolling with resistance involves responding to resistance or ambivalence in a nonconfrontational and collaborative manner. Rather than directly challenging or confronting resistance, MI recognizes it as a normal part of the change process and aims to better understand the source of resistance. Thus, the term *resistance* has been replaced by the less pejorative *sustain talk* in more recent editions of MI books. Sustain talk just refers to language that someone uses that expresses disinterest in or ambivalence about changing. It is contrasted by change talk, which is language indicating an interest in or intent to change. Here are some key features of rolling with resistance in MI:

a. Meet sustain talk with acceptance and empathy.
b. Rely on active and reflective listening.
c. Avoid arguing at all costs.
d. Look for words that signal change talk and reflect it or ask them to elaborate on it.
e. Try shifting your perspective.
f. Explore ambivalence to change.

The principle of rolling with resistance recognizes that all of us feel ambivalence about change and that the most helpful responses to this ambivalence are acceptance, empathy, and a collaborative approach. By doing so, MI and SMARTS seek to explore, understand, and resolve ambivalence toward change and spark increased internalized motivation to follow a goal for change.

USING THE SMARTS JAR OR SIMILAR TOKEN SYSTEM

A "SMARTS Jar" is a creative and constructive way to reinforce and acknowledge positive behaviors and achievements by SMARTS students during Phase I: SMARTS Student

Training. The SMARTS Jar can be a fun and motivating tool, albeit externally motivating (though fun is helpful to move a student from external toward integrating or internalizing their motivation for SMARTS). A SMARTS Jar is a great way to promote desired behaviors and encourage a sense of group cohesion and cooperation, especially in combination with the suggestions for group-behavior support, outlined in Form 6.7. Here is how to use the SMARTS Jar:

1. *Choose a SMARTS container and fill it.* In our studies of SMARTS, we used a 2-quart-sized mason jar or some other large, translucent container. It is important that the SMARTS Jars be translucent containers so students can see inside of them. We then placed one ring of tape around each jar at the midpoint and a second ring of colored tape at the top of each one. The two lines (see Figure 6.1) represent a finish line or mark that, when reached, indicate that a successful group goal has been achieved. For SMARTS Jar filler, we first opted to use glass beads. We did find that some students who were overstressed found the sound of the glass beads hitting the jar to cause some aggravation, so in those groups, we used cotton balls. The idea is that, when students engage in prosocial group behaviors or respond to questions or complement each other, the facilitator drops a glass bead or cotton ball into the SMARTS Jar. It is important to reward intergroup

FIGURE 6.1. SMARTS Jar. *Note.* Mark the sides of the SMARTS Jar at a few intervals with a reward. Check to make sure it won't take too many or too few tokens to reach each level so you can reasonably space out and reach goals as the lessons progress! Photo by authors.

prosocial behaviors as well as participation, though your groups may have other goals they want to work toward as well.

2. *Set clear criteria.* Determine what you are experiencing as a challenge for your SMARTS group. Each group can be different and will have different challenges. Then list those specific behaviors in a clear view. Or better yet, when having the initial SMARTS pre-lesson to talk with your SMARTS students about group expectations, list the groups' expectations from their SMARTS Constitution on a poster or a whiteboard where those expectations can be referenced throughout your group lessons. For example, when working with youth who are less apt to participate or speak up, commit to dropping a bead or cotton ball into the jar.

3. *Determine rewards.* The group should select group rewards—a pizza party, playing a game, or even an ice cream party. The goal should be motivating for the group as a whole. If reaching the goal is challenging, then determine a small goal at the halfway point and a larger goal for when the jar fill hits the jar's top ring of tape. Selecting rewards that have a social element to them is also a great idea, so with a pizza party, each student gets to share their favorite song or some other thing they really like. This gives students a chance to coalesce and build cohesion around a common but diverse set of interests.

4. *Celebrate victorious milestones.* Recognize at the end of each group how far along the group is to achieving its goal. Celebrate when they are halfway, project out the remaining time to goal success, and ask students if there is a way to excel their progress toward the group goal.

5. *Maintain consistency and fairness.* If the group values input and sharing as a group goal, then be sure to reward that at all times when students demonstrate it. And be ready to adjust the plan if you need to. For example, if one student seems keen on picking up the slack for others, then be sure to encourage participation and take a break from providing fill to the SMARTS Jar for the behavior(s) of just one or two group members. After all, it is a group goal. If needed, address this issue through an amendment to the SMARTS Constitution.

6. *Recognize and reinforce intrinsic motivation.* When your SMARTS students are displaying moments of genuine engagement with the activities, cooperation and togetherness, and enjoyment with each other and in your group, be sure to encourage that and reward your students in that moment. The reward can be a positive compliment to the group or a promise of a social reward later (e.g., lunch from the cafeteria with your group, extra group time to listen to music, or hanging out in your office). The point here is to exercise and reward your students' displays of intrinsic motivation by highlighting them when you see them and by recognizing the positive feelings, personal growth, and senses of achievement that come from positive interactions and achieving goals.

TABLE 6.4. Checklist of Posttest Data

Forms	Who receives/ completes	Distribute	Collected (completed)
SMARTS Intervention Checklist — Student Report (Form 6.11)	Student	☐	☐
SMARTS Intervention Rating Scale— Student Report (Form 6.12)	Student	☐	☐
SMARTS Intervention Rating Scale— Teacher Report (Form 6.13)	Teacher	☐	☐

Note. Reproducible versions of each letter or form are available at the end of this chapter and on the book's companion website.

MEASURING AND SHARING CHANGE

We live in a data-driven era. Collecting and sharing data is not only an ethical requirement of helping professions, but data will help you demonstrate the effectiveness of what you do with your students. The feedback forms in this chapter, which can be distributed to teachers and students for completion, can be downloaded and printed from the book's companion website (see the box at the end of the contents page). These fidelity tools can assist you with collecting information about what students and teachers find helpful in regard to SMARTS. Although these tools do not establish whether students are improving as an outcome, outcome improvement can be established through the use of simple pre- and posttest measures or through viewing the SMARTS self-monitoring and teacher daily-rating data that reflect whether or not students are following their goals. In addition, Table 6.4 lists several forms that will gauge student feedback about how involved and autonomy supportive they felt SMARTS to be, whether or not they liked SMARTS, and whether or not teachers also felt SMARTS to be helpful. Collecting this information will assist you with improving your delivery of SMARTS or any other intervention.

SUMMARY

In summary, when you are running groups that include dysregulated youth, the most important factor is to create a safe and predictable environment. Being organized and prepared is a big step in this process. In this chapter, we provided a list of strategies to help you prepare for introducing SMARTS. To help keep you organized, here is a summary of all that we covered:

- Introducing SMARTS school leadership, teaching colleagues, and students. See the forms included with this chapter for example letters and information about how to best introduce SMARTS.
- Selecting students for SMARTS: Use existing data or social-, emotional-, and behavioral-screening systems that may already be in place. Identify students with externalizing or self-regulation challenges first.
- We also provided several steps for you to consider as you prepare for SMARTS.
- Collecting consent and assent for student participation: See Forms 6.3 and 6.4 for example parent/caregiver consent and student assent forms.
- We discussed organizing your students into groups.
- Preparing a SMARTS Facilitator Binder for yourself as the implementer. The following items are helpful to prepare for implementing SMARTS and are included as reproducible forms in this manual:
  - Extra SMARTS punch cards/tokens (Form 6.8).
  - A set of SMARTS lesson guides (Lessons 0–9; see Chapter 7).
  - An extra copy of each SMARTS worksheet for students (see forms in Chapter 7).
  - A completed copy of the SMARTS Student–Teacher Goal Input Contract, completed by both teacher and student (Form 6.9). *One per student.*
  - Grade-appropriate SMARTS Phase II Goal Form for Teacher and Self-Monitoring (e.g., kindergarten, grades 1–3, grades 4–5). *Keep multiple copies on hand for students and teachers* (Forms 8.1–8.3).
  - SMARTS Phase III: SMARTS Data Processing and Goal Reformation Guide. *Keep multiple copies on hand for each student meeting* (Form 9.2).
  - SMARTS Process Fidelity Tracking Form (Form 6.10). *Keep one per student.*
  - SMARTS Intervention Checklist—Student Report (Form 6.11). *One per student.*
  - SMARTS Intervention Rating Scale—Student Report (Form 6.12). *One per student.*
  - SMARTS Intervention Rating Scale—Teacher Report (Form 6.13).
- Prepare a SMARTS folder for each student. These should include:
  - A copy of each lesson worksheet.
  - A SMARTS punch card or other token system in use at your school.
  - A few pieces of scrap paper and a pencil or a pen.
- Select and prepare at least two strategies to use during SMARTS student training in case of an overly challenging or reluctant student.
- Rely on the suggested SMARTS Jar and Mini-SMARTS Store behavior support plan (Form 6.7), or use your school's token economy system to promote appropriate behavior during groups.
- Collect pre- and posttest data as well as fidelity data to identify changes in your SMARTS student groups. Remember, daily student and teacher ratings can be used as an outcome to demonstrate change.

Preparing for your SMARTS groups demonstrates self-management and autonomy. Remember, the youth in your SMARTS groups are there to learn and practice self-management and self-regulation strategies, so it is good to demonstrate that from the start. And it is important to remember those youth developed their present dysregulated strategies by possible exposure to unorganized, unsafe, and unpredictable places and people. Indeed, rather than thinking of these youth as dysregulated or as lacking self-control skills, we should see them as overstressed. Youth who are hyperaroused or chronically spaced out are not lacking self-control or not trying hard enough; misbehavior is often a sign of stress overload. These youth need positive adult figures in their lives to model self-management and to share safe contexts with them in which to practice these skills. Being organized and prepared before your SMARTS groups will help your groups be successful. If you feel prepared and organized, the skills included in SMARTS will be important skills for your students to learn that will help them manage the normal and inevitable stresses throughout the rest of their lives.

SMARTS Summary for Principals, Teachers, and Caregivers

The *Self-Monitoring And Regulation Training Strategy (SMARTS)* was developed with input from students, teachers, and educational professionals to teach students skills in goal setting, self-monitoring, and self-regulation. SMARTS is best described in the following three phases for Student Training, Self- and Teacher Monitoring, and Data Processing.

Phase I: Student Training

Student training consists of 10 small group sessions (four to six students per group), each lasting 40–45 minutes and run by the SMARTS Facilitator. It is best to work through these lessons sequentially by holding at least two lessons per week. One thing we will need to determine is the best meeting time to pull SMARTS students from the classroom. For student training, the SMARTS Facilitator will lead the 10 lessons to train SMARTS students in the following concepts:

1. Pre-Group Meeting
2. Defining and Assessing Problems
3. Generating Alternative Solutions to Problems
4. Defining a Goal and Monitoring Goal Progress
5. Revisiting Goals and Replacement Strategies to Observe and Record Progress
6. Using Data and Graphs to Evaluate Goal Progress
7. Taking the Perspective of Others
8. Reframing Failure/Mistakes as Part of Learning
9. Recognizing Internal Responses to Problems
10. Managing External Responses to Problems

Phase II: Student Self- and Teacher Monitoring

Following Lesson 5, SMARTS students will have an individualized goal to monitor in the classroom throughout the day. It is important that teachers know what the students' SMARTS goals are and that they will be expected to rate students' performances toward those goals at each interval by selecting whether or not the students worked toward the goals during the previous interval.

It is essential that all teachers participate in the SMARTS intervention. To better facilitate teacher input, we have set up goal monitoring so that it can be quick and simple during the school day and so teacher participation will improve both their relationships with the individual SMARTS participants and the classroom atmosphere.

Phase III: Processing Self- and Teacher Data

During the processing phase, school support personnel will meet with SMARTS student groups once per week for approximately 10–20 minutes. Students' and teachers' daily observations collected through the week should be available on Form 9.1, SMARTS Phase III Processing: Self-Monitoring and Teacher Feedback Graphing Form.

Explain each person's role for successfully implementing SMARTS. These roles are defined here:

(continued)

SMARTS Summary for Principals, Teachers, and Caregivers *(page 2 of 2)*

SMARTS Facilitator: This role organizes, with teacher input, SMARTS groups and prepares and facilitates those groups; meets with students for 10 Phase I group-training sessions and then weekly during Phase II's self- and teacher-goal monitoring; and encourages students to consider classroom performance and appropriate goals that will assist them with improving classroom behavior and school success.

Teachers: Teachers check students' goals weekly by asking them about these goals or by reviewing the contract and goal sheet on the app or provided by the SMARTS Facilitator; consistently provides thoughtful ratings and comments on students' performances using the website or goal-rating form.

Students: Students attend group trainings, do their best to participate in group trainings, select goals that will help them improve in the classroom, and daily rate their performances on those goals, as well as thoughtfully consider how they are doing with their goals compared to their own ratings, their teachers' ratings, and their prior performances.

SMARTS Caregiver Letter

Date:

RE: Your child's participation in SMARTS at school

Dear Caregiver,

Our school is implementing a new program for students called the **S**elf-Monitoring **A**nd **R**egulation **T**raining **S**trategy **(SMARTS)**. SMARTS is a skills training program that provides instruction to students in goal setting, self-monitoring of goal performance, and self-regulation skills. Your child was selected for participation in this program because your child's teacher felt they may benefit from participating in SMARTS.

If you agree to allow your child to participate in the study, your child will participate in 10 small-group lessons that will focus on goal setting, self-monitoring of that goal, and self-regulation strategies. More specifically, SMARTS lessons include skills in identifying and defining problems, creating goals to solve problems, skills to monitor performance of those goals, and strategies for relaxation and dealing with stressful events. After the training, your child and the classroom teacher will monitor your child on the same goals that your child creates during the training. Your child will then attend a weekly meeting to compare the differences between their goal-monitoring data and the teacher's goal-monitoring data. These discussions will be helpful to assisting your child in rewriting new goals to succeed in school.

Should you agree to allow your child to participate, please sign and return one of the enclosed consent forms. You can keep the other form for your records. We hope you will agree to allow your child to participate in SMARTS. However, please know that you do not have to consent, and you can withdraw it at any time. Thank you and please contact me at the number below if you have any questions.

Sincerely,

SMARTS Facilitator

Phone: (   )   -

Email:

SMARTS Caregiver Consent Form

SMARTS Student: **Date:**

You are being asked to allow your child to participate in a support program at school—to participate is voluntary, and you or your child may refuse or you may withdraw your permission for your child to participate, for any reason, without penalty. Even if you give your permission, your child can still decide not to participate and they may decline participation at any time without penalty.

What is the program? The program is called *The **S**elf-**M**onitoring **A**nd **R**egulation **T**raining **S**trategy* (**SMARTS**).

Why is my child being asked to participate in SMARTS? Your child is being invited to participate in the SMARTS intervention because your child was nominated by the teacher as a student who could benefit from the program.

What will happen in SMARTS? SMARTS consists of three phases. In Phase I, SMARTS has 10 lessons in goal-setting, self-monitoring, and self-regulation skills that will be led/taught by _____ at your child's school. These meetings will take place on _____ each week. In Phase II, your child and the teacher will monitor or rate your child's performance on a goal your child selects each day. The data or ratings from each day will be graphed and your child will compare their data to their goal, prior performance, and their teacher's data as well. Then, your child will rewrite that goal and repeat Phases II and III.

What if you or your child has questions about SMARTS? If either you and your child have any questions, please contact _____ at (___) ___-_____ or email me at _____.

CAREGIVER'S Agreement: I have read the information provided above and my signature indicates that I have asked all the questions I have at this time and that I give permission to allow my child to participate in the SMARTS program.

Parent: _____   Date: _____

SMARTS Student Assent Form

You have been selected to participate in a program being offered at your school called The *Self-Monitoring **And** Regulation Training **S**trategy* **(SMARTS)**. You have been selected to participate because your teacher suggested you may benefit from training in goal-setting, self-monitoring, self-regulation skills.

What will happen?

- You will be asked to participate in 10 small-group activities.
- You will be asked to monitor your own goals using a daily SMARTS goal card.
- Your teacher will also monitor your goals using a similar card.
- At the end of each week, you and your SMARTS Facilitator will compare the differences between your scores and your teacher's scores.
- You will be asked to rewrite a goal to reduce the differences in the scores.
- We will continue to rewrite and monitor a goal until we feel we have successfully achieved that goal or another goal is selected.

Do my parents know I am participating in SMARTS?

Yes, your caregiver signed a consent form.

Do I have to participate in SMARTS?

You can quit participating at any time you wish.

Ask the student:

"Do you have any questions about anything I have said so far? *(Pause)* Would you like to participate in the SMARTS program?"

If yes, sign below:

_____   _____
SMARTS Student Signature   Date

_____   _____
Student-Support Personnel Signature   Date

SMARTS Teacher Nomination Form

Dear Colleague:

In order of priority, please list the students in your class who you believe could benefit from participating in SMARTS. SMARTS is a small group, targeted intervention that imparts skills in goal-setting, self-monitoring, and self-regulation skills and has been shown to be effective with helping elementary students learn better behavior-management skills. The students who may have some challenges with following rules, attentional control, or otherwise display externalizing behaviors would be the best students to nominate for participating in SMARTS.

List students here from most in need to least in need of SMARTS:

1. _____

2. _____

3. _____

4. _____

5. _____

6. _____

7. _____

8. _____

SMARTS Group Constitution

by and between

_____

(SMARTS Student Group Name)

and

_____

(SMARTS Group Facilitator Name)

SMARTS Constitution Preamble

This Memorandum of Understanding ("MOU") is entered into effective (date) _____, by and between the SMARTS Student Group henceforth named _____ and the SMARTS group facilitator to be known as, _____. Both undersigned entities shall be referred to collectively as the "Parties" or individually as "Party" for the purposes of this agreement.

SMARTS Constitution Background

Whereas the Parties did meet on ("effective date") _____ and agreed to abide by, respect, accept, discuss, and develop shared meaning agreeable to each Party, the following set of expectations for the explicit purpose of overseeing and executing the tasks, activities, and work needed to fulfill the SMARTS program goals, the specific set of expectations, roles, and responsibilities of each Party and collectively Parties are enumerated henceforth as:

1. _____   5. _____

2. _____   6. _____

3. _____   7. _____

4. _____

SMARTS Constitution Amendments and Duration

This MOU is subject to amendment subsequent to its signing if both Parties agree _AND_ the SMARTS Student Group agrees by a two-thirds majority that an above-listed expectation requires further clarification, or a new expectation is required to be added to facilitate the harmony and health of the Parties in pursuit of achieving the SMARTS program goals. The terms of this MOU shall commence on the effective date and end on _____.

Executed by the duly authorized Parties below:

SMARTS Student Group Name: _____

Student: _____   Student: _____

Student: _____   Student: _____

Student: _____   Student: _____

Student: _____   Student: _____

SMARTS Jar and Mini-SMARTS Store—Group Behavior Support

SMARTS Jar Behavior-Support System

In addition to positive teaching behaviors, SMARTS Facilitators may opt to use a token behavior-reinforcement system. Called the "SMARTS Jar," this tangible token system will help maintain motivation to participate in the SMARTS Phase I lessons along with the Mini-SMARTS Bucks Punch Card (Form 6.8). As students engage during lesson activities, the SMARTS implementer puts one or more marbles in the jar for student responses. The approach can be tailored to the unique needs of the group. If one student struggles with participation, they might receive two or three marbles for their responses. It can also be used as a behavior-management tool. If students have a hard time monitoring their volume, then they might receive a few marbles following several minutes of appropriate loudness. Marbles can be added for both individuals and group efforts, thus creating a sense of unity in the small group.

A common struggle with systems of reinforcement is that they often focus only on either immediate or long-term rewards. Some students might not have the maturity to connect immediate behavior with a long-term reward. The SMARTS Jar allows implementers to establish smaller rewards on the way to earning a larger group reward such as a pizza party.

The Mini-SMARTS Behavior Support Plan

Describe to students that they can receive Mini-SMARTS Bucks (fake dollars or tokens, you decide what works for you). Students earn Mini-SMARTS Bucks for respecting group expectations. When using the SMARTS behavior-support system, be sure to:

1. Start each SMARTS group by reviewing the agreed-upon expectations.
2. Emphasize expectations with SMARTS points consistently and highlight why.
3. Keep the group moving at a swift pace.
4. Ask students what they would like to have available in their Mini-SMARTS Store.
5. Set both individual student and a SMARTS group goals (student snacks after group, weekly SMARTS group donut party).
6. Provide immediate consequences for noncompliance in a clam manner.
7. Not take away SMARTS Bucks once a student earns that reward.

The Mini-SMARTS Store: How It Works

Student-support personnel work with students in the pre-meeting lesson to establish expectations for the SMARTS group. At each meeting, review with students in a positive and clear voice the expectations. Then, as you proceed through the lesson:

1. Have Mini-SMARTS Bucks punch cards ready to handout (see Form 6.8).
2. Work through the lesson and when a student observes a group expectation, say, "Thank you for . . ." (highlight the expectation) and offer the Mini-SMARTS token.
3. Permit students to trade the tokens at the end of the group for a small snack.
4. Count all student Mini-SMARTS Bucks punches toward the group goal.

Alternatively, if your school has a system in place for acknowledging and rewarding student behavior and positive social choices, it is suggested you integrate that system into your group.

Mini-SMARTS Bucks Punch Card

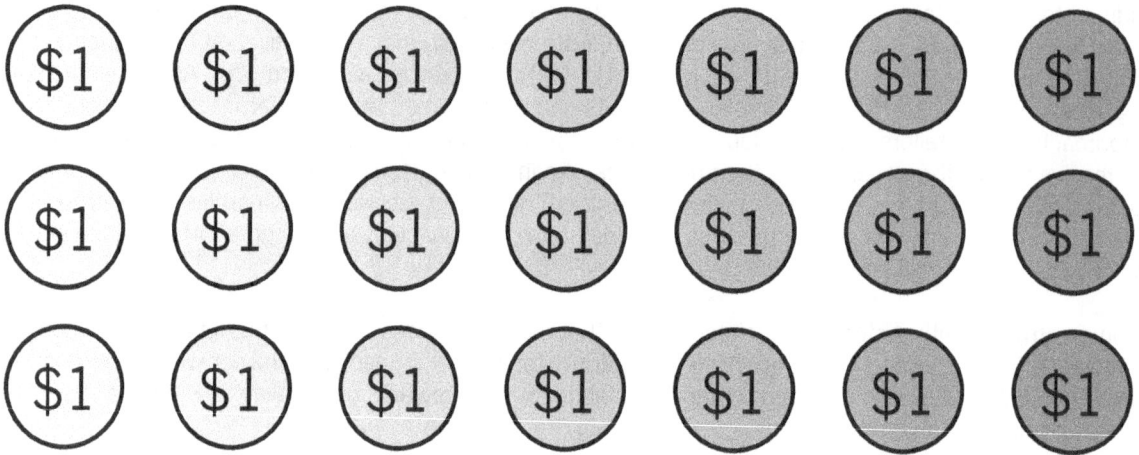

$1 $1 $1 $1 $1 $1 $1

$1 $1 $1 $1 $1 $1 $1

$1 $1 $1 $1 $1 $1 $1

SMARTS

Name: _____

SMARTS Student–Teacher Goal Input

SMARTS Student: _____   **Date:** _____

Teacher Input: Please list three of the top improvements that your student can select from to improve classroom performance.

1. _____
2. _____
3. _____

Student Input: Please list three of the top improvements that you feel you can do that will improve your classroom performance.

1. _____
2. _____
3. _____

Collaborative Input: Using the above information and language that describes a behavior that could be improved upon, write a goal that includes your teacher's input, your input, and that is something specific, measurable, achievable, realistic, and time bound.

Goal: _____

_____

_____

Teacher Name: _____

SMARTS Student: _____

SMARTS Fidelity Checklist

Phase I: Student Training. Place the start and stop time of each lesson in the boxes on days that students attend trainings.

Student Study ID	Comments	1	2	3	4	5	6	7	8	9

Phase II: Student Self-Monitoring

List only the dates that students did not self-monitor (i.e., no self- or teacher-monitoring data):

Phase III: Student Data-Review Meetings

a. List the date for each weekly data-processing form completed by students:

1	10	19	28
2	11	20	29
3	12	21	30
4	13	22	31
5	14	23	32
6	15	24	33
7	16	25	34
8	17	26	35
9	18	27	36

b. List the date for each weekly contract signed by students and teachers:

1	10	19	28
2	11	20	29
3	12	21	30
4	13	22	31
5	14	23	32
6	15	24	33
7	16	25	34
8	17	26	35
9	18	27	36

SMARTS Intervention Checklist—Student Report

Students complete this form after participating.

Please circle the answer the best expresses your experiences with SMARTS.

1. **The self-monitoring part of *SMARTS* was easy for me.**

    1-always   2-often   3-sometimes   4-rarely   5-never

2. **My *SMARTS* data was easy to compare to my teacher's data.**

    1-always   2-often   3-sometimes   4-rarely   5-never

3. **Writing goals was easy with *SMARTS* data.**

    1-always   2-often   3-sometimes   4-rarely   5-never

4. **I was involved in selecting my goals in *SMARTS.***

    1-always   2-often   3-sometimes   4-rarely   5-never

5. **I was involved in creating the definition of problems in *SMARTS*.**

    1-always   2-often   3-sometimes   4-rarely   5-never

6. **I got to help pick rewards with *SMARTS*.**

    1-always   2-often   3-sometimes   4-rarely   5-never

7. **I selected the percent of improvement on my goals with *SMARTS*.**

    1-always   2-often   3-sometimes   4-rarely   5-never

8. **I was responsible for recording my performance on my goals in *SMARTS*.**

    1-always   2-often   3-sometimes   4-rarely   5-never

9. **I was responsible for comparing my data with my teacher's data in *SMARTS*.**

    1-always   2-often   3-sometimes   4-rarely   5-never

Thank you for your SMARTS!

SMARTS Intervention Rating Scale—Student Report

Students complete this form after participating.

Please circle the answer the best expresses your experience with *SMARTS*.

1. *SMARTS* was fun.

       1-always   2-often   3-sometimes   4-rarely   5-never

2. *SMARTS* helped improve my behavior.

       1-always   2-often   3-sometimes   4-rarely   5-never

3. I wanted to monitor my own goals with *SMARTS*.

       1-always   2-often   3-sometimes   4-rarely   5-never

4. *SMARTS* helped me get along better with my teacher.

       1-always   2-often   3-sometimes   4-rarely   5-never

5. *SMARTS* made school more fun.

       1-always   2-often   3-sometimes   4-rarely   5-never

6. *SMARTS* caused problems for me with my friends.

       1-always   2-often   3-sometimes   4-rarely   5-never

7. I have more friends now that I participated in *SMARTS*.

       1-always   2-often   3-sometimes   4-rarely   5-never

8. I liked the activities in *SMARTS*.

       1-always   2-often   3-sometimes   4-rarely   5-never

9. I use the strategies I learned in *SMARTS*.

       1-always   2-often   3-sometimes   4-rarely   5-never

Thank you for your SMARTS!

SMARTS Intervention Rating Scale—Teacher Report

1. The intervention was appropriate for an elementary school.

   1-always   2-often   3-sometimes   4-rarely   5-never

2. The intervention was appropriate for elementary students.

   1-always   2-often   3-sometimes   4-rarely   5-never

3. I would suggest the use of this intervention to other teachers.

   1-always   2-often   3-sometimes   4-rarely   5-never

4. The intervention helped our school achieve schoolwide goals of positive behavior.

   1-always   2-often   3-sometimes   4-rarely   5-never

5. I will continue to use this intervention.

   1-always   2-often   3-sometimes   4-rarely   5-never

6. The intervention resulted in negative side effects for students.

   1-always   2-often   3-sometimes   4-rarely   5-never

7. The intervention was appropriate for all students who participated.

   1-always   2-often   3-sometimes   4-rarely   5-never

8. The intervention fit well into the schoolwide system of positive behavior support.

   1-always   2-often   3-sometimes   4-rarely   5-never

9. The intervention manual was clear in achieving intervention goals.

   1-always   2-often   3-sometimes   4-rarely   5-never

10. The intervention was reasonable to implement.

   1-always   2-often   3-sometimes   4-rarely   5-never

11. The monitoring procedures were reasonable for students.

   1-always   2-often   3-sometimes   4-rarely   5-never

12. The monitoring procedures were reasonable for teachers.

   1-always   2-often   3-sometimes   4-rarely   5-never

13. The monitoring data provide necessary data to change behavioral goals.

   1-always   2-often   3-sometimes   4-rarely   5-never

Thank you for your SMARTS!

CHAPTER 7

SMARTS Phase I
Student Training Lesson Plans

In this chapter, we have included all 10 lessons and student worksheets for Phase I: SMARTS Student Training. Each lesson plan is provided so that each should be presented to students. It is important to teach each lesson in Phase I in the order it is presented, as each lesson builds on the next, providing the foundation for sequential lessons. The pre-group guidelines are intended to provide facilitators with helpful considerations and pre-implementation steps that were identified from prior studies and participant feedback to introduce the intervention to elementary students and lay the groundwork for a successful group. Specifically, in this chapter, we review the following Phase I: SMARTS Student Training lessons in this order:

0. Pre-group meeting, clarifying expectations
1. Assessing and defining problems
2. Generating alternative solutions
3. Writing measurable goals to implement solutions
4. Observing and recording progress
5. Using data and graphs to evaluate progress
6. Taking the perspectives of others
7. Reframing mistakes as part of learning
8. Managing internal responses to problems
9. Managing external responses to problems

These lessons are presented in their entirety in this chapter, along with accompanying student worksheets for each lesson (Forms 7.1–7.15). Included in each lesson guide are the lesson objectives, recommended student activities, and an explanation of how each lesson builds on the skills presented in the prior lessons. On this book's companion website (see the box at the end of the contents page), you will find the lesson guides with implementor checklists that allow you to take notes and keep track of SMARTS tasks during the lessons. (In prior studies, we found that implementers really liked having the checklists in place to keep their pace.) The student worksheets for every lesson can also be viewed, downloaded, and printed from the companion website. Utilizing these resources, it should be easy to make your own implementation folder for each group, make copies of all the student forms, and make student SMARTS folders for each student in your group.

REVIEWING PHASE I:
SMARTS STUDENT TRAINING LESSON STRUCTURE

SMARTS lessons have a predictable structure, which increases the likelihood of engagement and understanding for students and the ease of implementation for you. It is helpful to explain the lesson structure to students in the SMARTS group. Briefly explain that the components of each lesson include an introduction, activity, and reflection. Explain that each lesson will take 40–50 minutes. Also explain that each lesson will build upon prior lessons, even though each lesson is different. Figure 7.1 shows the elements of a basic SMARTS lesson plan.

SMARTS FOLDERS

Before the first lesson, it is a good idea to make a SMARTS folder for each student in your group. We would recommend that all lesson materials be kept in these folders. Prior to each lesson, you can make copies of the worksheets and place them in each student's folder so students will have their lesson materials at the start of the group. All the worksheets can be found following each lesson plan. They are also available to be downloaded and printed on this book's companion website (see the box at the end of the contents page). Any type of folder works, or you may decide to make a packet of worksheets with a plain cover. Having all the worksheets together and keeping the folders in one place is very helpful for keeping students on track and ready to learn. Do not let students take the folders with them back to their classrooms, lockers, or desks. This prevents students from having to search for the materials and wasting meeting time.

Lesson X: SMARTS Lesson Title Goes Here
(15–20 minutes)

Materials
- A complete list of materials

Objectives
1. **Statements of what students will learn in this lesson**

Introduction
1. A primer script for what the lesson topic is about

Activities
1. Students will first:
   a. Explain the activity in specific detail

Reflection
1. Ask students clarifying questions.
   a. What just happened?
   b. Why did it happen?
   c. What does it mean?

Wrap-Up
- Details about cleanup
- Tell students the day and time of the next meeting for Lesson 1.

FIGURE 7.1. SMARTS lesson plan template.

CREATE GROUP EXPECTATIONS

In the pre-group meeting, work with students to establish expectations for the group. Ask students to name rules or expectations for the group and then write these expectations on paper or a whiteboard. Display the paper or whiteboard so the expectations can be seen during every lesson. If a student offers a "strange," unclear, or silly expectation, try to reframe it as a useful expectation. Student understanding and buy-in can be increased by guiding a discussion to produce a list of group expectations. If these general group expectations have not been generated by students, group leaders should help facilitate a discussion about including them.

General expectations for the group may include the following:

- Respect others' personal space.
- One person talks at a time.
- Respect yourself and others.
- Be on time.
- Have a positive attitude.

- Follow directions the first time.
- What happens at the group stays in the group (i.e., keep discussions confidential).

GROUP SIZE

We recommend that you limit group sizes for training and processing sessions to between three and seven students. Our observations from studies suggest that smaller groups of three or four students work best. With slight modifications to the lesson plans, SMARTS can also be used with individual students.

SMARTS JAR BEHAVIOR-SUPPORT SYSTEM

This tangible token system will help maintain motivation to participate throughout the SMARTS Phase I lessons. Tangible rewards can motivate students, but many reinforcement systems focus only on either immediate or long-term rewards. This can be problematic for some students. For example, if the reward is a pizza party after completing all nine lessons, some students might not have the maturity to connect immediate behavior with a long-term reward. The SMARTS Jar allows counselors to establish smaller rewards on the way to earning a bigger reward.

How It Works

Student-support personnel or SMARTS Facilitators put a token in a jar following each student response during the reflection part of the lesson. All student contributions will be reinforced, regardless of their value. SMARTS implementers can add an additional variable (e.g., high-quality responses during an activity, respectful behavior, students referencing a previous lesson objective).

The Jar

Any container will work as long as students can see their progress as the tokens accumulate. Along the side of the jar, each group facilitator should mark two lines at different levels on the jar and then write one word on each line that denotes an appropriate/intermediate reward (e.g., snacks, iPad time, outdoor lessons).

> **SMARTS Jar Tip**
>
> Check to make sure it won't take too many or too few of the tokens to reach each line on the SMARTS Jar so you can reasonably space out and reach goals as the lessons progress! For more details on the SMARTS Jar and Mini-SMARTS behavior-support system, along with other tips and suggestions for running small groups, see suggested practices listed in Chapter 6.

The Tokens

Any kind of feasible token will work—marbles, puffy cotton balls, or flat stones. We have observed in our studies that some students do not like the noise of the marbles in the glass jars, but others do! Let your group decide what the filler will be, then test out the number of items (e.g., marbles and cotton balls are different sizes) it will take to fill the jar. If your students select a group reward, put a piece of tape on the jar for the expected line that must be reached before the goal is achieved.

LESSON 0: SMARTS Pre-Group Meeting
(15–20 minutes)

Materials

- Chart paper
- SMARTS Jar and tokens
- Markers
- SMARTS folders, one for each student

Objectives

1. **Students will understand the purpose and structure of the SMARTS program.**

2. **Students will understand short- and long-term rewards for the group (Mini-SMARTS).**

3. **Students will create group expectations that will be reviewed at the start of each lesson.**

Introduce the Group

1. Thank everyone for being there and for agreeing to participate in the SMARTS program.

2. Explain: This will be our SMARTS group for the next several weeks.

3. Talk about the purpose of this group. Explain: We are going to meet _____ times per week for the next _____ (#) weeks for about an hour to talk about setting goals and to work on skills that will help everyone be successful in school and life.

Activities

1. **Students will understand the purpose and structure of the SMARTS program.**

   a. Explain that there will be nine lessons, not including today's.

   b. Lessons will be around 35–45 minutes and will include activities and chances to earn rewards. Let students know what day of the week and what time you will meet and how they will know when to come (e.g., Will you come pick them up in their classrooms or will their teachers send them down?).

   c. Following the lessons and training, explain that each student will have a goal on which they will rate their progress each day and that their teachers will rate their progress too.

    d. After 5 days of rating your progress, explain that you will then meet again to review their ratings and compare them to their goals and to their teachers' ratings as well. Then you might rewrite their goals or keep them as they are.

2. **Students will understand short- and long-term rewards for the group (Mini-SMARTS).**

    a. Show students the SMARTS Jar and tokens.

    b. Explain: The tokens will keep track of responses and positive participation in the group.

    c. Explain: Share what will happen when the tokens reach the different lines. Let students brainstorm what rewards they would like to receive as a group.

3. **Students will create group expectations that will be reviewed at the start of each lesson.**

    a. Explain: For the group to work, we have to set expectations or rules that we all agree on.

    b. Ask: What are some expectations around the way we speak? Act? Respond? Listen?

    c. Record answers on a whiteboard or on sticky notes.

    d. Supplement student answers with examples like "one person speaks at a time," "use inside voices," "listen while someone else is talking," "keep a safe/calm body," and so on. See tips and tools.

Reflection

1. How will our group earn rewards?
2. What questions do you have about how the group will run?
3. How can we help each other be successful and follow the agreed-upon group rules?
4. What can you learn from our group? What is in it for you?

Wrap-Up

- Pass out individual folders with worksheets.
- Tell students the day and time of the next meeting for Lesson 1.

LESSON 1: Defining and Assessing Problems
(40–45 minutes)

Materials

- Poster paper and markers
- SMARTS folders, one for each student
- Form 7.1, Problem Reflection Worksheet
- SMARTS Jar and tokens

Objectives

1. **Students list behaviors that cause problems in the classroom.**

2. **Students select most frequent behaviors, define these behaviors using measurable terms.**

3. **Students list their own common behaviors that may cause problems in the classroom.**

Introduction

Today we are going to learn to recognize problems so that we can better understand how to solve them. What does it mean to recognize a problem? Answer: It means to understand what's causing trouble. (Start discussion using tokens to reward participation and continue to reinforce answers with tokens.)

Tell a story about a time you had to recognize a problem before you could solve it. For example: The water in your sink won't go down the drain. What would happen if you didn't recognize the problem and kept the faucet on? Answer: The sink would overflow. To solve the problem, first turn off the sink to stop the water from getting higher. Then you must learn what's blocking the pipe so you can figure out how to unblock it.

Activities

1. **Students list behaviors that cause problems in the classroom.**

   a. Discuss/list school and classroom expectations. Record these on poster paper or a whiteboard.

   b. Discuss examples of behaviors that do not meet expectations; discuss how these behaviors disrupt the classroom.

   c. Students brainstorm/list 5–10 problematic classroom behaviors (e.g., shouting out answers, tapping pencils, poking other students on the way to the pencil sharpener). Record these on poster paper.

2. **Students select most frequent behaviors; define behaviors using measurable terms.**

   a. Define frequency (e.g., how often) and intensity (e.g., how strong) and write down these answers.

      • Example: Using the sink example, you can say that first it was getting clogged every month, then every week, then every day, and then then every morning and night. These are examples of the *frequency*, or how often the problem occurs.

      • If a little water could get down the drain, then it would be *less intense*. If the sink was so clogged that no water could go down at all and it overflowed every time, the clog would be *more intense*.

   b. Students rate each listed behavior's frequency and intensity on a scale from 1 to 10; discuss how behaviors are disruptive in class.

   c. Students take turns role-playing a behavior from the list.

      • Ask: Have you seen similar situations in your classroom? How does the teacher respond? How do other students react? What happens to the other students when this happens?

3. **Students identify their own problem behaviors in the classroom.**

   a. Hand out Form 7.1, Problem Reflection Worksheet. Model how to fill it out, then either read the questions aloud or support students reading them individually. Use the sink example to review frequency and intensity.

   b. Students complete Problem Reflection Worksheet.

Reflection

Give a lot of praise here for the hard work of thinking about problems. Normalize that we all have problems; problems are clues to help us be successful, and to be successful, we must get better at recognizing what we can do to minimize problems. Make sure to emphasize that next week, the group will be working on thinking of solutions and different ways to think about the challenges they may be experiencing.

1. What tools do you already use to work through a problem?

2. Are there any specific classes or times of day you experience more problems?

3. Are there people or strategies that help you work through those problems?

Wrap-Up

• Students hand in folders to use again at the next meeting.

• Remind students of the time and date of the next meeting.

Problem Reflection Worksheet

Part 1: Identifying Problems

Name three problems or challenging behaviors that you experience. Circle the frequency (how often: 1 = *not often* to 10 = *often*) and intensity (how strong; 1 = *not strong* to 10 = *strong*) of each behavior.

Part 2: Reflecting on Problems and Challenging Behaviors

Behavior	Frequency (*how often*)	Intensity (*how strong*)
1.	1 2 3 4 5 6 7 8 9 10	1 2 3 4 5 6 7 8 9 10
2.	1 2 3 4 5 6 7 8 9 10	1 2 3 4 5 6 7 8 9 10
3.	1 2 3 4 5 6 7 8 9 10	1 2 3 4 5 6 7 8 9 10

How do you feel about yourself when you are struggling with a problem behavior? _____

_____

How would school be different for you if you **seriously** decided to change a behavior? _____

_____

What's the **worst** thing that could happen if you changed a behavior? _____

_____

What's the **best** thing that could happen if you changed a behavior? _____

_____

On the following scale, **how ready are you to change** your behavior? (circle one)

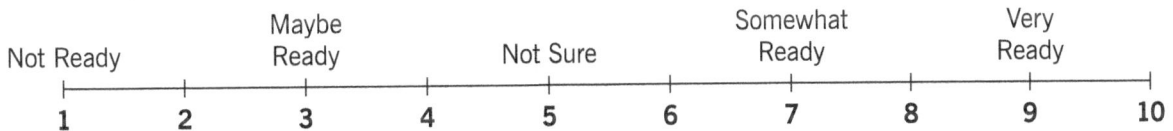

Not Ready		Maybe Ready		Not Sure		Somewhat Ready		Very Ready	
1	2	3	4	5	6	7	8	9	10

Recognize where you rated yourself above. Write one or two reasons you rated yourself at this level.

_____

_____

_____

_____

Thank you for your SMARTS today!

LESSON 2: Generating Alternative Solutions to Problems
(40–45 minutes)

Materials

- Form 7.2, Replacement Behavior Worksheet
- Examples of Problem Behaviors and Replacement Strategies (Form 7.3) cut into strips
- SMARTS Jar and tokens

Objectives

1. Students examine the drive behind their behaviors (what they "get" out of it).
2. Students discuss and suggest replacement behaviors for their problem behaviors.

Introduction

Tell a story to the group about figuring out reasons for behaviors and replacement behaviors. Example story: I had a dog named Texas. Texas was such a sweet puppy, and our family loved him so much. But there was one problem: Every time my family left the house to go to school or work, Texas would pick one shoe and eat it. Pretty soon, everyone in the family had a ruined pair of shoes, and everyone was angry. Finally, when I was complaining to a friend about how my favorite running shoes were ruined, my friend told me that the dog had a reason for doing this. (You can let students guess the reason or just keep going.) The reason is that Texas got scared and sad when we left him alone in the house. We got him a special toy and gave it to him only when we left the house, and he stopped chewing our shoes.

Follow-up questions to get ready for the activity: (Reinforce answers with marbles.)

- What was Texas's behavior doing that made the family angry or didn't follow their expectations of how a dog should act?
- Why was Texas doing it? What was he getting out of it?
- What was the replacement? What did Texas learn to do instead?

Activities

1. Students examine the drive behind their behaviors (what they "get" out of it).
   a. Each student chooses a slip of paper with a problematic behavior written on it.
   b. Students take turns performing the problematic behavior.

c. After each performance, ask:

- What expectation is not being followed? (Refer to the list from the Lesson 1 poster paper.)

- Why would someone *not* follow this expectation? What do they get out of it?

  o Supplement students' responses with answers like: attention, laughs, getting out of work, distracting yourself from something else, or being bored, frustrated, stressed, angry, or sad. Record these responses on poster paper.

d. Repeat steps (a) and (b) with replacement-behavior slips so each student gets to act out a problem behavior and a replacement behavior.

e. After each performance of a replacement behavior, ask:

- How is the need/purpose of the problematic behavior filled by the replacement behavior? Refer to the recorded list from (c) and the story about Texas the dog. Encourage students to generate more replacement behaviors if they struggle with connecting a replacement behavior to the purpose of the behavior. (Example: You also could have given Texas a pillowcase or the T-shirt of a family member to lie with when the family left to make him not miss the family. The idea is that there can be more than one replacement behavior that would fulfill the same need.)

- What do people get out of following expectations?

  o Supplement student responses with: keeping a routine, better relationships with teachers and friends, better grades, and feeling happy, calm, or peaceful. (Example from the lesson introduction: When Texas used the toy or the blanket, the family didn't get angry every time they came home to see ruined shoes. Instead, Texas got a treat when they came home.)

2. **Students discuss and suggest replacement behaviors for their problem behaviors.**

a. Students should look at Form 7.1, Problem Reflection Worksheet, from the last lesson, located in their SMARTS folder.

b. Find Form 7.2, Replacement Behavior Worksheet, in your SMARTS folder. Model how to fill out the form by putting a behavior in the box and rating the intensity and its frequency.

c. Students should fill out their worksheets. Support the students as needed.

Reflection

1. What are your feelings about changing your behavior?

2. If your friend were trying to change a behavior, what advice would you give them?

3. Who is responsible for finding solutions to your problems?

4. Who can help us find solutions for problems in class?

Wrap-Up

- Remind students of the date and time of the next meeting.
- Check the level of the SMARTS Jar.

Replacement Behavior Worksheet

Directions: Use Form 7.2, Problem Reflection Worksheet, from the last lesson. When we need to change one behavior, we should find a replacement strategy. A replacement strategy will help you get what we want. Let's be sure the behavior we chose last time is the right one. It should be one that others also find problematic. For help, review Form 7.3, Examples of Problem Behaviors and Replacement Strategies.

Choose one problem behavior from the last lesson: _____

List two things you think you get out of this problem behavior (the reasons behind it).

1. _____

2. _____

List two replacement strategies (that are OK for school) that still get you what you want.

1. _____

2. _____

If you try a replacement strategy listed above, list the **worst** thing that could happen. _____

_____

_____

If you try a replacement strategy listed above, list the **best** thing that could happen. _____

_____

_____

On the following scale, **how ready are you to change** your behavior? (circle one)

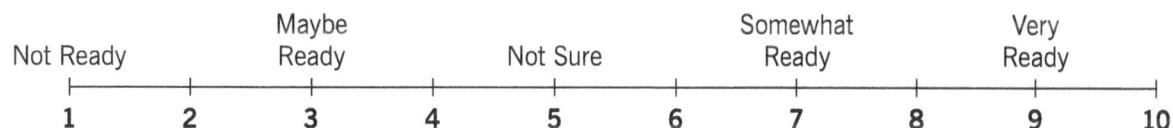

Not Ready		Maybe Ready		Not Sure		Somewhat Ready		Very Ready	
1	2	3	4	5	6	7	8	9	10

Recognize where you rated yourself above. Write one or two reasons you rated yourself at this level.

_____

_____

_____

_____

Thank you for your SMARTS today!

Examples of Problem Behaviors and Replacement Strategies

Problem Behaviors	Replacement Strategies
Kennedy interrupts others during reading group because she wants the other kids to know how smart she is.	Kennedy will share her thoughts and ideas with a classmate and help others who might need it.
Keith taps his pencil loudly on his desk because he feels fidgety after lunch.	Keith will tap his pencil quietly on his leg.
Wendy makes rude comments to other students to make them laugh.	With the help of examples, Wendy will write down and practice positive compliments that are funny.
Aaron is out of his seat 10 times during math because he doesn't know fractions and doesn't know how to do the worksheet.	Aaron will ask for help from the teacher or a classmate when he doesn't understand.
Olive is out of her seat 10 times during math because she feels full of energy at the end of the day.	Olive asks permission to get out of her seat once an hour. Olive uses a stress ball or fidget square to help with her energy.

Thank you for your SMARTS today!

LESSON 3: Defining a Goal and Monitoring Goal Progress
(40–45 minutes)

Materials

- Form 7.4, Practice Goal Monitoring Worksheet
- Form 7.5, Defining a Goal Worksheet
- Form 7.6, Observable Behavior Goal Bank
- Completed worksheets from Lessons 1 and 2
- Clock
- SMARTS Jar and tokens
- Computer or device to watch a short video

Objectives

1. **Students define a goal to monitor.**
2. **Students practice observing and measuring someone else's behavior.**
3. **Students record results from behavior observation.**

Introduction

1. Review: What did we talk about in the last lesson?
   - Answer: Things we can do differently to get what we want and need instead of using a problem behavior.

2. Say: Today we are going to learn how to make a goal and to monitor progress.
   - Ask: What are ways in real life that people monitor progress toward a goal? (Possible answers: weighing yourself to see if you lost weight, writing down how fast you can run a mile, how many sit-ups you can do in a minute as you train to get in shape, or writing down how many pages you read each night until you finish a book.)
   - Ask: Why is monitoring a goal helpful? (Possible answers: to see how you are doing, to see if you make changes, to confirm whether or not what you are doing is working.) For example, if you wanted to finish a 100-page book in a week but read only two pages a day, you can see that this goal won't be accomplished and that you should read more.

   Use your SMARTS Jar and tokens to encourage participation.

Activities

1. **Students practice observing and measuring someone else's behavior.**

    a. Define *interval*. Example: An interval is a defined period, like a time slot. For example, from 8:00 to 9:00 A.M. is a 1-hour, or 60-minute, interval.

    b. Open folders to Form 7.4, Practice Goal Monitoring Worksheet.

    c. Explain: We will watch a Steph Curry clip and observe and record how many times he jumps in each interval. Watch the clock or timer and say "Next" when each 30-second interval is over.

    Links: *www.youtube.com/watch?v=P5_xgip67ac* or Google "Steph Curry highlights" and pick a video.

    d. Repeat (c) to provide students with more opportunities to practice.

2. **Students record results from behavior observation.**

    a. Students share data about Steph's goal.

    b. Explain: Students will be doing the same thing (monitoring their own behaviors in intervals throughout the day).

3. **Students define a goal to monitor.**

    a. Explain: To make a goal about a behavior you want to change, you must first define the goal. We are going to set goals about behaviors (instead of feelings) because we can monitor those kinds of goals.

    -   Ask: Could we have monitored if Steph was happy or sad in this game?

    -   Answer: No, we can only measure what we see, which is his behavior. So if a problem behavior involves a feeling, like getting angry, for example, ask yourself, "What does my body look like or do when I have this problem? What am I doing with my body when I have this problem?" Refer to Form 7.6, Observable Behavior Goal Bank, for concrete examples.

    b. Give students Form 7.5, Defining a Goal Worksheet. Review the directions and, if needed, do a sample one together using the story of Texas the dog from Lesson 2 or your own example.

To set their goals, have students identify their own problems/replacement behaviors using their completed worksheets from Lessons 1 and 2 or the examples from Form 7.3, Examples of Problem Behaviors and Replacement Strategies.

Reflection

1. How did you decide *yes* or *no* or *sometimes* for how often Steph achieved his goal of jumping?

2. Could you tell how Steph Curry was feeling when he jumped? (Answer: No, not for sure; even if he is smiling, he could be nervous or something else because feelings are not an observable behavior. You can observe the action, not the feeling; that is why we choose behavior goals—because we can observe them and see them change.)

3. How did your Form 7.4, Practice Goal Monitoring Worksheet, data compare to your peers' sheets?

4. How confident are you in observing your own behavior? What would make you more confident?

Wrap-Up

- Students turn in sheets or keep them in their folders.
- Remind students of the time and date of the next meeting.
- **Preparation Note:** For next week's lesson, each student needs to bring a packet of three Goal Self-Monitoring Worksheets (Form 7.7) with them to class.

FORM 7.4

Practice Goal Monitoring Worksheet

Directions: Every 30-second interval, count the number of times Steph jumps.

Steph's goal: "I will jump three or more times every 30 seconds."

Interval (30 seconds each)	Number of Jumps (use tally marks)	Did he succeed in his goal?		
1		Yes	No	Sometimes
2		Yes	No	Sometimes
3		Yes	No	Sometimes
4		Yes	No	Sometimes
5		Yes	No	Sometimes
Total number of jumps:				

Thank you for your SMARTS today!

Defining a Goal Worksheet

Directions: Look at the Problem Reflection Worksheet from Lesson 1 and the Replacement Behavior Worksheet from Lesson 2. Using these sheets, write out a behavior goal. List your identified problem behaviors and your replacement behaviors, then combine that information into a single goal that you can observe and monitor—just like we practiced today!

From the Problem Reflection Worksheet in Lesson 1, name the problem you want to focus on.

_____

From the Replacement Behavior Worksheet in Lesson 2, list two behaviors that will replace the problematic behavior you wrote previously. These behaviors must be observable (i.e., someone else should be able to see them).

1. _____

2. _____

Fill in the blanks below.

I will reduce (problem behavior) _____

by (replacement behavior #1) _____

or by (replacement behavior #2) _____

Rate how ready you are to try these replacement behaviors. (circle one)

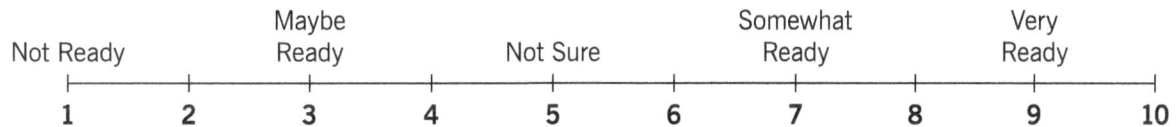

	Maybe			Somewhat	Very
Not Ready	Ready	Not Sure		Ready	Ready

1	2	3	4	5	6	7	8	9	10

What would be the **best** thing that could happen to you if you tried these replacement strategies? _____

_____

What would be the **worst** thing that could happen if you tried these replacement strategies? _____

_____

Recognize where you rated yourself above. Write one or two reasons you rated yourself at this level.

_____

_____

_____

_____

Thank you for your SMARTS today!

Observable Behavior Goal Bank

Example	Non-Example
Raise my hand before I share in class	Be quiet
Look at the teacher when he or she is speaking	Focus more
Keep my body facing forward when the teacher is teaching	Be good
Use an indoor voice in the classroom	Be respectful
Tap on my leg instead of tapping on the desk with a pencil	Be still
Ask for a break when I'm angry or stressed	Be responsible
Put schoolwork in my desk or backpack as soon as possible	Be more organized

Thank you for your SMARTS today!

LESSON 4: Revising Goals and Replacement Strategies to Observe and Record Progress

(40–45 minutes)

Materials

- Form 7.7, Goal Self-Monitoring Worksheet. *Note: Each student needs three copies in their SMARTS folder to take to class and rate a goal at the end of group.*

- Form 7.8, List of Sample Goals

- Optional: your own Goal Self-Monitoring Worksheet as an example

- Form 7.5, Defining a Goal Worksheet

- SMARTS Jar and tokens

Objectives

1. **Students revise goals (specific, realistic, and measurable).**

2. **Students revise goals ("I will" statements).**

3. **Students revise replacement behavior to fit goal.**

4. **Students observe/measure their behavior for 3 days.**

Introduction

1. Ask students to revisit or state their goals from the last lesson.

2. Tell students a story about a specific, realistic, and measurable goal.

   - Example: Since we have been talking about goals, I decided to set one for myself. I had a goal for the weekend of cleaning my closet. There were clothes on the floor, boxes of stuff piled to the ceiling, and old shoes everywhere. So, I put the old shoes in a box to give away and told my family/roommate/friend the closet was clean. They didn't think so! My goal was not specific enough because we all had to agree what clean looked like. (Define *specific*; give examples, such as taking all the clothes off the floor or having shoes lined up).

   - Then, my family/roommate/friend said they thought the closet should be so clean that nothing was in it. We needed that closet to put our clothes in, so that was not realistic either. (Define *realistic*; give examples, such as the floor could be kept free of clothes or all towels could be neatly folded.)

   - Finally, my family/roommate/friend said part of the goal should be that we are always happy to put our coats on hangers when we are in the closet. But how would we know if everyone is happy every time we go into the closet? That is not measurable. (Define *measurable* as something that can be counted or seen, not a feeling.) In the end, the closet was clean, and we kept the goal of having a closet with all our clothes hung on hangers and with all our shoes lined up every day.

3. Explain: In our last lesson, we talked about defining a goal. Today we practice revising goals, just like my family did with the closet, as well as replacement behaviors and measuring our own behaviors.

Activities

1. **Students revise goals (specific, realistic, and measurable).**

   a. Write the words *specific*, *realistic*, and *measurable* on white paper. Discuss what these words mean.

   b. Go through several examples on Form 7.8, List of Sample Goals. Ask students if they are specific, realistic, or measurable.

   c. Students should look back at their goals from Form 7.5, Defining a Goal Worksheet, share goals, and determine if they meet the criteria.

2. **Students revise goals ("I will" statements).**

   a. Explain: Your goal should be phrased as "I will" statements, not "I won't." Use the closet example. Instead of, "I won't throw my clothes on the floor," use "I will hang up my clothes."

   b. Pass out Form 7.7, Goal Self-Monitoring Worksheet packets.

   c. Students write revised goals (that meet criteria from Activity 1) on all three of the Goal Self-Monitoring Worksheets (Form 7.7).

3. **Students revise replacement behaviors to fit the goal.**

   a. Students each choose one replacement behavior that will let them satisfy their revised goals and write them on the sheets.

4. **Students observe/measure their own behaviors.**

   a. Explain: Just like when we observed how much Steph Curry jumped in 30-second intervals, you will record when you follow your goals every hour, over 3 days. Walk students through the use of the worksheet.

   b. Optional: Fill out a Goal Self-Monitoring Worksheet about your closet being cleaned. Show students how you measured the goal every day.

   c. Explain: We will graph the results in our next lesson to better understand our data.

Reflection

1. Why is it important to have specific, realistic, and measurable goals?
2. How does it feel to change the way you look at your behavior?
3. Why do you think it's good to use "I will" versus "I won't" statements?
4. How confident do you feel in observing your own behavior?

Wrap-Up

- Make sure everyone has their packets to self-monitor themselves each hour over 3 days before the next meeting. Note: If possible, remind students about this in the next few days.
- **Preparation Note:** For Lesson 5, you will need three completed sample Goal Self-Monitoring Worksheets (Form 7.7). For Lesson 6, you will need suggestions and feedback from students' teachers about their goals. See Student–Teacher Goal Input (Form 7.10).

Goal Self-Monitoring Worksheet

You will need three copies of this paper, one for each day of goal-monitoring practice.

1. Start by circling what day today is, either day 1, day 2, or day 3.

2. Next, write down the goal you have been working on.

3. List your replacement strategy.

4. Monitor your goal progress by circling *yes* (Y), *no* (N), or *sometimes* (S) at the end of each interval. If you forget or are late adding your rating, that is OK. Take time, think about how you did with following your goal, and go ahead and mark it at a later time. Add some notes about your progress, like why you did or did not follow your goal.

_____

_____

_____

- **Circle which day is today:**   **Day 1**   **Day 2**   **Day 3**
- **My goal:** *I will* _____
- **Replacement strategy:** *I will* _____ *instead.*

Rating Intervals	Goal Monitoring (Y = 2; S = 1; N = 0)	Notes
Start of day–9:00	Did I follow my goal? **Y** **S** **N**	
9:00–10:00	Did I follow my goal? **Y** **S** **N**	
10:00–11:00	Did I follow my goal? **Y** **S** **N**	
11:00–12:00	Did I follow my goal? **Y** **S** **N**	
12:00–1:00	Did I follow my goal? **Y** **S** **N**	
1:00–2:00	Did I follow my goal? **Y** **S** **N**	
2:00–End of day	Did I follow my goal? **Y** **S** **N**	
Add up the score at each interval to get your **Daily Total** _____		

Thank you for your SMARTS today!

List of Sample Goals

Samples of specific/unspecific goals

- Nonspecific Goal = I will spend more time studying for math tests.
- **Specific Goal = I will spend 1 hour after school each day studying math.**
- Nonspecific Goal = I am going to make new friends at school.
- **Specific Goal = I will talk to one new person at school each day for 1 week.**

Samples of realistic/unrealistic goals

- Unrealistic Goal = I am going to be the most popular person in the school.
- **Realistic Goal = I will make friends with two people at school before the end of the year.**
- Unrealistic Goal = I am going to lose 10 pounds this week.
- **Realistic Goal = I am going to lose 10 pounds over the next 8 weeks by not eating sugar.**

Samples of measurable/immeasurable goals

- Unmeasurable Goal = I am going to get good grades in science this school year.
- **Measurable Goal = I am going to get at least a score of 85% or higher on all my science class assignments this school year.**
- Unmeasurable Goal = I am going to be a nicer person.
- **Measurable Goal = I am going to speak to my teachers in a respectful tone.**

Thank you for your SMARTS today!

LESSON 5: Using Data and Graphs to Evaluate Goal Progress
(40–45 minutes)

Materials

- Pencils
- Three completed Self-Monitoring Goal and Record Sheets (Form 7.7) for each student
- Form 7.9, Self-Monitoring Graph
- Example Self-Monitoring Goal and Record Sheets
- Example Self-Monitoring Graph
- SMART Jar and marbles

Objectives

1. **Students graph daily goal data.**
2. **Students use data and graphs to assess their goal progress.**
3. **Students understand the use of self-monitoring to work toward a goal.**

Introduction

1. Remind students about your goal of keeping your closet clean, which you discussed in the last meeting. Tell them you decided to self-monitor, or keep track of, whether or not you were meeting your goal every day, just like they did in the past week. Show them the filled-out example monitoring sheets of your closet progress. Point out how you made the goal on some days and you didn't on others, and explain what happened (e.g., you were in a rush on Tuesday, so you didn't hang up your coat; on Thursday, you were really angry and forgot to put your shoes on the shoe rack).

2. Explain: We are going to look at your Goal Self-Monitoring Worksheets and use those data to make graphs to see your progress easier.

Activities

1. **Students graph daily goal data.**
   a. Model how to tally their points for each day from the Goal Self-Monitoring Worksheets.
   b. Using the percentage key on the Self-Monitoring Graph (Form 7.9), calculate the percentage for each day. Use the data to make the graph.

c. Discuss what your model graph shows about your progress in meeting your goal. Ask: What does it mean when the line goes up? What does it mean when it goes down? What does it mean when the line goes straight across?

d. Support students in tallying points, finding percentages, and completing the Self-Monitoring Graph (Form 7.9) with the data they collected about themselves. If students did not collect data, they can use your data or make a guess about their progress each day to create the data to graph.

2. **Students use data to assess goal progress.**

a. Explain: Look at your data from your graph and decide if you should keep working on this goal, adjust your goal, or choose a new goal.

3. **Students understand the use of self-monitoring to work toward a goal.**

a. Explain: Self-monitoring is a way for you to work on a goal on your own. It helps you keep that goal in the front of your mind. It can be easy to forget to keep working on a goal. (For example, you keep this chart on the closet door so you remember to hang up your coat.)

b. Ask: What are some other ways people use self-monitoring?

   • Supplement students' responses with examples like exercise, health, diet, saving money, and reducing bad habits.

c. Explain: In a few weeks, you will start self-monitoring every day. You will use an app on your iPad or device to keep track of how you are doing toward your goal. The app will help remind you what your goal is and to self-monitor throughout the day. Your teacher will be keeping track on their own app too, so you will have two graph lines to compare instead of just one like today.

Reflection

1. If you are working to improve a goal, in which direction should your line be going?

2. If you are not improving on your goal, in which direction will the line go?

Wrap-Up

• Review when students will start using the app and answer any other questions.

• **Preparation Note:** For Lesson 6, you will need suggestions and feedback from students' teachers about their goals. See Form 7.10, Teacher Goal Input.

Self-Monitoring Graph

Directions: Use the data from your Goal Self-Monitoring Worksheets to graph your progress. To calculate your percentage (if you haven't already), use the key on the next page to add up your score for each day, then divide the total by 14.

- Add up the total number of Y (2), S (1), or N (0) for each of the 3 days.
- Estimate the percentage for each day by dividing the total for each day by the total possible (e.g., for a Day 1 score of 9, divide: 9 ÷ 14 = 64%).
- You can double-check your math using the score/percent conversion chart below.
- Place an x in the approximate place that corresponds to your percentage.
- Connect all three of your x's by drawing a line between them.

Place an x for each day's total.				Daily Score	Percentage
	Day 1	**Day 2**	**Day 3**	1/14 =	7%
100%				2/14 =	14%
90%				3/14 =	21%
80%				4/14 =	29%
70%				5/14 =	36%
60%				6/14 =	43%
50%				7/14 =	50%
40%				8/14 =	57%
30%				9/14 =	64%
20%				10/14 =	71%
10%				11/14 =	79%
0%				12/14 =	86%
				13/14 =	93%
				14/14 =	100%

Looking at the graph of your progress, answer the following questions:

1. What was the percentage stated in your goal? _____

2. What day(s) were your percentages higher than your goal? _____

3. What day(s) were your percentages lower than your goal? _____

4. Will your goal stay the same?   YES   NO

If it needs to change, what will your revised goal be?

- I will _____

- Replacement strategy: _____

Thank you for your SMARTS today!

LESSON 6: Taking the Perspective of Others
(40–45 minutes)

Materials

- Completed Form 7.10, Teacher Goal Input, for each student
- Copies of Form 7.11, Values Cards
- Paper with either pencils or pens
- SMARTS Jar and tokens

Objectives

1. **Students define what perspective is for humans.**

2. **Students understand that the perspective of others is based on unique life experiences.**

3. **Students practice looking at their teachers' and classmates' perspectives.**

Introduction

1. Write the word *space* on your whiteboard. Ask students to close their eyes and list (either written or mentally note) the first three words that come to mind that express their thoughts on space.

   a. How are these things different? How do they express different feelings, images, and perceptions of what you think of when you hear the word *space*?

2. Share a copy of the Values Cards (Form 7.11) with the students.

3. Explain that you will allow each student, one at a time, to select a word to read aloud.

   a. Once read, each student should either write down or mentally note two or three words or a sentence that defines the word from their perspective.

   b. Each student will get a few moments to jot down or mentally note the words.

   c. When everyone is done generating ideas, quickly share the words each student wrote.

4. Ask students to identify the two most different words associated with the Values Card words. Then ask them to identify the most similar words their peers came up with.

   a. If there is time, students can ask each other questions to clarify why they chose certain words.

5. Explain: People can see the same thing and interpret it in different ways. This is because everyone has their own unique perspective, or point of view, shaped by their own experiences, and everyone's experience and point of view is legitimate.

Activities

1. **The group defines perspective.** Perspective is a particular attitude or way of seeing something, a point of view. Write definition on poster paper or board.

   a. Say: We are going to look at some examples of how we can see things from different perspectives.

      - Read scenario: A woman is walking down the street with five children.
      - Ask students: What's the relationship between the woman and the children?
      - Students write down or discuss their different responses. Each time a student shares an idea, ask why they imagined that scenario.

   Example 1:

   STUDENT: I thought the woman was a day care teacher.

   LEADER: Why did you decide that was the situation?

   STUDENT: I went to day care at a lady's house with four other kids, and we used to take walks a lot.

   Example 2:

   STUDENT: I figured it was a family.

   LEADER: Why did you decide that was the situation?

   STUDENT: I always used to go places with my aunt and cousins, so when I see five kids together, I always think it's sisters and brothers and cousins.

(If students don't come up with similar answers, you can share your perspective and the life experience that informed this idea to help guide the conversation.)

2. *The key here is to show that everyone might have a different perspective on a situation, and these perspectives are rooted in their life experience or something they have seen or heard.*

   Students practice looking at their teachers' and peers' perspectives.

   a. Explain: Remember, we have been working on setting a goal for behavior.

   b. Ask: Who else might have a perspective of your behavior in class? (Answer: teachers and classmates)

   c. Explain: We are going to think about how your teachers or classmates might have the same or different perspectives on your behavior in class. I've asked your teachers to write out an individual goal for you to work on in school.

   d. Pass out individual student goal slips.

   e. Ask students: What do you think about the goals your teachers chose for you? Do their perspectives make sense to you? How would your teacher's day be different if you worked on this goal? How would the day be different for the whole class?

Reflection

1. How were your perspectives similar to your teachers'?
2. How were your perspectives different from your teachers'?
3. What can you learn from your peers and their different perspectives?
4. What can you learn from your teachers and their different perspectives?

Wrap-Up

- Ask students to observe one interaction with another person, stop and try to see that person's perspective, and then ask that person if your perspective is different from theirs.

Teacher Goal Input

Teacher instructions: Think about one observable, positively stated ("He or she will . . .") behavioral goal for this SMARTS student to work on in your classroom.

SMARTS Student: _____

Teacher: _____

Goal: _____

_____

Teacher instructions: Think about one observable, positively stated ("He or she will . . .") behavioral goal for this SMARTS student to work on in your classroom.

SMARTS Student: _____

Teacher: _____

Goal: _____

_____

Teacher instructions: Think about one observable, positively stated ("He or she will . . .") behavioral goal for this SMARTS student to work on in your classroom.

SMARTS Student: _____

Teacher: _____

Goal: _____

_____

Teacher instructions: Think about one observable, positively stated ("He or she will . . .") behavioral goal for this SMARTS student to work on in your classroom.

SMARTS Student: _____

Teacher: _____

Goal: _____

_____

Thank you for your SMARTS today!

Values Cards

Fairness	Communication	Courage
Tolerance	Forgiveness	Peach
Environment	Family	Courage
Creativity	Respect	Stability
Belonging	Tradition	Helpfulness
Friends	Environment	Acceptance

Thank you for your SMARTS today!

LESSON 7: Reframing Failure/Mistakes as Part of Learning
(40–45 minutes)

Materials

- Michael Jordan Nike commercial (*www.youtube.com/watch?v=JA7G7AV-LT8*; also search for "Michael Jordan Nike commercial failure")
- Michael Jordan's Story of Failure (Form 7.12)
- Reframing Failure/Mistakes as Part of Learning Worksheet (Form 7.13)

Objectives

1. Students use a mistake/failure as an opportunity.
2. Students learn strategies to be proactive rather than reactive.

Introduction

1. Ask: Tell me something you know about Michael Jordan. Record answers.
2. Ask: Was he *always* successful?
3. Explain: He actually made mistakes and had some hard times. We are going to talk about using mistakes and failure as part of learning.

Activities

1. **Students use a mistake or a failure as an opportunity.**
   a. Review or add to information students knew about Michael Jordan: He is the most famous player in history, won the NBA Championship six times, won the MVP trophy five times, played a dozen All-Star games, and won NCAA titles and two Olympic gold medals.
   b. Show Nike commercial (*www.youtube.com/watch?v=JA7G7AV-LT8*) or Google "Michael Jordan Nike commercial failure."
   c. Read Michael Jordan's story to students (Form 7.12).
      - Before you read, ask students to listen for what goal and what replacement behaviors Michael Jordan set, and what he did to reach his goal. Ask them to listen for how he feels when he makes a mistake or fails.
      - Pause while reading and have students ask and answer questions or notice when his goals or replacement behaviors are mentioned.

2. **Students learn strategies to be proactive, not reactive.**

    a. After you read, use the worksheet to go through discussion about Michael Jordan.

    b. Define *proactive*. Being proactive means using an experience to think about changing something in the future, making things different for next time, creating, or controlling a situation by causing something to happen rather than responding to it after it has happened.

        • Ask: What are some examples of when Michael Jordan was proactive in his life?

    c. Define *reactive*. Being reactive means that you don't take any initiative or make strategic decisions in life; you just go where life kicks you, and then you react to what happens to you.

        • Ask: What would it have looked like if Michael Jordan was reactive when he didn't make the basketball team the first time?

    d. Students turn to Reframing Failure/Mistakes as Part of Learning Worksheet (Form 7.13) in their SMARTS folders. Assist students in answering questions.

Reflection

1. If we fail at a task once, what are some ways we can learn how to do it better?
2. How is it solving problems when you are angry/stressed/frustrated?
3. Who is in charge of how we feel about what others say to us?
4. Why is it important to be proactive versus reactive?
5. How can we learn from plans that didn't work the first time?

Wrap-Up

• Remind students that they are going to self-monitor their progress in reaching their goals in class.
• Remind them that they will not have a perfect score or graph every time and that they can use those times to learn.

Michael Jordan Succeeded Because He Failed

Michael Jordan (MJ) developed a competitive spirit from being one of five children in a home with high expectations. MJ's spirit and desire to play basketball was driven by a rivalry with his brother Larry. Every day they played a one-on-one game in the backyard, and Larry usually dominated MJ. Larry was considered the true family athlete, but Michael didn't like losing to his brother—or anyone.

MJ played basketball on the playground nearly every day, and he would score more points than anyone. Though others noticed that MJ had some skills and could shoot the ball, Michael did not have mastery over basics like dribbling, rebounding, and playing defense. Also, MJ rarely passed the ball. MJ's high school coach knew him through his brother, and the coach invited MJ to try out for the junior varsity team, even though he was only a freshman. At the tryout, the coach saw that MJ lacked basic skills and that he was not a team player. So, the coach decided MJ would benefit from a year of practicing on the freshman team. When the list of names for the junior varsity team was announced, many of MJ's friends made the team, but he did not. He stared at the list, reading it over and over. When he did not see his name, he felt crushed.

This moment was very important in MJ's life. When he got home that day, he remembered crying. Despite this setback, his mother encouraged him to ask his coaches for specific tips, to continue practicing, to maintain his work ethic, and try to become more of a team player. Leaving disappointment behind, MJ followed her recommendations and practiced the drills his coaches taught him to improve his dribbling, free throws, layups, and defensive stances.

MJ and his coaches monitored his progress and noticed that, before long, he was improving. His P.E. teacher typically arrived at school around 7:00 a.m. to find MJ already there practicing, no matter the season or his other circumstances. MJ was so committed that the teacher would have to ask him to leave each morning so that he could start class.

MJ returned to try out for the varsity team the following year much better prepared thanks to strong basic skills and a positive attitude. Although MJ was barely six feet tall as a sophomore, he gave everything he had and made the team. His newfound skills, coupled with his cooperative spirit, taught MJ to pass the ball to teammates who scored points. MJ was viewed by his teammates as a leader because he was a team player and a hard worker. He led by example, insisting that the team could achieve anything through hard work, goal-setting, and practicing with a positive attitude.

Behind MJ's competence and spirit lies the secret: He was willing to try and fail, to ask for help, and to treat failures as clues to areas he needed to practice to be successful.

Through the years, MJ used failure to motivate himself. Although he continued to feel an impulse to give up whenever he flubbed or lost a game, he learned to fight that impulse by closing his eyes and recalling the painful day when his name didn't show up on the junior varsity team list. The memory of that sense of failure would revive his spirit and remind him that only hard work and practice could lead him back to victory. Thanks to this way of thinking, MJ became one of the greatest players in the history of basketball, winning six NBA Championships, being awarded the MVP trophy five times, playing in six NBA All-Star games, winning the NCAA championship, and playing on two U.S. Olympic teams, where he won two gold medals. Through it all, MJ remained convinced that he achieved his success through his willingness to fail, to use failure as a clue to success, and to practice hard.

Reframing Failure/Mistakes as Part of Learning Worksheet

Reframing Failure/Mistakes as Part of Learning—Michael Jordan

In the story "Michael Jordan Succeeded Because He Failed," we see that Michael Jordan took his failure to make the varsity basketball team as an opportunity to improve.

1. What was Michael's failure? _____

_____

2. How did Michael Jordan feel when he did not see his name on the list? _____

_____

Reframing for Success: Being Proactive = Making Things Happen

3. What was Michael Jordan's goal? _____

_____

4. How did Jordan use the failure to help him be successful? _____

_____

5. What replacement behaviors helped Michael Jordan be successful? _____

_____

Reframing Failure/Mistakes as Part of Learning—You

How can you be proactive?

1. Think of a situation where you were disappointed or felt like you failed and were reactive.

2. How did you react? _____

_____

3. How could you have been more proactive? _____

_____

On the following scale, ***how ready are you to change*** your behavior? (circle one)

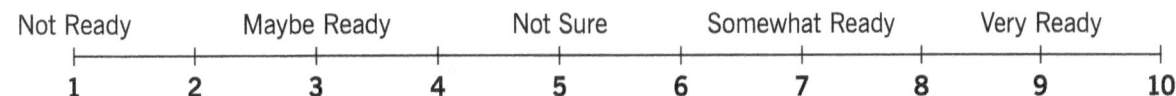

Not Ready		Maybe Ready		Not Sure		Somewhat Ready		Very Ready	
1	2	3	4	5	6	7	8	9	10

Recognize where you rated yourself above. Write one or two reasons why you rated yourself at this level.

_____

_____

Thank you for your SMARTS today!

LESSON 8: Recognizing Internal Responses to Problems
(40–45 minutes)

Materials

- Form 7.14, Deep Breathing and Heart Rate Recording Worksheet
- "Houston, we have a problem" clip (*www.youtube.com/watch?v=C3J1AO9z0tA*; also search "Houston we have a problem, Apollo 13," which is a 3-minute clip)
- SMARTS Jar and tokens

Objectives

1. **Students learn about physiological responses to external stimuli.**
2. **Students learn to take their own pulses.**
3. **Students learn to breathe as a stress-reduction strategy and to monitor effects on the heart.**

Introduction

1. Ask: Who remembers what it means to monitor something? What are some situations when you would monitor your heart rate? Make sure students understand what monitoring your heart rate means (e.g., this is a typical practice at the doctor).
2. Ask: Why do people monitor their heart rates? Answer: To make sure they are healthy or not too stressed.
3. Before the clip: Ask students to look for things being monitored and to look for clues about how the astronauts were feeling. Watch the clip *www.youtube.com/watch?v=C3J1AO9z0tA* or Google *Apollo 13* movie, "Houston, we have a problem."
   - After the clip: List all the things being monitored (e.g., oxygen tank levels, fuel cell levels, all the buttons and red alerts, thrusters, heart rates). Explain: Astronauts must wear heart rate monitors on space flights. Their heart rates are constantly transmitted to the engineers on the ground.
   - Ask: What do you think the astronauts felt like in their bodies when all the failures happened? Why would their heart rates go up (e.g., if they were working hard, if they were worried or in trouble)? Is it hard to think clearly when you feel like that?
   - Explain: We have various responses to problems. Problems affect our ability to think, what we feel, and our physical systems. (On a poster pad, write "Think, Feel/Emotions, Body/Physical State") Today we are going to take our heart rates and pay attention to the way our bodies respond to stress.

Activities

1. **Students learn about physiological responses to external stimuli.**

   a. Explain: Internal responses to stress, like your heartbeat speeding up, affect our physical state, ability to think, and how we feel. Today we are going to learn about how our brain and body work together to respond to events outside ourselves—like loud noises, stressful situations, and even positive things like a hug from a friend. Understanding these responses help us make sense of and manage our emotions.

   b. Example: Giving an oral report in front of class.

      • We could sweat, turn red, and feel our heart rate increase (physical state).

      • We might forget what we were going to say (ability to think).

      • We could feel lost, embarrassed, or scared (feel/emotions).

2. **Students learn to take their own pulses.**

   a. Show/model how to take a pulse at the wrist or neck (see Figures 7.2 and 7.3).

3. **Students learn to breathe as a stress-reduction strategy and to monitor the effects on their heart rates.**

   a. Pass out the Deep Breathing and Heart Rate Recording Worksheet (Form 7.14).

   b. Assist students as they find their pulses, count beats for 10 seconds, and fill out #2 on their worksheets.

   c. Fill in the Deep Breathing and Heart Rate Recording Worksheet (Form 7.14).

   d. Students do short exercises for 1 minute (e.g., jumping jacks, burpees, running in place, squeezing hands, wringing a towel in their hands).

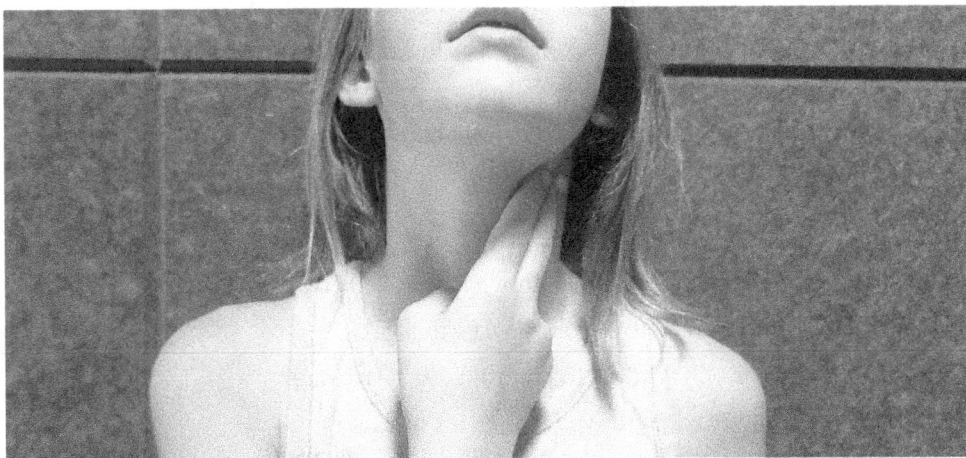

FIGURE 7.2. Pulse checking at neck. Photo by author.

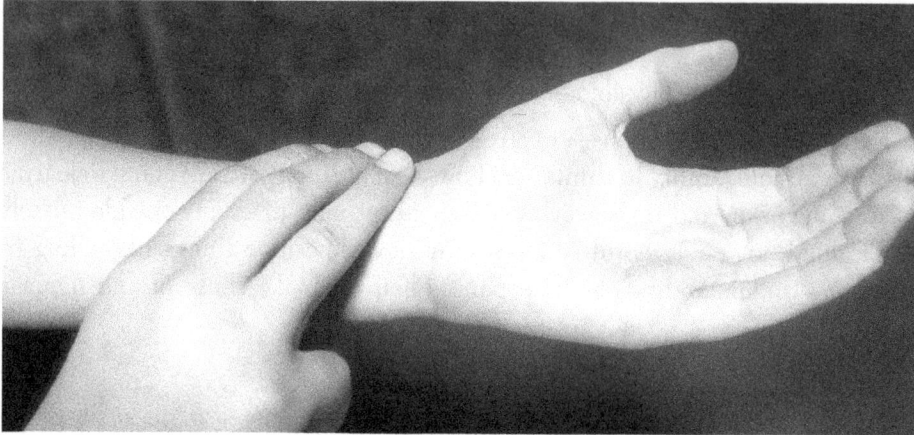

FIGURE 7.3. Pulse checking at wrist. Photo by author.

   e. Immediately afterward, record their heart rates on #3 on the Deep Breathing and Heart Rate Recording Worksheet (Form 7.14).

   f. Practice a breathing exercise from #4 of the Deep Breathing and Heart Rate Recording Worksheet (Form 7.14) for 1 minute.

- Students record post-breathing heart rate on #3 on the Deep Breathing and Heart Rate Recording Worksheet (Form 7.14). Tell students that we will complete the worksheet at next week's session.

   g. Ask students:

- What was your first heart rate?
- What happened when you exercised?
- Was your heart rate different after the breathing exercise?
- What does the breathing exercise do for your physical state? What about for your ability to think or feel?

   h. Say: You have the power to breathe yourself into a relaxed state.

Reflection

1. What happens to our heart rates when we are scared? Angry? Happy?
2. Does it feel powerful to control your heart rate?
3. When are the times you will try to control your heart rate?
4. What does this have to do with your behavior in class?

Wrap-Up

- Challenge students to pay attention to times in the coming week that their heart rates speed up. Ask them to try to use the breathing exercises one time in real life before the next meeting.

- Optional: Give students a copy of the breathing exercises directions to take home.

Deep Breathing and Heart Rate Recording Worksheet

1. **First, practice deep breathing as a stress reduction technique. Read to students in a moderate to slow cadence and calm tone. Practice this for 1–2 minutes.**
   - Sit comfortably with your back straight. Put one hand on your chest and the other on your stomach.
   - Breathe in through your nose. The hand on your stomach should rise. The hand on your chest should move very little.
   - Exhale through your mouth, pushing out as much air as you can while contracting your abdominal muscles. The hand on your stomach should move in as you exhale, but your other hand should move very little.
   - Continue to breathe in through your nose and out through your mouth. Try to inhale enough so that your lower abdomen rises and falls. Count slowly as you exhale.

2. **Next, ask students to take their pulse and record the number of beats per minute.**
   - If possible, partner students. Instruct partners that there are two ways to do this.
   - Place two fingers on your lower neck, on either side of your windpipe (left-hand photo).
     - Place one finger of one hand on opposite wrist just below thumb on arteries (right-hand photo).
     - Press lightly and feel around until you feel your heartbeat/pulse.
   - Once you find it, use a watch or clock with a second hand.
   - Count the beats you feel for 10 seconds. Multiply this number by six to get your heart rate (pulse) per minute.

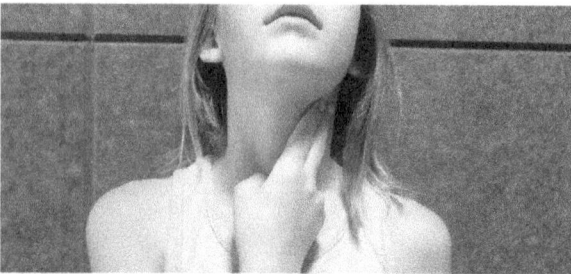

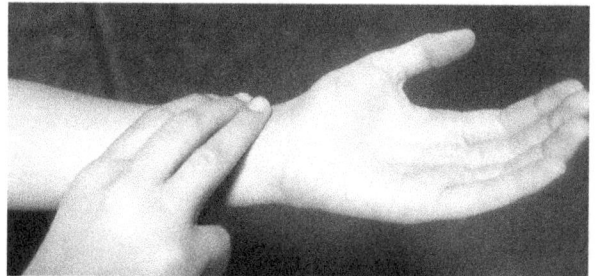

Check your pulse: _____ × 6 = _____ BPM (beats/minute)
                        (for 10 seconds)   *(your pulse)*

3. **After you have taken your pulse:**
   a. Run in place next to your desk for 30 seconds or
   b. Do 25 jumping jacks or
   c. Bend over to touch your toes and stand up 10 times
   d. Check your pulse, as explained above, and record it on the grid on the next page

Check your pulse: _____ × 6 = _____ BPM (beats/minute)
                        (for 10 seconds)   *(your pulse)*

4. **Now, practice the breathing technique.** Practice for 1 minute. Then, check your pulse.

Check your pulse: _____ × 6 = _____ BPM (beats/minute)
                        (for 10 seconds)   *(your pulse)*

(continued)

Deep Breathing and Heart Rate Recording Worksheet *(page 2 of 2)*

Repeat #3 and #4 (or until you are asked to stop) and record your results below.

5. **Exercise for 10 seconds** _____ × 6 = _____ BPM

6. **Breathing for 10 seconds** _____ × 6 = _____ BPM

Stop here.
Save #s 7–10 for Lesson 9:

7. **Exercise for 10 seconds** _____ × 6 = _____ BPM

8. **Muscle relaxation for 10 seconds** _____ × 6 = _____ BPM

9. **Exercise for 10 seconds** _____ × 6 = _____ BPM

10. **Muscle relaxation for 10 seconds** _____ × 6 = _____ BPM

Thank you for your SMARTS today!

LESSON 9: Managing External Responses to Problems
(40–45 minutes)

Materials

- Deep Breathing and Heart Rate Recording Worksheet (Form 7.14) in SMARTS folder
- Muscle Relaxation Script (Form 7.15)
- Clock/Timer
- SMARTS Jar and tokens

Objectives

1. Students learn muscle-relaxation techniques.
2. Students learn internal responses to external stressors.

Introduction

1. Remind students about last week's challenge. Ask them to share stories about if they remembered to take their pulse or if they tried breathing exercises since your last meeting.

2. Tell students about a time when you were stressed or nervous. Tell them to listen for how you felt and what your body did in response to the situation. You could look at the chart you made in Lesson 8 that listed Physical State, Ability to Think, How We Feel.

   - Example: When I was six or seven, my dad and I were at an amusement park. We got in a long line. I didn't really pay attention to which ride it was, but when we got close enough, I realized it was for a giant roller coaster. I got so scared! It was a cloudy and cool day, but I started sweating, and my heartbeat was really fast. When we got into the roller coaster car, my hands were slippery when I held onto the bar. My dad kept telling me it was going to be fun, but I didn't believe him. We went up, up the first hill, and then the ride started going really fast. At first, I was yelling, but soon I was laughing and screaming for fun. We went back and rode it again and again.

3. Have students help fill in the answers about your physical state, your ability to think, and how you felt in line and at the beginning of the ride.

4. Explain: Last week, we practiced paying attention to your heartbeat and the way your body responded to stressful situations. This week, we will practice another strategy to reduce stress in the moment.

Activities

1. **Students review physical skin responses to stress.**

   a. Ask students to open their folders to the Deep Breathing and Heart Rate Recording Worksheet (Form 7.14) from Lesson 8.

   b. Explain: We are going to try another technique to learn to relax in the moment.

2. **Students learn muscle-relaxation techniques.**

   a. Start with #3 on the Deep Breathing and Heart Rate Recording Worksheet. Students exercise for 1 minute (e.g., jumping jacks, burpees, running in place).

   b. Students take their pulse for 10 seconds.

   c. Read the Muscle Relaxation Script (Form 7.15) using a calm tone and an even rhythm.

   d. Repeat once or twice using the short or long script.

3. **Students learn about muscle and skeletal responses to stress.**

   - Ask: Do you feel the relaxation technique helped? What could you feel physically, mentally, or emotionally during it?

   - Explain: These techniques can help you relax, and no one will know that you are doing them. You can do some of the process or all of it—whatever works best for you in the situation.

   - Have students compare the results from the breathing exercises last week (#s 1–5 on the worksheet) to the muscle relaxation script (#s 6–9 on the worksheet) this week.

   - Ask: Does one work better for you than another? Which do you think you would be more likely to use in a stressful situation?

   - Ask students to recall the goals they have set to monitor. Ask them to imagine or share with the group when they could use one of these techniques to help meet their goals.

     Example: My goal is to stay in my seat in math class. When I want to get up, I am going to try to tensing and then relaxing my arms and legs instead of getting up.

     Example: My goal is to not tap my pencil on my desk or make other disruptions, so when I hear myself tapping, I am going to breathe in my nose and out of my mouth three times.

Reflection

1. Explain: This is our last group lesson. We will keep meeting individually to process your weekly data.

2. What has been your favorite part of these lessons?

3. What is one thing that has stuck with you the most?

Wrap-Up

- Students can either hand in folders or take them home with them. Check in about the next phase of self-monitoring and remind students of the schedule.

Muscle Relaxation Script

Recall the breathing exercise from the last lesson. Let's practice again.

- Sit comfortably with your back straight. Put one hand on your chest and the other on your stomach.
- Breathe in through your nose. The hand on your stomach should rise. The hand on your chest should move very little.
- Exhale through your mouth, pushing out as much air as you can, while contracting your abdominal muscles. The hand on your stomach should move in as you exhale, but your other hand should move very little.
- Continue to breathe in through your nose and out through your mouth. Try to inhale enough so that your lower abdomen rises and falls. Count slowly as you exhale.

The next exercise focuses on intentional and purposeful relaxing of the muscles in your body. It is hard work but be sure to continue your breathing practice while doing this!

1. Begin with the large muscles of your legs. Tighten all the muscles of your legs, hold the tension for 5 seconds, and squeeze hard. Feel the muscles wanting to give up this tension. And now relax. Let all the tension go. Feel the muscles in your legs going limp, loose, and then relaxing. Notice how relaxed the muscles feel now. Feel the difference between tension and relaxation.

2. Now focus on the muscles in your arms. Tighten each muscle when I mention them. Hold them as I mention other muscles. Start with your shoulders, then tighten your upper arms. Now tighten your lower arms and hands. Squeeze your hands into tight fists. Tense the muscles in your arms and hands as tightly as you can. Squeeze harder, harder, and hold the tension in your arms, shoulders, and hands. Feel the tension in these muscles. Hold it for a few moments more—and now release. Let the muscles of your shoulders, arms, and hands relax and go limp. Feel the relaxation as your shoulders lower into a comfortable position and your hands relax at your sides. Allow the muscles in your arms to relax completely.

3. Focus again on your breathing. Slow, even, regular breaths. Breathe in relaxation and breathe out tension. In relaxation, out tension. Continue to breathe slowly and rhythmically.

4. Now tighten the muscles of your back. Feel your back tightening, pulling your shoulders back and tensing the muscles along your spine. Arch your back slightly as you tighten these muscles. Hold and then relax. Let all the tension go. Feel your back comfortably relaxing into a good and healthy posture.

5. Turn your attention now to the muscles of your chest and stomach. Tighten and tense these muscles. Tighten them further, hold this tension, and release. Relax the muscles of your trunk.

6. Finally, tighten the muscles of your face. Scrunch your eyes shut tightly, wrinkle your nose, and tighten your cheeks and chin. Hold this tension in your face and then relax. Release all the tension. Feel how relaxed your face is.

7. Notice all the muscles in your body. Notice how relaxed your muscles feel. Allow any last bits of tension to drain away. Enjoy the relaxation you are experiencing. Notice your calm breathing, your relaxed muscles. Enjoy the relaxation for a few moments.

8. When you are ready to return to your usual level of alertness and awareness, slowly begin to reawaken your body. Wiggle your toes and fingers. Swing your arms gently. Shrug your shoulders and take a big stretch.

Thank you for your SMARTS today!

CHAPTER 8

SMARTS Phase II
Student Self- and Teacher Monitoring

This chapter explores key SMARTS steps, processes, and helpful hints to successfully support students and teachers with Phase II of SMARTS—the self-monitoring and teacher-monitoring stage. Specifically, in this chapter, we:

- Present a history of the use of self-monitoring as a behavioral-change support strategy.
- Discuss how SMARTS takes advantage of the principle of reactivity to help us be successful.
- Impart tips from our work with students to assist you with helping them successfully self-monitor their goals.
- Work through different SMARTS goal-monitoring sheets for students of differing abilities and ages and how to set up your students' goal sheets for both the students and their teachers.
- Discuss a range of tips for overcoming challenges during student self-monitoring.

BACKGROUND AND RATIONALE FOR SELF-MONITORING: A METACOGNITIVE STRATEGY

The purpose of SMARTS is to scaffold student training and shape student experiences that (1) provide students with skills needed for goal development, (2) increase motivation and engagement by directly involving students in the self-monitoring phase of SMARTS, and (3) enhance the effectiveness of self-monitoring by increasing students' sense of input, ownership, autonomy, and responsibility for their own goal-directed behaviors. When we commit to acting in an autonomous, supportive manner and allow students increased ownership and input over the goals and the skills needed to monitor performance, we engender students to engage in patterns of socialized behaviors that are valued in the school context. We, the adults at school, also model for students the kinds of engaging behavioral patterns that are valued in the school context to solve problems: communication, collaboration, prosocial interactions, and other skills needed to be successful at school and in other areas of life.

Self-monitoring has a long history rooted in behavioral psychology and, as noted in Chapter 1, has been extensively studied as a behavior-support practice across many different fields and with many different people, age groups, and goal types. The origins of self-monitoring can be tied back to B. F. Skinner's seminal work on operant condition and behavioral modification (Skinner, 1953). Skinner's research emphasized the role of reinforcement in shaping and maintaining behavior. The concept of self-monitoring and self-regulation gained prominence in the 1970s with the work of Albert Bandura, who presented his model of social learning theory (Bandura, 1977). Bandura (1977) emphasized the importance of self-regulation in socialization and that for a person to successfully socialize into groups, they must also be successful at self-monitoring, self- and social awareness, and engaging in a reflection process as a key element of learning adaptive interactive behaviors.

The term *self-monitoring* was first coined by Mark Snyder in 1974 as a "process of attending to and recording one's own behavior" (p. 659). Since then, self-monitoring has been widely studied and applied in various fields, including education, psychology, health care, substance abuse, diabetes research, and in other ways where professionals seek to engage others in positive behavior-change strategies and promote autonomy in the pursuit of goal attainment. Its effectiveness has been supported by empirical research in school settings most extensively, and self-monitoring has been shown to be effective at improving both challenging behaviors and academic performances (Kazdin, 2017; Zimmerman, 2008).

Self-monitoring can be used as both an assessment and an intervention. Typically, with children, self-monitoring is viewed as a strategy to affect behavior change rather than as an assessment. As an assessment strategy alone, the byproduct of a well-designed self-monitoring system naturally produces data to help describe the level at which a student is functioning, such as the total number of problems they get right or the number of letter sounds made in an interval. This is a needed byproduct of a self-management intervention, as we are all required to collect data to appraise the improvement of a specific practice or to signal the need for a change. As a behavior assessment, self-monitoring can tell us how many times a

Self-Monitoring Fact

Self-monitoring can be used as both an assessment and an intervention and produces data that can be used to evaluate whether a student is being responsive to the self-monitoring plan.

student speaks out of turn in class or engages in some other challenging behavior. As an academic assessment, self-monitoring is a direct assessment and can assist teachers in knowing what the next step might be in a student's learning. As an intervention strategy, self-monitoring is designed to function as a method to alter behaviors through the simple act of collecting data on a performance goal.

As we briefly mentioned in Chapter 1, self-monitoring as a practical process has a *reactive effect* that makes it a metacognitive strategy (Shapiro & Cole, 1994). Reactivity is a metacognitive principle referring to behavioral changes that occur as a function of simply observing one's own behavior—irrespective of the reliability or accuracy of those observations (Nelson & Hayes, 1981). For example, observed in studies of self-regulated learning (Bandura, 2005; Cleary & Zimmerman, 2004), students who self-monitor their math performance systematically gain an increased awareness of the number of problems they have done correctly. *Simply observing and recording one's own performance informs and stimulates cognitive reward centers, which increases motivation and improves self-governance.* The reactivity principle has also been observed in studies examining the self-monitoring of daily caloric intake and the types of foods eaten where weight loss is observed without any other dietary intervention (Boutelle & Kirshenbaum, 2012; Butryn et al., 2007). Although it may appear, at least on the surface, that no discernible extrinsic support is present during a self-monitoring process, the very act of setting a goal to alter a behavior changes the target behavior in and of itself. If you couple this simple, reactive effect with the training and practice designed to increase a student's awareness and intentionality to reflect upon a challenging behavior with appraising the behavior against a stated goal, recording those reflections, and gaining insight into progress over time, we begin to see how change can happen through this metacognitive strategy.

> **Self-Monitoring Fact**
>
> Reactivity is a metacognitive principle referring to behavioral changes that occur as a function of simply observing one's own behavior, irrespective of the reliability or accuracy of the observations.

KEY TIPS FOR STUDENTS TO SUCCESSFULLY SELF-MONITOR GOALS

Helping elementary students successfully self-monitor their goals involves providing them with guidance and support to develop the needed skills. Fortunately, decades of research help us organize the basic skills in the Phase I: SMARTS Student Training. Key elements for successfully helping students to self-monitor include the following.

Teach Goal Setting

SMARTS includes lessons that directly teach the skills and strategies students need to learn to successfully self-monitor. SMARTS Lessons 1–5 impart skills to identify problem behaviors, recognize alternative strategies, write goals that directly address the problem behaviors, self-monitor one's progress on those goals, and graph and adjust those goals following several days of self-monitoring. Once students have successfully completed Lessons 1–5, they should have goals that are relevant to the challenges they are experiencing and can be ready to self-monitor that goal in the classroom. Several of our research studies have had students being able to self-monitor after they were exposed to Lessons 1–5; following Lesson 5, students have a goal and the knowledge to self-monitor their goal performances. We continued to provide them with Lessons 6–9, but in tandem with self- and teacher-goal monitoring.

SMARTS Lessons 6–9 include other relevant and important social and emotional learning skills needed to understand the perspectives of others. Most important to the SMARTS process is for students to better understand and appreciate the content of Lesson 6, or what their classroom teachers perceive as expected behaviors. Not only is this important to compare self- and teacher data during Phase III's data-review meetings, but practicing this skill can assist students with simply becoming more aware of the general expectations at school. Lesson 7 addresses the idea that because none of us are perfect and that we all need to view mistakes as an essential part of learning. This understanding of failure as a part of the process is crucial, as not all students will achieve their goals. The important part at this point in the intervention is for them to see errors or shortcomings as clues to success. This may translate to SMARTS students adjusting their goals from week to week, depending upon the data. Finally, Lessons 8 and 9 focus on self-regulation skills and provide opportunities to practice being more aware of internal processes. The goal for these lessons is not only for students to increase awareness but to also gain a sense of control over these processes and more successfully learn to manage their responses during the school day.

Summarized in Table 8.1, following are some tips and practices described in more detail to help you implement Phase II successfully with your students.

Encourage Collaboration on Goal Setting

Although we really want to support and promote student autonomy in the goal-setting process, the success of the intervention depends on setting the right goals. For this to happen, students also need to collaborate with others on challenges they have in the classroom or in other areas of the building. Lesson 6 includes teacher collaboration on student-goal development. There is also a contract that can be used to gather some teacher input. Simply put, teachers and others can be powerful advocates in helping students hone their goals to focus on the important skills they need to be successful.

Model Self-Monitoring

Each lesson includes activities and introductions where you, the facilitator, can model your own use of each skill for students. Demonstrate your own self-monitoring by think-

TABLE 8.1. Phase II Self-Monitoring Tips

SMARTS Phase II tips	Practices
Encourage collaboration on goal setting	Peer support! Have your students collaborate on similar goals where they can.
Model self-monitoring	Monitor your own goals with students. Talk about why your goal is important to you and share progress.
Use visual tools	Graph your own progress and help students view their progress through graphs.
Establish regular routines and checkpoints	Set up a checkpoint at the same time and place each day. Develop one or two checkpoint questions that are MI related: 1. On a scale of 1–10, how ready are you to accomplish your goal today? 2. On a scale of 1–10, how confident are you that you can accomplish your goal today?
Encourage self- and social awareness and thoughtful reflection	In group and when reviewing progress, encourage students to stop and really think and reflect on how they feel they did overall.
Provide and receive regular performance feedback	Provide feedback—use the MI and autonomy-supportive tactic by asking permission to provide feedback.
Celebrate milestones	Keep a special treat handy for when students have made progress. Even if they fall short of a goal, progress is progress.

ing aloud during lessons and training, showcasing how to assess progress during SMARTS Phase III's data-processing meetings, and adjusting your goals dependent on the data or changing the details that affect goal attainment. Model the use of self-monitoring tools and language as students begin to self-monitor as well. Doing it with them not only helps them see that self-monitoring is a useful habit and that you value it as well but communicating this makes the SMARTS intervention matter!

Use Visual Tools

Studies have shown that using visual aids for students and others to understand progress is a valuable feedback tool. Feedback is an important part of the SMARTS process, and graphing student performances week to week serves many purposes. Lessons 5 and 6 ask students to collect several days' worth of self-monitoring data, to graph those data, and to compare their graphs with their goals to appraise performances. The graphs help students reflect on their efforts over time and understand and practice basic math functions as a relevant means to calculating a percent or graphing on an x and y chart. Seeing the data charted helps students engage more meaningfully with the data.

Establish Regular Routines and Checkpoints

Work with classroom teachers to set regular check-in times for students to gather their self-monitoring sheets and turn them in each day. Also set regular checkpoints with students to aggregate, graph, and evaluate their progress after 5 days or one school week. If behaviors are more intense and frequent, Phase III's data-review meetings might need to occur more frequently.

Encourage Self- and Social Awareness and Thoughtful Reflection

Encourage students to evaluate their own performances. Highlight for students the practices and content in Lessons 8 and 9 and encourage them to practice self-reflection. If students need more detail to evaluate their own performances, consider helping students use more descriptive terms in their goals. Ask students to stop for 5 seconds before rating themselves and fully reflect on the last interval they are rating. Be sure to ask students open-ended questions about their progress, what strategies they find useful or not useful, and what they think they need to improve. Also, be sure to encourage them to identify what might need to be different and what they have control over to change in an effort to reach their goals. These issues are also covered in the script and forms for Phase III's processing.

Provide and Receive Regular Performance Feedback

One of the greatest tools in facilitating behavioral change among all of us is regular, accurate, and meaningful feedback. SMARTS encourages students to reflect weekly on their own self- and teacher-monitoring data. Again, if the behavior at the focus of the SMARTS goal is more intense or more frequent, monitoring times may need to be more frequent, and data-review meetings may need to occur more often as well. When reviewing the data with your students, do your best to let them interpret and add meaning to their data. The data help to depersonalize the performance, but it is important that students experience the feedback as constructive, actionable, and focused on growth or goal attainment.

Celebrate Milestones

It is important to acknowledge effort in work as much as it is for us to recognize when a student achieves a goal. It is also important to encourage students to set new goals once they reach a goal. SMARTS is truly about the journey; SMARTS is about the goal as a process and not the goal as a product. Encourage students to see both the process itself and their efforts to observe the process as the important point, but let's also always pause to celebrate achievement!

PHASE II: SMARTS SELF-MONITORING AND TEACHER-MONITORING PROCESS AND FORMS

In Phase II, we are ready to monitor goals; this is the meat of the matter. But before we get there, we want to share with you a few process factors that have been helpful in our experience. For starters, the whole point of SMARTS is not only to engage students in the process of changing behavior, monitoring data, and promoting student autonomy and involvement; it is also to share the workload between teachers and student-support personnel who are working in schools. We know the burden placed on teachers to be all things in school settings, so SMARTS was deliberately designed to lessen the teacher workload and implement an intervention, utilizing the collaborative skills of social workers, counselors, special educators, or others to train and support students as they transition into the self-monitoring phase. That said, when we collaborate on these matters, it can create some challenges. Here are a few process suggestions we have for Phase II that we have found helpful.

> **SMARTS Fact**
>
> SMARTS is designed to share the behavior-support workload between teachers and student-support personnel. Teachers can have more input, but all they need to do on a daily basis is rate how well a student followed their SMARTS goal.

- *Tip 1.* Create an emotionally safe routine for each morning check-in. Choose an area with easy access for students but with adequate privacy so that they will feel safe sharing their feelings at the start of their day.
- *Tip 2.* Prime your students' motivational engines each day by asking:
  o *On a scale of 0 to 10, how ready are you to follow your goal?*
  o *On a scale of 0 to 10, how confident are you that you can meet your goal?*
- *Tip 3.* If time permits, ask the students to elaborate their readiness and confidence ratings by asking, "Why are you at a [whatever number they rated themself] and not at a [any number below that number]?" For instance, if a student rates themself with a 5 on readiness, you would ask, "Why are you at a 5 and not a 1?" Their response will be about reasons that they are feeling ready, and this is a type of change talk.
- *Tip 4.* In the case that your SMARTS students answer these inquiries with low responses, it's a good idea to check your SMARTS students' basic engine needs each day by asking:
  o *How well did you sleep last night?*
  o *How would you rate your mood, with 0 = bad and 10 = good?*
  o *Did you eat breakfast this morning?*

- *Tip 5.* Be sure all SMARTS players (student-support person, students, teachers) know their roles. Table 8.2 lays out key roles and duties to make sure everyone knows their responsibilities.

For Phase II's self- and teacher-goal-monitoring process, two processes are central to success: observing and recording. This is true for both teachers and students. The first part, observation, requires a student and a teacher to determine whether an event occurred or did not occur (i.e., the student stayed in their seat, raised their hand before speaking). This event should be clearly outlined or "operationalized" in the goal itself. That is, the goal should aptly describe the event itself using terms that are observable

TABLE 8.2. Phase II Key Roles and Responsibilities

Role	Responsibility

SMARTS Facilitator
• School psychologists
• School social worker
• Counselor
• Specials teacher
	• Prepare SMARTS self-monitoring sheets based on Phase I training goals for next 5 or so days.
	• Schedule an initial 10-minute Phase II meeting where you review the students' goals and practice rating their performances.
	• Check in with your SMARTS students each morning.
	  ○ Greet and compliment them on being there.
	  ○ Review goals.
	  ○ Prime students' readiness for following their goals.
	  ○ Check in with them if they appear to be having a tough morning.
	• Ensure that each teacher gets a copy of the students' SMARTS goal-monitoring sheet.
	• Collect SMARTS teacher-monitoring sheets each day.
	• Check in with SMARTS students at the end of the school day and collect their self-monitoring sheets.

SMARTS student	• Check in with your SMARTS Facilitator each day.
	• Remember your goal.
	• Remember to rate yourself as close to each rating interval as possible.
	• If you forget to rate yourself, it is OK; do it anyway!
	• Before you rate yourself:
	  ○ Stop—reread your goal!
	  ○ Pause—reflect and think about how you did.
	  ○ Go—circle the best response option that reflects how you did.
	• Reflect on your SMARTS lessons for help if you feel stuck.
	• Ask for help if you need it.

SMARTS teachers	• Review each SMARTS student's goal. • Record the students' performances on the SMARTS goal sheets. • Provide notes to contextualize any *no* ratings. • Speak to the SMARTS Facilitator and/or student if the goal is not accurate or not focused on the areas where the student needs to focus.

and measurable. In all honesty, this is the hardest part of self-monitoring for students. Students do not always agree with what the problem is, or they struggle to explain it accurately in a goal. Honestly, this is often the hardest part for all of us! Be gentle and encourage your students and their teachers to be patient on the goal-development part, to collaborate and ask each other for input, and to agree to continue working on modifying the goal.

The second part, recording, requires both the student and the teacher to decide and record whether or not the event outlined in the goal occurred. Seems simple, right? Did they stay in their seat for the last 30 minutes? Yes! Done. It *is* simple, so long as the recording sheet or device is not complicated. Though different formats and styles of goal-recording forms can be used for different students, behaviors, and school factors (e.g., schedules, start times), these forms should have some very basic and simple features. At its most simple, the form should have:

1. Basic identifying information like the student's name or nickname
2. Dates that the student self-monitored
3. Student's goal
4. Clearly defined rating intervals that are mutually exclusive
5. Clearly defined and exhaustive rating scale

Self-monitoring forms may have other details, such as student, teacher, and parent signature lines, areas for totaling scores, calculating accuracy, and other details, such as external reinforcers or other elements.

Rating Scale Considerations

Determining the optimal number of rating options for a self-monitoring form for elementary students is a critical consideration in designing an effective self-monitoring tool. Research suggests that a moderate number of rating options tends to yield more reliable and valid data, while still allowing students to differentiate their responses accurately. For elementary students, some research has suggested that a 5-point, Likert-type scale with clear descriptors is effective (Lane, 2007). A 5-point scale provides enough response options to capture nuanced distinctions in behaviors without overwhelming students. The goal is to strike the right balance between simplicity and sensitivity and to allow students to select a rating that expresses their performance accurately (Sanford et al., 2011). Underlying this decision is the importance in considering students' individual differences and developmental factors. Some research has suggested that younger students benefit from a simpler scale, such as a 3-point scale or smiley-face scales (Chafouleas, et al., 2009). Ultimately, selecting an appropriate number of rating options involves considering the cognitive and linguistic abilities of your students and having clarifying conversations about what the scales mean, as well as practicing with students who will be filling the scale out.

Forms 8.1 and 8.2 represent two formats we have used with students in grades K–3. Form 8.1 is a form for kindergarten students. In the first column, we often talked to students about their day and used either stickers or pictures drawn inside the boxes for each subject or break in the day. For example, for student time at recess, we used stickers or pictures of balls, a swing, or two friends playing together. For math, you would write the numbers 1, 2, and 3. For reading, a sticker or picture of a book. For writing, you guessed it: A, B, C. Lunch is a sticker of an apple or a lunch box. You can do the same for each period by using Form 8.2, or you can insert times or the names of classes for students who are reading or use stickers if that is what your students need. You get the idea. If your students in grades 1–3 feel challenged by differentiating between three response options, simplify and reduce the degrees of freedom by using Form 8.1 instead of Form 8.2.

Form 8.3 is for upper-elementary students. In our experience, upper-elementary students are not fans of using smiley faces to denote how they are doing. The example provided in Figure 8.1 has periods listed to define an interval of 1 hour, but you may also elect to replace the time frames with times that align with your school's schedule or to list specific courses or natural breaks in the school day (e.g., math, P.E., recess, reading) using Form 8.3. It is also good to practice communicating what the scale means to students in the context of their goals.

OVERCOMING CHALLENGES IN SELF-MONITORING

When we think about self-monitoring and self-management, almost all of us are talking about the ability to plan a goal and to carry out the necessary actions to achieve it. Part of success in any process is to monitor our progress along the way to know if we need to change, adjust, or reconsider our goals altogether. Successfully achieving any goal requires strategies (e.g., SMARTS replacement strategy), attention to the goal and self-monitoring (e.g., attention to my goal, attention to rate myself), and completion of tasks that are part of the goal itself (e.g., practicing deep breathing when stressed). Through practice and over time, students will learn to use these skills successfully. When teaching elementary students to self-monitor behavior goals, there are endless ways to experience challenges. These challenges can vary based on individual students, their developmental stages or any limitations, and students' and

Troubleshooting Tip

If a student experiences stress, practice the self-regulation strategies discussed in SMARTS Lessons 6–9 on perspective taking, deep breathing, and visualization, as well as being aware of internal and external responses to stressors.

Student Name: _____   Date: _____

SMARTS Goal: _____

_____

Replacement Strategy: _____

Interval	Class/Activity	Goal Monitoring *(Circle)*	Notes
Start–9:00		Did I follow my goal? *Y = 2 S = 1 N = 0*	
9:00–10:00		Did I follow my goal? *Y = 2 S = 1 N = 0*	
10:00–11:00		Did I follow my goal? *Y = 2 S = 1 N = 0*	
11:00–12:00		Did I follow my goal? *Y = 2 S = 1 N = 0*	
12:00–1:00		Did I follow my goal? *Y = 2 S = 1 N = 0*	
1:00–2:00		Did I follow my goal? *Y = 2 S = 1 N = 0*	
2:00–End		Did I follow my goal? *Y = 2 S = 1 N = 0*	
Add up the score at each interval to *Y = 2; S = 1; N = 0*			**Today's Total:** ___/14

Student: _____   Teacher: _____

FIGURE 8.1. SMARTS Self-Monitoring Form for Students in Grades 4–5, with 1-hour time intervals.

teachers' prior experiences with the process. Many of the challenges to the SMARTS self-monitoring program can be overcome during Phase I: SMARTS Student Training or by revisiting Phase I's training lessons when a student is struggling. We discuss a few common barriers here that we have seen over the years while watching school personnel implement SMARTS.

Lack of Understanding of SMARTS

At first, elementary students may struggle with the process of SMARTS or understanding the concept of self-monitoring altogether. Our recommendation here is to keep working with students through practice. Keep goals limited to one at a time. Over time, students will get it, will successfully monitor goals, and, with practice, will be able to monitor increasingly more complex goals.

Limited Student Self-Awareness

Elementary students are often short on self-awareness. This can make it challenging to accurately assess and rate their behaviors in a timely way. The best way to promote quality self-monitoring practices is to encourage students to stop, read the goal, think about what it means, and then think about specific events or examples of how they did or did not follow their goal. We must be certain that a student has selected an achievable goal and a replacement behavior. If the student is not capable of achieving the goal, back up and either build their skills or help them select a replacement behavior that they have the skills to use effectively.

Inconsistent Implementation

The solution to this challenge is to dedicate a person who is the SMARTS Facilitator. That way, this person is the expert in the process, can help troubleshoot poor implementation with solution-focused strategies presented in this book, and can work with students to ensure that they are following training and SMARTS practice guidelines.

Goal Isn't Targeting the Problem

Clearly defining the goal is the most challenging part of a self-monitoring program. The goal must target the problem area. The goal should be positively stated—that is, the goal should suggest students do something ("I will . . .") as opposed to stopping something ("I will stop . . ."). This is the purpose of the replacement behavior or the replacement strategy in SMARTS. The goal must also focus on a behavior that occurs frequently enough to be captured throughout the school day. If the behavior is of low frequency, then decrease the frequency or the number of intervals at which the student is self-monitoring. It is also important to work with teachers to ensure that the goal is something they reasonably agree will help the student while still supporting the student's autonomy and ability to select and craft their own goal.

> **Troubleshooting Tip**
>
> SMARTS sets students up with goals and self-monitoring practices and is designed to be practiced. Validate your students if they forget to rate themselves. Help them remember and create ways to remind themselves to monitor their goals. Overall, it takes time to learn a skill, and sometimes we make mistakes as a part of learning. Encourage this thinking in your students.

Teachers Aren't Rating SMARTS Goal Sheets

This is perhaps one of the most detrimental aspects of SMARTS. Indeed, prior studies have suggested that a self-monitoring plan will not only fail but may also do harm to students if teachers are not able to uphold their end of the intervention and provide feedback and ratings to students. We have watched as students have spent a good deal of time in SMARTS training, crafting a goal that targets classroom behaviors, dedicating themselves to improving, and monitoring that goal for a week, but then when they enter their Phase III data-review meeting, they learn that their teacher did not rate how well the student was doing on the goal all week. It is like taking the wind out of their sails. In these cases, work with the teacher to craft meaningful work-arounds. Some suggestions include flexibility for teachers in when they should rate students (e.g., just complete all ratings at the end of day), reminders (e.g., automated text messages or emails at the end of each day), and simply asking teachers to rate the charts only for students when they fail to meet their goals for the prior interval and then defaulting all other responses to be an assumed *yes*. This allows teachers to mark sheets only when they see students not following their goals. If you sense the teacher is disengaged or unmotivated to complete the ratings, it may be helpful to set up a time to discuss the program with them and refer to some motivational, enhancement conversation strategies reviewed in Chapter 5.

> **SMARTS Fact**
>
> In a prior study of SMARTS, for students who completed fewer than 80% of SMARTS self-monitoring intervals, the most predictive factor of why students were not completing ratings were because teachers were not completing SMARTS ratings. If it does not matter to the adults, students will not invest in the strategy either.

Students Aren't Rating SMARTS Goal Sheets

This may be a motivation issue. Not all of them are going to be jazzed about participating in this process. In these cases, it is important to have a conversation with students and discuss the problem, what they are not getting out of the solution, and what they would like out of a solution. This may be a good time to review the motivational interviewing strategies discussed in Chapter 5 to elicit change talk and motivation from the student. It is OK to consider external rewards for simply complying with the rating piece or to select a peer to help the rating. Select something the two of them can do together if they complete those ratings for a week.

Inaccurate Self-Assessment

While many think this is a real problem, it is not. Most of us know if we are following a goal. Despite some students not being entirely genuine with rating their own performances, the truth is that we all attempt to game our own goals from time to time. Science will tell you this about self-monitoring: Irrespective of the accuracy of the self-assessment ratings, student behaviors can and do still improve through the simple act of students having created a goal. If accuracy is an issue and you feel you need to address it, start by pairing up students to rate goals together. It is always good to work with pals, so pick someone whom your student is motivated by.

Addressing these challenges requires tailored approaches to the problem. It is important to scaffold your students during Phase I's training. If you need to, go back and revisit the specific skills that students need more practice and time to understand. By recognizing and proactively addressing these issues, we can help students develop effective self-monitoring skills and achieve their goals.

SUMMARY

The SMARTS program aims to change the behavior-support experience by embedding self-monitoring and teacher-monitoring practices into students' daily routines. By equipping students with the skills to set and monitor their own goals, we can foster a more autonomous and engaged environment. This approach not only enhances students' academic performance but also builds critical life-coping skills such as self-awareness, responsibility, and effective problem solving. As you implement these strategies, remember that consistency, collaboration, and celebration of achievements are key to sustaining motivation and achieving long-term success. Following is a brief checklist of items that we have covered and that can be referred to when you are engaging students in Phase II of SMARTS with self- and teacher-goal monitoring.

SMARTS Phase II Checklist

- **Scaffolding Student Training**
  - Introduce goal-development skills early.
  - Encourage student participation in self-monitoring.
- **Promoting Autonomy and Engagement**
  - Foster student ownership and responsibility.
  - Model positive social behaviors and problem-solving skills.
- **Implementing Phase II**
  - Begin self- and teacher monitoring after initial lessons.
  - Utilize provided goal sheets and tips for different grade levels.
- **Understanding Self-Monitoring**
  - Acknowledge its roots in behavioral psychology and social learning theory.
  - Recognize its effectiveness across various fields.
- **Applying the Reactivity Principle**
  - Encourage self-observation to induce behavioral changes.
  - Use self-monitoring to increase awareness and motivation.

- **Successful Self-Monitoring Tips**
  - Teach and model goal setting.
  - Use visual feedback tools.
  - Establish regular routines and checkpoints.
  - Foster self- and social awareness.
  - Celebrate milestones and achievements.
- **Creating Effective Routines**
  - Ensure emotionally safe environments.
  - Use motivational prompts and check basic needs.
  - Define clear roles for participants.
- **Key Monitoring Processes**
  - Use simple and clear behavior recording forms.
  - Use age-appropriate rating scales.
- **Addressing Challenges**
  - Ensure proper understanding and implementation of SMARTS.
  - Accurately target problems with goals.
  - Engage both teachers and students in monitoring.
  - Correct inaccurate self-assessments.

SMARTS Self-Monitoring Form for Kindergarten Students

Student Name: _____ Date: _____

SMARTS Goal: _____

_____

Replacement Strategy: _____

_____

Class/Activity	YES	NO
	☺ = 1	☹ = 0
	☺ = 1	☹ = 0
	☺ = 1	☹ = 0
	☺ = 1	☹ = 0
	☺ = 1	☹ = 0
	☺ = 1	☹ = 0
	☺ = 1	☹ = 0
	☺ = 1	☹ = 0
	☺ = 1	☹ = 0
Add the # of ☺ =		

Student: _____ Teacher: _____

Thank you for your SMARTS today!

SMARTS Self-Monitoring Form for Students in Grades 1–3

Student Name: _____ Date: _____

SMARTS Goal: _____

_____

Replacement Strategy: _____

_____

Class/Activity	YES	SOMETIMES	NO
	☺ = 2	😐 = 1	☹ = 0
	☺ = 2	😐 = 1	☹ = 0
	☺ = 2	😐 = 1	☹ = 0
	☺ = 2	😐 = 1	☹ = 0
	☺ = 2	😐 = 1	☹ = 0
	☺ = 2	😐 = 1	☹ = 0
	☺ = 2	😐 = 1	☹ = 0
	☺ = 2	😐 = 1	☹ = 0
	☺ = 2	😐 = 1	☹ = 0
Add the # of ☺ and 😐 =			

Student: _____ Teacher: _____

Thank you for your SMARTS today!

_____

SMARTS Self-Monitoring Form for Students in Grades 4–5

Student Name: _____ Date: _____

SMARTS Goal: _____

_____

Replacement Strategy: _____

_____

Interval	Class/Activity	Goal Monitoring (Circle)	Notes
Start–9:00		Did I follow my goal? Y = 2 S = 1 N = 0	
9:00–10:00		Did I follow my goal? Y = 2 S = 1 N = 0	
10:00–11:00		Did I follow my goal? Y = 2 S = 1 N = 0	
11:00–12:00		Did I follow my goal? Y = 2 S = 1 N = 0	
12:00–1:00		Did I follow my goal? Y = 2 S = 1 N = 0	
1:00–2:00		Did I follow my goal? Y = 2 S = 1 N = 0	
2:00–End		Did I follow my goal? Y = 2 S = 1 N = 0	
Add up the score at each interval to Y = 2; S = 1; N = 0			**Today's Total:___/14**

Student: _____ Teacher: _____

Thank you for your SMARTS today!

CHAPTER 9

SMARTS Phase III
Processing Self- and Teacher Data

In this chapter, we discuss Phase III of SMARTS, the processing phase. Once students and teachers have rated student-goal progress for several days to a week, these data can be translated into daily percentages. Those percentages can then be graphed for visual comparison. Students can compare their own ratings alongside their original goals, compare their performances alongside their prior performances, and compare their own data alongside that of their teachers' data. Quality feedback and processing with students facilitates growth, confirms efforts or illuminates new strategies, enhances motivation to improve, and is a necessary component for anyone to improve goal performance. Performance feedback combined with self-monitoring has emerged as an evidence-based approach to promote academic engagement and self-regulation practices among students, and it is an important step to making SMARTS matter and work to help students learn new skills. In this chapter, we:

- Discuss the impact of performance feedback within the context of self-monitoring, including some history and evidence for why we know performance feedback works.
- Consider the benefits and implications that MI can bring to the SMARTS Phase III data processing and feedback for students and share effective strategies to enhance the self-monitoring experience.
- Provide an example of Mac and Alex walking through a week's worth of goal-monitoring sheets from Mac and their teacher and also completing the graphing form and goal-reformation guide used in the SMARTS Phase III feedback process.

BACKGROUND AND RATIONALE FOR DATA REVIEW AND PROCESSING: PERFORMANCE FEEDBACK

The act, process, and procedures encased in the educational practice of providing performance feedback has been the subject of extensive research within the field of education. Many studies have examined the effects of various approaches to providing feedback and its effects on subsequent student academic achievement, motivation, and classroom instructional practices. Performance feedback in education settings refers to the provision of information to students (and/or teachers and school leaders) about their performances and what they might do differently to achieve better outcomes and goals. Early studies in the 1960s and 1970s explored the effects of performance feedback on academic achievement. These seminal studies often employed simple feedback systems, such as providing students with grade cards and scores. Research during this time did establish a connection between feedback and improved student outcomes (Bloom, 1968; Kulik & Kulik, 1988).

> **What Is Performance Feedback?**
>
> Performance feedback is the process of providing individuals with information about their performances on a task in relation to a specific goal or set of expectations. Often, performance feedback involves communicating observations and assessments or evaluations of how an individual's efforts or work toward meeting a goal or set of expectations is progressing and may also include conversations about strategies to more effectively achieve that goal.

In the 1980s and 1990s, educational researchers evolved their collective inquiries into the effects of performance feedback to differentiate between the types of feedback and the varying effects on motivation and academic achievement. This period of research highlighted that supportive, constructive, and positive feedback plays an important role in shaping a student's academic and social self-concept, perceptions of academic competence, and that those approaches enhanced intrinsic motivation (Ceci & Kumar, 2016; Hattie & Timperley, 2007). The emergence of formative assessment research in the late 1990s brought increased attention to the potential of feedback as a tool for improving both learning for students and instructional practices for teachers. These studies explored the characteristics of effective feedback such as how specific the feedback should be, the optimal timeliness of feedback events, and the effects of providing actionable guidance (Black & William, 1998; Shute, 2008). In the 2000s, researchers applied the concept of performance feedback to better understand its role in enhancing self-regulated learning with studies showing how feedback promoted increased metacognitive skills, self-monitoring, self-reflection, and self-regulatory practices (Panadero & Jonsson, 2013). Today, we know that the importance of feedback and research, particularly around the area of motivational interviewing, provides new insights into the power of performance feedback, the style of the coach or facilitator leading the performance feedback session, and key language that facilitators can cue in on with students to optimize their ability to resolve ambiguity toward goal achievement and growth.

To summarize, decades of research have shown the power of quality performance feedback and its impact on academic (Koziol et al., 2017), behavioral, and self-regulation performance of students (Thompson et al., 2012, 2014, 2021). Feedback that is supportive and non-judgmental, specific and concrete, timely yet brief, and focused on actionable behaviors or strategies to achieve goals enables students to track their progress, see improvement over time, and make modest adjustments in behaviors that help to optimize goal-oriented success (Weber et al., 2016). The process and the rewarding improvements in performance will not only reinforce these practices but also help students gain a deeper understanding of the learning process.

> **Feedback Tip**
>
> Supportive and nonjudgmental feedback that is specific, concrete, timely yet brief, and focused on actionable behaviors or strategies allows students to track their progress, observe improvements over time, and make small adjustments to optimize goal-oriented success.

KEY TIPS FOR SMARTS FACILITATORS TO PROVIDE QUALITY PERFORMANCE FEEDBACK

MI strategies and quality performance feedback best practices are essential components of SMARTS as a self-monitoring intervention for students. Here, we list key tips or effective practices for SMARTS Facilitators to strengthen the impact of SMARTS goal development and monitoring processes. The key tips included and listed in Table 9.1 are certainly not meant to be exhaustive, but they reflect research-supported practices and the spirit of MI to improve skills for facilitators to deliver high-quality performance feedback, promote student engagement, strengthen students' capacity for self-regulation, and encourage positive behavior change.

Tip 1: Establish and Maintain a Supportive and Trusting Relationship

There is a reason this is the first tip we offer; it is perhaps the most meaningful and important thing we can all do for our students in education settings. We cannot state this enough: It is the reason why we are there as teachers. As teachers and educators, our studies increasingly show that students report having a hard time finding trusted adults at school. Many students report that they do not have an adult at school they can go to if they have a problem, and that is an issue. We acknowledge that it can be challenging to build strong relationships with every student, especially those who are disruptive and challenging. But there are still small, concrete steps that can be taken.

TABLE 9.1. Research-Supported Strategies to Enhance SMARTS Phase III Feedback

Tips	What it looks like
Establish and maintain a supportive and trusting relationship to enhance feedback.	• Show genuine interest and empathy; find common interests. • Give full attention, maintain eye contact, and use understanding cues. • Validate emotions, recognizing their illogical nature. • Model calmness and respect, even when students are unregulated.
Utilize effective MI techniques.	• Express empathy: Understand and validate the student's feelings. • Identify discrepancy: Ask questions that highlight the gap between current performance and SMARTS goals. • Roll with resistance: Avoid arguing; acknowledge and explore any resistance from your students. • Support self-efficacy: Recognize change talk and encourage belief in the ability to change.

Establish realistic goals from the start.	• Remember our SMARTS goals guidelines:
	  ○ Specific: Define clear and precise goals.
	  ○ Measurable: Ensure that progress toward goals can be quantified.
	  ○ Achievable: Set goals the student has the skills to accomplish.
	  ○ Realistic: Set an attainable goal.
	  ○ Timely: Establish deadlines for goal completion.

Provide specific and actionable feedback.	• Be concise and clear. • Focus on behavior—what can we do? • Provide an example. • Do not tell a student what they "ought to do." • Explore next steps.
Provide feedback in a timely manner.	• SMARTS studies suggest that feedback should occur each week on the last day of school.
Provide individualized feedback.	• Rely on a student's SMARTS data. • Explore how the data reflect the stated goal. • Examine any comments left by teachers. • Incorporate student perspectives on why the data look the way they do.
Be constructive.	• Praise effort, not outcomes. • Start with the positives, move to constructive critiques, then end on a positive note. • Ask students what they think happened.
Cultivate self-reflection.	• Demonstrate your own ability to reflect on mistakes as clues to success. • Rely on the SMARTS processing guides to help the student reflect.

- Show genuine interest and empathy for students' perspectives, feelings, and experiences. Find common experiences/interests to talk about at school, no matter how big or small.
- Give students your attention, maintain eye contact, and use verbal and nonverbal cues that show you understand and value their thoughts and opinions.
- Validate emotions. This is important, as students experience a range of emotions that are not always logical.
- Co-regulate. No matter how unregulated your students can get and no matter how much that may rattle you, it is important to always model and maintain a calm and respectful demeanor—particularly when a student's seemingly out-of-control emotions are directed at you.

Tip 2: Utilize Effective MI Techniques

Use scientifically supported MI strategies to encourage student autonomy, ownership, intrinsic motivation for change, and self-directed and goal-oriented behavior. Using open-ended questions, exploring ambivalence to change, and evoking students' own reasons and ideas for change are solid ways to show your students that you care and support them and believe they are capable of change. Remember to use your OARS and resist the righting reflex. Little can undermine a relationship with a student more than telling them what do, whereas supporting student autonomy strengthens trust. Consider a student who says, "I'm not sure SMARTS is the right thing for me." One type of educator response might be to say, "It's in your best interest. You need to do this, or else you aren't gonna make it out of fifth grade." This response would illustrate the righting reflex and would almost certainly cement the student's disinterest in the program, undermine their autonomy, and lower their trust in this adult. An alternate response would be to directly acknowledge the student's concerns, emphasize their choices, and invite further conversation. "I appreciate your honesty and your interest in being sure this is a good fit. While I do hope you stay, it's ultimately your choice. You seem like you're feeling discouraged."

Tip 3: Establish Clear and Realistic SMARTS Goals from the Start

Work collaboratively with students and teachers to ensure that students can set clear and realistic self-monitoring goals. There is no magic trick here; it truly requires effort, dedication, and time to ensure that the student craft the right goals to be successful in the classroom. Goals that are Specific, Measurable, Attainable, Relevant, Time-bound, and Strategy-focused (SMARTS goals!) will help once we find the correct issues to target. Being descriptive and providing concrete examples to enhance students' input, ownership, understanding, and autonomy around goal creation will encourage a successful SMARTS experience.

Tip 4: Provide Specific and Actionable Feedback

Deliver performance feedback that is actionable and specific. Studies have shown that students who receive strategy-laden feedback between testing sessions improve performance. An unhelpful thing we see educators say to students is, "Nice job" or "Great work." These are generic statements. Do not be generic; be specific. Provide details about exactly what went well. Suggest alternative strategies or ways to accomplish any task. Be curious with your student; ask them what they think could result in a better outcome. If you have an idea about a strategy, ask your student for their permission to suggest it. Saying something like, "Hey, do you want any beta on how I might approach that?" will get an affirmative response, and students will be more likely to try it than if you say, "What you ought to do is. . . ." Focus on both strengths and areas of improvement related to their SMARTS goals. Where students may lack understanding, use concrete examples and stories to explain things in a way that enhances student understanding.

Tip 5: Provide Feedback in a Timely and Incremental Way

Provide feedback in a timely way. Our studies have shown SMARTS to be more effective when students and teachers self-monitor for a typical school week from Monday to Friday before processing their self- and teacher-goal-monitoring data on Friday afternoons when possible.

Tip 6: Individualized Feedback for All Students

When we recognize that students all have individualized learning styles, preferences, and needs, we know we also need to provide them with individualized feedback about their performances. Some students need more scaffolding and performance feedback than others. Invite them to see that it is OK to support people in a differential and needs-based way. Personalizing feedback and connecting it to each student's goal will help them maintain their own engagement and sense of intrinsic motivation toward trying something new to achieve that goal.

Tip 7: Provide Specific Praise, and Provide Critical-Yet-Constructive Feedback

Strive for a balanced approach when providing feedback. We all know the importance of providing positive reinforcement and feedback about effort and progress. Be sure to always praise effort, even more than a successful outcome. The outcome is important, don't get us wrong, but research clearly indicates that we need to praise student effort and hard work toward that outcome. Equally as important, be sure to provide students with critical-yet-constructive feedback to promote constructive communication, growth, and improvement. Start with positive feedback. This helps facilitate a receptive atmosphere in the student to hear the constructive criticism later. When giving constructive feedback, be matter-of-fact, specific, and objective. Critique is not personal; it is intended to foster a growth mindset. Use the MI "Columbo" technique: "I am confused. You worked so hard all week, and then on Thursday afternoon, your ratings seemed to decline. What do you think happened?" Listen actively and with empathy when you ask students what might have gone wrong. Meet one-word answers with open-ended questions. Accept resistance if encountered, recognize it, and ask why it might be present.

Tip 8: Encourage Self-Reflection and Self-Evaluation

Encourage ownership over the processing of self- and teacher-monitoring data. The first few processing sessions will be you, the SMARTS Facilitator, leading most of the discussion and processing of the data. Use the SMARTS processing guides. Once students learn the process by the second or third meeting, they will be familiar with the data, ways to view the data, and the prompts on the SMARTS Phase III processing forms (see Forms 9.1 and 9.2 for examples), and this knowledge of the processing routine will free you as the facilitator to have more of a conversation with students, where you can ask questions about what they see in their data and ways they might try to alter their goals for the following week.

SMARTS PHASE III: DATA REVIEW, PROCESSING, AND PERFORMANCE FEEDBACK

The Phase III: SMARTS Data Review, Processing, and Performance Feedback phase of the SMARTS intervention is perhaps the most important. Following a Phase II period of data collection, it will then be time to meet with your SMARTS groups and review the student self- and teacher-goal progress ratings from the prior days. The purpose of the review is to appraise performance against the student's goal and review, revise, or maintain that goal going forward. The Phase II self- and teacher-monitoring phase will produce behavioral data that will be the subject of the Phase III review meeting. During the processing phase, SMARTS Facilitators will meet with SMARTS student groups for approximately 30–35 minutes. With support, students will plot the total percentages on a graph, review the graph, and respond to several

Establishing a Phase III Routine

Keep SMARTS Phase III processing and data-review meetings moving quickly. Establish a routine and maintain that routine. Data-review meetings should not last more than 30–35 minutes and can be done with the same group as Phase I: SMARTS Student Training. As students get more familiar with the process, promote their autonomy by transferring the duties to them and supervise their work.

prompts in the Data Assessment and Goal Reformation Guide (Form 9.2). The prompts ask students to consider their data in several ways, such as:

- Compare your current self-monitoring data to your current goal.
- Compare your current self-monitoring data to your prior progress.
- Compare your current self-monitoring data to your teacher's data.

Many of the skills covered in the lessons are also useful during the Phase III data-processing stage. Be sure to remind students of lessons on perspective taking, discussions on goal setting and problem solving, and of the various replacement strategies they may have identified early on but have overlooked at this stage. This ability to access materials from earlier lessons is another benefit of keeping a SMARTS student folder and maintaining all worksheets from Phase I's student training, Phase II's daily goal self-monitoring and teacher-monitoring forms, and any prior Phase III graphs and processing documents. During these meetings, if students work well together, encourage them to discuss their data, identify areas of discrepancy from their goals or their teachers' data, and identify any specific events that may have contributed to the discrepancies.

When students show several weeks' worth of success in maintaining behaviors in the classroom according to the data, they experience success from SMARTS. Successful and consistent goal attainment and increased agreement between students and teachers will signal the need for students to either fade the intervention (see Chapter 10 for a discussion on fading) or to select a new goal.

It is important to create a routine for Phase III's processing with SMARTS students. Setting regular meeting times will create expectations that this work matters and will ensure that time is used well as students get comfortable with the routine. It is also important to let the student- and teacher-goal-monitoring data speak for itself—or rather that students' interpretations of the data are the leading insight. Consider yourself as a guide to the process rather than the sage on the stage with the answers. It is also OK to rely on your schoolwide reinforcement systems or token systems to reward students for achieving their SMARTS goals. Providing external rewards for success will not undermine internal motivation; it will highlight that students did a good thing that is valued by you and others at the school.

Rely on the SMARTS Data

Focus on the data and rely on the SMARTS processing forms. In observations of students who present challenging behaviors, suggest that these two strategies help depersonalize or decouple the feedback from the educators providing the feedback and focus students on how they are doing and how they could do better.

Table 9.2 details key roles and responsibilities for Phase III's data review and processing. As shown in Table 9.2, it is important to understand that Phase II and Phase III repeat iteratively for students on the SMARTS self-monitoring plan. The Phase II roles

TABLE 9.2. SMARTS Phase III Key Roles and Responsibilities

Role	Responsibility

SMARTS Facilitator
• School psychologists
• School social worker
• Counselor
• Specials seacher
• Para support person
	PHASE II continues
	• Prepare SMARTS self-monitoring sheets based on Phase I training goals for the next 5 or so days.
	• Schedule an initial 10-minute Phase II meeting where you review the students' goals and practice rating performances.
	• Check in each morning with you SMARTS students.
	• Greet and compliment them on being there.
	• Review goals.
	• Prime students' readiness for following their goals.
	• Check in with them if they appear to be having a tough morning.
	• Ensure that each teacher gets a copy of the students' SMARTS goal-monitoring sheet.
	• Collect SMARTS teacher-monitoring sheets each day.
	• Check in with SMARTS students at the end of the school day and collect their self-monitoring sheets.
	
	PHASE III
	• **Meet weekly with SMARTS students in small groups.**
	• **Prepare SMARTS folders with data-processing handouts from Chapter 9:**
	   ○ **Data Assessment Guide**
	   ○ **Goal Assessment Guide**
	   ○ **Goal Reformation Guide**

SMARTS student	PHASE II continues
	• Check in with your SMARTS Facilitator each day.
	• Remember your goal.
	• Remember to rate yourself as close to each rating interval as possible.
	• If you forget to rate yourself, it is OK; do it anyway!
	• Before you rate yourself:
	   ○ Stop—reread your goal
	   ○ Pause—reflect and think about how you did.
	   ○ Go—circle the best response option that reflects how you did.
	• Reflect on your SMARTS lessons for help if you feel stuck.
	• Ask for help if you need it.
	
	PHASE III
	• **Meet weekly with SMARTS Facilitator in a small group to complete:**
	   ○ **Data Assessment Guide**
	   ○ **Goal Assessment Guide**
	   ○ **Goal Reformation Guide**

(continued)

TABLE 9.2. *(continued)*

Role	Responsibility
SMARTS teachers	PHASE II continues • Review each SMARTS student's goal. • Record the student's performance on the SMARTS goal sheet. • Provide notes to contextualize any *no* ratings. • Speak to the SMARTS Facilitator and/or student if the goal is not accurate or not focused on the areas where the student needs to focus. **PHASE III** • **Provide suggestions to improve goal formation for SMARTS students.**

continue, while Phase III duties will begin to occur weekly. Phase III duties are listed in **bold** in Table 9.2.

At your first and subsequent data-review meetings, it is recommended that students' SMARTS folders are prepared ahead of time to save effort and dedicate time to group work. For each data-review meeting, we have developed a series of forms that help students walk through their data, compare their weekly self-monitoring and teacher-feedback data to each other, and compare the data to their goals as well as prior performances. It is important to know that students do not need to write all responses by themselves; they can work in pairs and their partners can take notes, or they can work verbally through the form. It is helpful to keep track of these forms and why changes are made over time, so taking some notes is helpful. Here is the process and the order in which the Phase III forms should be used:

1. **Weekly goal-monitoring sheets.** Students need their completed daily goal-monitoring sheets and teacher-monitoring forms (see Chapter 8). Request that students add up the totals each day to expedite the data-review process. When they add the totals for each day, not only are they practicing math, but they can also then use the total number of points for each day of self-monitoring and teacher-rating forms to enter the percentages provided on the SMARTS percentage key charts.

2. **SMARTS Graphing Form (Form 9.1).** Once students have their self-monitoring and teacher-rating forms for the week, they can use the SMARTS Graphing Form. If each student adds up the total for each day, they can then refer to the percentage key chart for the type of form they are using (kindergarten, or grades 1–3 and 4–5 forms) and mark the graph with an *x* on the approximate place corresponding to each day.

    a. **Pro SMARTS Tip 1: Foster independence.** Depending on their developmental levels, students will likely need additional help with these steps. For kindergarten and grades 1–3 students, they will need more direct support. For grades 4–5, suggest pairing students together and guiding them through this step. They can often help each other. Once they do this once or twice, most students can then do it on their own.

b. **Pro SMARTS Tip 2: Use color.** Using different-colored pencils for marking the student and teacher ratings on the graph form will be a helpful way to help students distinguish between the two percentages or perspectives on the graph and will assist them with comparing the two lines and answering questions in the next step.

3. **SMARTS Data Assessment and Goal Reformation Guide (Form 9.2).** Using the SMARTS Graphing Form and any weekly notes from students or teachers to contextualize the ratings, request that students complete the SMARTS Data Assessment Guide. The guide will ask students to review their data and graphed line and their teacher's data and graphed line, and then compare the data against the goal, as well as compare their own data to that of their teachers. Finally, the form will prompt students to reflect on what was happening on days where they did well and on days where they may have fallen short before asking students to determine whether they will keep their current goals, alter them, or change them altogether. This is where comments and notes are helpful.

4. **SMARTS Goal Forms (Forms 8.1–8.3).** Once students have completed the goal-assessment form, they can then determine if they need to keep the same goal or alter the goal slightly (i.e., change the percentage of performance, change the replacement strategy, tweak the wording to be more specific), and then they are good to go back and repeat Phase II: SMARTS Student Self- and Teacher Monitoring. As discussed in Chapter 8, kindergarten students should use the simpler and more straightforward rating found in Form 8.1, students in grades 1–3 should use Form 8.2, and students in upper-elementary grades should use Form 8.3.

a. **Pro SMARTS Tip 3: Stay organized.** Request that students complete one goal sheet and then make 10 copies (five for the student for the next week and five for the student's teacher). Keep these in their SMARTS folders for the following days' self-monitoring morning check-ins.

After 4–5 days of self-monitoring, you will again meet with students and review their progress. Repeated practice will help students do this step quicker each time, and obtaining feedback from teachers on the goal-reformation process will help to hone their goals from week to week. Now that we have introduced the basic process and forms to you, let's sit in while Mac and Alex review a full week of Mac and a teacher called Mr. Smith rating Mac's goal and see how these forms are filled out, how MI and autonomy support is used as a conversational tool to support Mac's engagement and motivation for their goal, and how they use the forms as a tool for a conversation to help Mac move toward an important goal.

Example: Progress Review Meeting with Alex and Mac

In the example below, we highlight an exchange between our school social worker, Alex, and our student, Mac D, in which Alex begins processing Mac's goal progress for the current week. The two meet every Friday afternoon, right before school ends for the week. During this exchange, we note different MI strategies that Alex utilizes while processing with Mac.

The following exchange is broken down into sections that focus on different elements of the processing meetings. This first section focuses on greetings exchanged between Alex and Mac.

> **What You Need for Phase III**
>
> Alex will be prepared before the meeting with Mac's SMARTS folder and copies of:
>
> - Mac's completed Phase II self- and teacher-rating forms for the week (Figures 9.1–9.5)
> - A blank Phase III SMARTS Graphing Form (Form 9.1)
> - A clean Phase III SMARTS Data Assessment and Goal Reformation Guide (Form 9.2)

ALEX: Happy Friday, Mac. How's it going today? (*Open-ended question*)

MAC: It's OK. I'm going to the movies tonight!

ALEX: That sounds like fun, Mac! You will have to let me know how the movie is next week.

MAC: OK!

ALEX: I am hoping we can process through you and your teacher's progress monitoring on your goal this week. Does that sound alright with you? (*Setting agenda, asking permission*)

Engagement is the priority in every meeting. Stephen Rollnick once commented that the first 20% of every meeting should be spent on rapport building. Here, we see Alex check in about Mac's weekend plans and show genuine interest in them. Alex then transitions to the focus on their meeting for the day by setting a brief agenda and getting Mac's agreement.

MAC: That sounds good to me.

ALEX: Great. Let's look at what days you believe you met or were working toward your goal and let's review your daily forms for the last week, the ones you filled out on your own goal and the ones Mr. Smith completed. We can mark the Phase III SMARTS Graphing Form with the data.

MAC: Sounds good. Can I do it?

ALEX: Absolutely. We have practiced in the past, and I know you know how to do it. Let me know if you want help.

Mac proceeds to lay out the self-monitoring and teacher-monitoring forms that Mr. Smith completed regarding Mac's goal performance for the week (Figures 9.1–

(a)

Student Name: _Mac_ Date: _3/4/2024_

SMARTS Goal: _I will work on not yelling or getting into arguments with my classmates and teacher. I know I am working on my goal by not getting into trouble with my teacher and not missing out on recess._

Replacement Strategy: _I will use box breathing when I feel angry and will write down my thoughts and feelings in a journal. I will also count to three and take deep breaths._

Interval	Class/Activity	Goal Monitoring *(Circle)*	Notes
Start–9:00	Morning announcement	Did I follow my goal? (Y = 2) S = 1 N = 0	Conflict with my classmates that I walked away from
9:00–10:00	Specials	Did I follow my goal? (Y = 2) S = 1 N = 0	Other students tried to distract me in P.E.
10:00–11:00	Math	Did I follow my goal? (Y = 2) S = 1 N = 0	Used my journal to express frustration
11:00–12:00	Lunch/recess	Did I follow my goal? (Y = 2) S = 1 N = 0	Fun at lunch
12:00–1:00	Reading	Did I follow my goal? (Y = 2) S = 1 N = 0	Enjoyed reading group with friends
1:00–2:00	Science	Did I follow my goal? Y = 2 (S = 1) N = 0	Argued with a peer
2:00–End	Social Studies	Did I follow my goal? (Y = 2) S = 1 N = 0	Fun group project
Add up the score at each interval to Y = 2; S = 1; N = 0			**Today's Total:** _13_ /14

Student: _Mac_ Teacher: _Andy Smith_

(continued)

FIGURE 9.1. (a) Mac's Goal Self-Monitoring Worksheet and (b) Mr. Smith's Goal Monitoring Worksheet for Mac—Monday.

(b)

Student Name: _Mac_   Date: _3/4/2024_

SMARTS Goal: _I will work on not yelling or getting into arguments with my classmates and teacher. I know I am working on my goal by not getting into trouble with my teacher and not missing out on recess._

Replacement Strategy: _I will use box breathing when I feel angry and will write down my thoughts and feelings in a journal. I will also count to three and take deep breaths._

Interval	Class/Activity	Goal Monitoring (*Circle*)	Notes
Start–9:00	Morning announcement	Did I follow my goal? Y = 2 (S = 1) N = 0	A classmate interrupted Mac a few times and Mac snapped at them.
9:00–10:00	Specials	Did I follow my goal? Y = 2 (S = 1) N = 0	Gym teacher shared that Mac started to get into arguments during a game and was redirected.
10:00–11:00	Math	Did I follow my goal? (Y = 2) S = 1 N = 0	Upset and wrote what was upsetting him. Shared with me during transition time. Great work, Mac!
11:00–12:00	Lunch/recess	Did I follow my goal? (Y = 2) S = 1 N = 0	Lunch monitor was good.
12:00–1:00	Reading	Did I follow my goal? (Y = 2) S = 1 N = 0	Mac did very well and complimented another classmate during small-group reading.
1:00–2:00	Science	Did I follow my goal? Y = 2 (S = 1) N = 0	Got upset with a peer during worktime and took several attempts to redirect.
2:00–End	Social Studies	Did I follow my goal? (Y = 2) S = 1 N = 0	Mac worked well with the rest of his table to complete a mini-group project.
Add up the score at each interval to Y = 2; S = 1; N = 0			**Today's Total:** _11_ /14

Student: _Mac_   Teacher: _Andy Smith_

FIGURE 9.1. (*continued*)

9.5). Mac reviews each day, starting with his own ratings from Monday through Friday, and then enters Mr. Smith's ratings from Monday through Friday on the Phase III SMARTS Graphing Form. Then Mac connects each data point for each day using two different-colored pencils, black for their own ratings and gray for Mr. Smith's ratings, to help distinguish the two perspectives (Figure 9.6 on p. 218). Mac enters a few summary comments from the rating forms over the week and then shares the form with Alex.

Support Autonomy in SMARTS Phase III

Alex will be prepared with Mac's Phase II self- and teacher-monitoring forms for the week and will work with Alex to review each and enter the data into the Phase III SMARTS Graphing Form. The first few times Mac enters the data, Alex will provide more guidance and support. With practice, Mac will soon be able to complete this task on their own in just a few minutes. Comments from the Phase II student- and teacher-monitoring forms can be noted on the graphing form for context as to the totals offered in the overall daily ratings.

(a)

Student Name: _Mac_   Date: _3/5/2024_

SMARTS Goal: _I will work on not yelling or getting into arguments with my classmates and teacher. I know I am working on my goal by not getting into trouble with my teacher and not missing out on recess._

Replacement Strategy: _I will use box breathing when I feel angry and will write down my thoughts and feelings in a journal. I will also count to three and take deep breaths._

Interval	Class/Activity	Goal Monitoring *(Circle)*	Notes
Start–9:00	Morning announcement	Did I follow my goal? Y = 2 S = 1 (N = 0)	Did not sleep well and did not want to be at school
9:00–10:00	Specials	Did I follow my goal? Y = 2 (S = 1) N = 0	Started slow in gym but by the end felt better
10:00–11:00	Math	Did I follow my goal? (Y = 2) S = 1 N = 0	Math was fun and I got extra credit today
11:00–12:00	Lunch/recess	Did I follow my goal? (Y = 2) S = 1 N = 0	Sat by my favorite people for lunch
12:00–1:00	Reading	Did I follow my goal? (Y = 2) S = 1 N = 0	Felt really tired and did not want to do work but did not cause problems
1:00–2:00	Science	Did I follow my goal? Y = 2 (S = 1) N = 0	Mad after my teacher yelled at me but did my science work
2:00–End	Social Studies	Did I follow my goal? (Y = 2) S = 1 N = 0	Group project was fun
Add up the score at each interval to Y = 2; S = 1; N = 0			**Today's Total:** _10_ /14

Student: _Mac_   Teacher: _Andy Smith_

(continued)

FIGURE 9.2. (a) Mac's Goal Self-Monitoring Worksheet and (b) Mr. Smith's Goal Monitoring Worksheet for Mac—Tuesday.

(b)

Student Name: _Mac_   Date: _3/5/2024_

SMARTS Goal: _I will work on not yelling or getting into arguments with my classmates and teacher. I know I am_
working on my goal by not getting into trouble with my teacher and not missing out on recess.

Replacement Strategy: _I will use box breathing when I feel angry and will write down my thoughts and feelings in_
a journal. I will also count to three and take deep breaths.

Interval	Class/Activity	Goal Monitoring *(Circle)*	Notes
Start–9:00	Morning announcement	Did I follow my goal? Y = 2 (S = 1) N = 0	Came into class with a scowl but improved and did well
9:00–10:00	Specials	Did I follow my goal? (Y = 2) S = 1 N = 0	Gym went well today, no problems
10:00–11:00	Math	Did I follow my goal? (Y = 2) S = 1 N = 0	Completed assignment and extra credit
11:00–12:00	Lunch/recess	Did I follow my goal? (Y = 2) S = 1 N = 0	Lunch monitor said Mac had a good lunch
12:00–1:00	Reading	Did I follow my goal? Y = 2 S = 1 (N = 0)	Mac was distracted and argued when confronted over not doing task at hand
1:00–2:00	Science	Did I follow my goal? (Y = 2) S = 1 N = 0	Recovered well and completed assigned work
2:00–End	Social Studies	Did I follow my goal? (Y = 2) S = 1 N = 0	Continued on group project and contributed
Add up the score at each interval to Y = 2; S = 1; N = 0			Today's Total: _11_ /14

Student: _Mac_   Teacher: _Andy Smith_

FIGURE 9.2. *(continued)*

MAC: Hmm, I know Monday and Thursday were good, but from the looks of it, Thursday and Friday I did not do so well, and it looks like Mr. Smith agrees with that. So all the days but those two I feel like I followed my goal.

ALEX: So, you met your goal on Monday, Tuesday, and Wednesday? (*Focus on success*)

MAC: (*nods*)

ALEX: How were you able to meet your goal these days? (*Open-ended question*)

MAC: Those were days I didn't get in trouble and my teacher didn't have to talk to me. I marked down that I was asking questions, and I got my work done, so I didn't have any homework!

ALEX: That's really impressive, Mac. (*Affirmation*) You were able to complete your assignments on your own, and you didn't have any homework? (*Support self-efficacy*)

MAC: (*smiling*) Yeah! I felt like I did really well. Mr. Smith even let me cash in some reward tokens, and I got a new desk pet.

ALEX: That is exciting. When you think about Thursday and Friday, what do you remember? (*Open-ended question*)

(a)

Student Name: _Mac_   Date: _3/6/2024_

SMARTS Goal: _I will work on not yelling or getting into arguments with my classmates and teacher. I know I am working on my goal by not getting into trouble with my teacher and not missing out on recess._

Replacement Strategy: _I will use box breathing when I feel angry and will write down my thoughts and feelings in a journal. I will also count to three and take deep breaths._

Interval	Class/Activity	Goal Monitoring *(Circle)*	Notes
Start–9:00	Morning announcement	Did I follow my goal? (Y = 2) S = 1 N = 0	Felt good this morning, had fun on the way to school
9:00–10:00	Specials	Did I follow my goal? (Y = 2) S = 1 N = 0	Gym was fun
10:00–11:00	Math	Did I follow my goal? (Y = 2) S = 1 N = 0	Math was easy and quick in groups.
11:00–12:00	Lunch/recess	Did I follow my goal? (Y = 2) S = 1 N = 0	Brought my lunch and traded with friends
12:00–1:00	Reading	Did I follow my goal? (Y = 2) S = 1 N = 0	Enjoyed reading silently today
1:00–2:00	Science	Did I follow my goal? Y = 2 (S = 1) N = 0	Building models but my partner would not help and I got frustrated and did it all
2:00–End	Social Studies	Did I follow my goal? (Y = 2) S = 1 N = 0	Played Oregon trail in social studies class with good partners, we won!
Add up the score at each interval to Y = 2; S = 1; N = 0			**Today's Total:** _13_ /14

Student: _Mac_   Teacher: _Andy Smith_

(continued)

FIGURE 9.3. (a) Mac's Goal Self-Monitoring Worksheet and (b) Mr. Smith's Goal Monitoring Worksheet for Mac—Wednesday.

(b)

Student Name: _Mac_   Date: _3/6/2024_

SMARTS Goal: _I will work on not yelling or getting into arguments with my classmates and teacher. I know I am working on my goal by not getting into trouble with my teacher and not missing out on recess._

Replacement Strategy: _I will use box breathing when I feel angry and will write down my thoughts and feelings in a journal. I will also count to three and take deep breaths._

Interval	Class/Activity	Goal Monitoring *(Circle)*	Notes
Start–9:00	Morning announcement	Did I follow my goal? (Y = 2) S = 1 N = 0	Showed up in a good mood, seemed well rested
9:00–10:00	Specials	Did I follow my goal? (Y = 2) S = 1 N = 0	No problems
10:00–11:00	Math	Did I follow my goal? (Y = 2) S = 1 N = 0	Worked quickly and had no conflicts
11:00–12:00	Lunch/recess	Did I follow my goal? (Y = 2) S = 1 N = 0	
12:00–1:00	Reading	Did I follow my goal? (Y = 2) S = 1 N = 0	Silent reading
1:00–2:00	Science	Did I follow my goal? (Y = 2) S = 1 N = 0	Nice science class. Mac worked with challenging peers
2:00–End	Social Studies	Did I follow my goal? (Y = 2) S = 1 N = 0	Again worked well with others
Add up the score at each interval to Y = 2; S = 1; N = 0			Today's Total: _14_ /21

Student: _Mac_   Teacher: _Andy Smith_

FIGURE 9.3. *(continued)*

MAC: I was bad. I was really tired Thursday. I felt sick, and then Friday started out well and I thought I was doing fine, but it looks like Mr. Smith didn't think so. I tried to keep to myself and avoid others. I did not want to be at school, and my classmates were also annoying.

ALEX: You were frustrated because you had been sick and tired, and then your classmates were doing things that bothered you, even though you were trying to keep to your own business? *(Reflection)*

MAC: Exactly! Then my dad got mad that I didn't want to do my homework Thursday, but we worked it out and he helped me and it got done.

ALEX: Well, it looks like on Thursday you felt you did not follow your goal, but it looks like Mr. Smith thought you did just fine. What do you think was happening there?

MAC: I don't know. On Thursday I just did not feel good, so maybe that was it. Apparently, Mr. Smith thought I did OK, though. I did not know that at the time. I thought I was having a horrible day.

ALEX: Good for you—even though you feel your day was not great, you appeared to maintain and take care of business in class. (*Affirmation*) After your difficult day at school, it would have been easy to get stuck and give

> **MI and SMARTS Strategy**
>
> Focus on the good days that students meet or exceed their goals before focusing on the days that students did not meet their goals or that they differed from their teachers' ratings. Explore these discrepancies with the student; rely on the comments to provide any context.

(a)

Student Name: _Mac_   Date: _3/7/2024_

SMARTS Goal: _I will work on not yelling or getting into arguments with my classmates and teacher. I know I am working on my goal by not getting into trouble with my teacher and not missing out on recess._

Replacement Strategy: _I will use box breathing when I feel angry and will write down my thoughts and feelings in a journal. I will also count to three and take deep breaths._

Interval	Class/Activity	Goal Monitoring *(Circle)*	Notes
Start–9:00	Morning announcement	Did I follow my goal? Y = 2 S = 1 (N = 0)	Don't feel well today and I don't want to be here
9:00–10:00	Specials	Did I follow my goal? Y = 2 S = 1 (N = 0)	Hate gym today
10:00–11:00	Math	Did I follow my goal? Y = 2 (S = 1) N = 0	Did not do my math
11:00–12:00	Lunch/recess	Did I follow my goal? Y = 2 (S = 1) N = 0	Kept to myself
12:00–1:00	Reading	Did I follow my goal? (Y = 2) S = 1 N = 0	Read by myself
1:00–2:00	Science	Did I follow my goal? Y = 2 S = 1 (N = 0)	
2:00–End	Social Studies	Did I follow my goal? Y = 2 S = 1 (N = 0)	
Add up the score at each interval to Y = 2; S = 1; N = 0			**Today's Total:** _4_ /14

Student: _Mac_   Teacher: _Andy Smith_

(continued)

FIGURE 9.4. (a) Mac's Goal Self-Monitoring Worksheet and (b) Mr. Smith's Goal Monitoring Worksheet for Mac—Thursday.

(b)

Student Name: Mac _____ Date: 3/7/2024 _____

SMARTS Goal: _I will work on not yelling or getting into arguments with my classmates and teacher. I know I am_ _working on my goal by not getting into trouble with my teacher and not missing out on recess._

Replacement Strategy: _I will use box breathing when I feel angry and will write down my thoughts and feelings in_ _a journal. I will also count to three and take deep breaths._

Interval	Class/Activity	Goal Monitoring *(Circle)*	Notes
Start–9:00	Morning announcement	Did I follow my goal? Y = 2 (S = 1) N = 0	Mac seems out of sorts today and does not want to be here but did not have peer problems
9:00–10:00	Specials	Did I follow my goal? Y = 2 S = 1 (N = 0)	Did not participate and argued with several peers
10:00–11:00	Math	Did I follow my goal? Y = 2 S = 1 (N = 0)	Did not do work and argued with me when I asked
11:00–12:00	Lunch/recess	Did I follow my goal? Y = 2 (S = 1) N = 0	Was fine during lunch
12:00–1:00	Reading	Did I follow my goal? Y = 2 S = 1 (N = 0)	Refused to get into reading groups and read alone
1:00–2:00	Science	Did I follow my goal? Y = 2 (S = 1) N = 0	Did not argue and did work, but would not work in group
2:00–End	Social Studies	Did I follow my goal? (Y = 2) S = 1 N = 0	Worked in group for trivia game
Add up the score at each interval to Y = 2; S = 1; N = 0			**Today's Total: _5_ /21**

Student: Mac _____ Teacher: Andy Smith _____

FIGURE 9.4. *(continued)*

up, but Mr. Smith saw that you had a great day and, it seems at the end of the day, you somehow found a way to turn it into a positive by getting your work done at home and getting along with your dad. (*Agreement with a twist*)

MAC: Yeah. It was better to not cause myself problems or argue about the homework with my dad. It was better to get along and get it done.

ALEX: That makes good sense. (*Affirmation*) Can you tell me more about your Thursday? (*Open-ended question*)

MAC: We had a short day, and every time I started to get into the zone, we moved onto something new, so I kind of just stopped paying attention. What was the point if I couldn't keep up? (*Sustain talk*)

ALEX: That's frustrating. It's hard to stay interested when things keeping shifting. (*Empathy*) Were there any downsides that happened when you stopped paying attention? (*Open-ended question to elicit change talk*)

MAC: Well, I had a ton of homework that night that I didn't understand, and then I got into a fight with my mom. She said I couldn't go to the movies today if I didn't get my homework done yesterday.

ALEX: How might it be helpful if we found a way for you to stick with it even when it gets frustrating when topics are shifting in class? (*Open-ended question to elicit change talk*)

(a)

Student Name: *Mac*   Date: *3/8/2024*

SMARTS Goal: *I will work on not yelling or getting into arguments with my classmates and teacher. I know I am working on my goal by not getting into trouble with my teacher and not missing out on recess.*

Replacement Strategy: *I will use box breathing when I feel angry and will write down my thoughts and feelings in a journal. I will also count to three and take deep breaths.*

Interval	Class/Activity	Goal Monitoring *(Circle)*	Notes
Start–9:00	Morning announcement	Did I follow my goal? (Y = 2) S = 1 N = 0	*Ready for the day to be over but want to be here and have fun*
9:00–10:00	Specials	Did I follow my goal? (Y = 2) S = 1 N = 0	*Gym was fun first thing*
10:00–11:00	Math	Did I follow my goal? (Y = 2) S = 1 N = 0	*Did my work, peer giving me trouble, but I ignored them*
11:00–12:00	Lunch/recess	Did I follow my goal? (Y = 2) S = 1 N = 0	*Ate with friends and no problems*
12:00–1:00	Reading	Did I follow my goal? (Y = 2) S = 1 N = 0	*Worked on report with peer*
1:00–2:00	Science	Did I follow my goal? (Y = 2) S = 1 N = 0	*Finished group project and started on next week's work*
2:00–End	Social Studies	Did I follow my goal? (Y = 2) S = 1 N = 0	*Worked with peer to write quiz questions and answers*
Add up the score at each interval to Y = 2; S = 1; N = 0			**Today's Total:** *14* /14

Student: *Mac*   Teacher: *Andy Smith*

(continued)

FIGURE 9.5. (a) Mac's Goal Self-Monitoring Worksheet and (b) Mr. Smith's Goal Monitoring Worksheet for Mac—Friday.

(b)

Student Name: _Mac_   Date: _3/8/2024_

SMARTS Goal: _I will work on not yelling or getting into arguments with my classmates and teacher. I know I am_
working on my goal by not getting into trouble with my teacher and not missing out on recess.

Replacement Strategy: _I will use box breathing when I feel angry and will write down my thoughts and feelings in_
a journal. I will also count to three and take deep breaths.

Interval	Class/Activity	Goal Monitoring *(Circle)*	Notes
Start–9:00	Morning announcement	Did I follow my goal? Y = 2 S = 1 (N = 0)	Snapped at two peers when Mac walked in the room, was confronted
9:00–10:00	Specials	Did I follow my goal? Y = 2 (S = 1) N = 0	Was loud and disruptive with two others during gym
10:00–11:00	Math	Did I follow my goal? Y = 2 (S = 1) N = 0	Argued with neighbor about assignment
11:00–12:00	Lunch/recess	Did I follow my goal? Y = 2 S = 1 (N = 0)	Sat with a loud group during lunch, would not move away when asked
12:00–1:00	Reading	Did I follow my goal? Y = 2 (S = 1) N = 0	Worked with others but argued over book report
1:00–2:00	Science	Did I follow my goal? Y = 2 (S = 1) N = 0	Worked ahead, and when asked not to, Mac argued with me
2:00–End	Social Studies	Did I follow my goal? Y = 2 S = 1 (N = 0)	Was tearing up peer's paper and not working with them on assignment
Add up the score at each interval to Y = 2; S = 1; N = 0			Today's Total: _4_ /21

Student: _Mac_   Teacher: _Andy Smith_

FIGURE 9.5. *(continued)*

MAC: It would feel good to tell my parents I had a good day, and I would been proud of myself for continuing to try even when I get frustrated. (*Change talk*)

ALEX: Those are some good points, Mac. (*Affirmation*). You did the work to be able to go to the movies! (*Support self-efficacy*)

MAC: I did, and it felt good. (*Change talk*)

Notice how Alex checks in with Mac about both successful and less successful days, first focusing on the positives and drawing their sense of self-efficacy through open-ended questions (e.g., "How did you do that?"), affirmations, and reflections. When exploring less successful days, Alex withholds judgment and advice giving. Instead, Alex

Date	Day 1	Day 2	Day 3	Day 4	Day 5
	3-4-24	3-5.24	3-6-24	3-7-24	3-8-24
100%					
90%					
80%					
70%					
60%					
50%					
40%					
30%					
20%					
10%					
0%					
Notes:	close	close	Slightly off this day but did OK	Off this day, argued with peers	Off this day, argued a lot with teacher

Kindergarten Form

Daily Score	Percentage
1/9 =	11%
2/9 =	22%
3/9 =	33%
4/9 =	44%
5/9 =	56%
6/9 =	67%
7/9 =	78%
8/9 =	89%
9/9 =	100%

Grades 1-3 and 4-5 Forms

Daily Score	Percentage
1/14 =	7%
2/14 =	14%
3/14 =	21%
4/14 =	29%
5/14 =	36%
6/14 =	43%
7/14 =	50%
8/14 =	57%
9/14 =	64%
10/14 =	71%
11/14 =	79%
12/14 =	86%
13/14 =	93%
14/14 =	100%

FIGURE 9.6. SMARTS Phase III Processing: Self-Monitoring and Teacher Feedback Graphing Form—Mac and Mr. Smith.

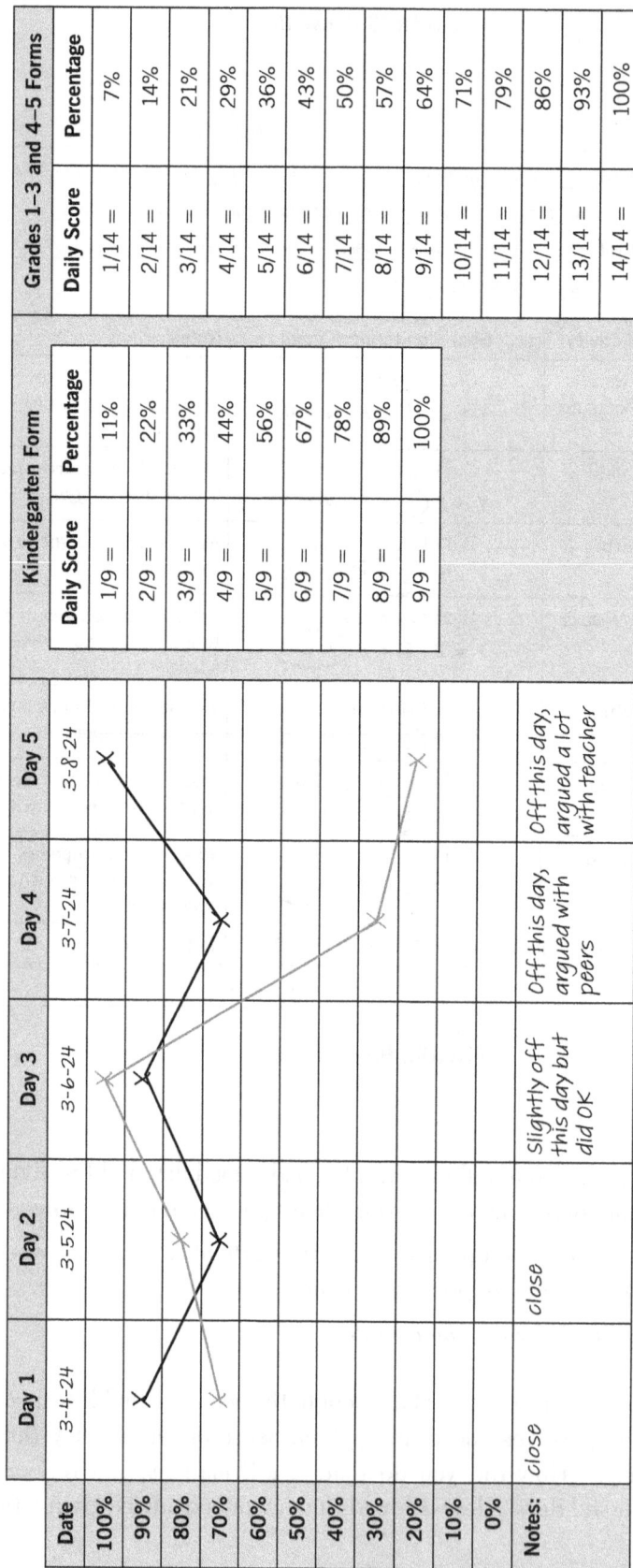

Note: Mac = X and —, Mr. Smith = X and —

uses complex reflections to convey empathy and then explores the disadvantages of Mac's choices and potential advantages of making new choices.

Alex opens Mac's SMARTS folder and takes out the SMARTS Phase III Processing: Data Assessment and Goal Reformation Guide (Figure 9.7) and begins to review the form with Mac. Mac circles the days they feel that they met their goal, the days Mac sees that Mr. Smith rated Mac as meeting the stated goal, and the days on which they both agreed or disagreed. As they talk about each area on the sheet, Alex makes a few notes along the way about why Mac selects the ratings that are circled.

ALEX: When we look at what your teacher said, it appears there is some disagreement between which days you met or did not meet your goal.

MAC: That is not surprising.

ALEX: How so? (*Open-ended question*)

MAC: I kinda think my teacher doesn't like me much and always gets on me for not paying attention or something.

ALEX: It looks like your teacher rated Thursday and Friday a little lower than you. However, he said he observed you trying to use skills, but you were having some disagreements with your peers.

MAC: Thursday was hard, but I don't think it was that bad. Friday was a bit tougher. I kinda forgot I was trying to use skills. (*Change talk*) I'm happy he noticed I was trying. (*Change talk*) Sometimes I feel invisible in class. (*Sustain talk*)

ALEX: It feels good to know when your teacher notices the good things you are doing. (*Reflection*) On Wednesday, he noted you showed up to school ready, that you had an excellent day, and got along well with classmates while getting your work accomplished.

MAC: I did that! He saw me? Maybe he really doesn't dislike me. (*Change talk*).

ALEX (*with a smile*): It would be difficult being in a class with a teacher who didn't like you. (*Reflect with empathy*) I think it would be hard for someone to dislike you, Mac. (*Affirmation*) It also feels good to know that your teacher is on your

MI and SMARTS Strategy

Complete the Phase III SMARTS Data Assessment and Goal Reformation Guide alongside students. Have students circle the days they feel they did well, the days they did not do so well, and the days they differed from their teachers. If you disagree, remember to use your MI skills and explore those discrepancies through curiosity—for example: "I don't understand. Your goal was _____ and your graphing sheet says _____, but your assessment of your performance seems different. Can you tell me more about that?" Use the form as a conversational driver; explore student responses using questions that ask for more information.

Name _Mac_   **Today's Date** _3/8/2024_

1. **Look at your data (SMARTS graphs and percentages)**

   Circle days where the data show you met your goal.   (M) (Tues) (Wed)   Th   Fr

   Notes. _Mac commented that he was interested in the class lessons on Monday, Tuesday, and Wednesday._
   He also noted going to bed early Monday night and said he was not tired on Tuesday, but did not feel well
   Thursday and Friday.

   Circle days where the data show you did not meet your goal.   M   Tues   Wed   (Th) (Fr)

   Notes. _Mac noted that it was difficult to get back into the school routine on Thursday, as he felt ill and did_
   not want to be at school. This led into Friday as well as Mac noting being distracted.

2. **Look at your teacher's data (SMARTS graph and percentages).**

   What days did your teacher rate you met your goal?   (M) (Tues) (Wed)   Th   Fr

   Notes. _Mac's teacher noted that he observed Mac trying to use skills throughout the week and noted_
   improvement on Monday, Tuesday, and Wednesday, but on Thursday and Friday, the ratings differed between
   Mac and Mr. Smith.

   What days did your teacher rate you low on the goal?   M   Tues   Wed   (Th) (Fr)

   Notes. _Mac's teacher shared in his notes that Thursday and Friday were hard days for Mac. There was an_
   early dismissal that may have impacted the time spent on each lesson and Mac did not feel his best.

3. **Compare your data with your teacher's data.**

   What days did you and your teacher agree?   M   (Tues) (Wed) (Th)   Fr

   Notes. _After discussing this feedback with Mac, they agreed with their teacher on Monday, Tuesday, and_
   Wednesday, but disagreed Thursday and Friday. Mac expressed surprise that Mr. Smith thought Mac had a
   better day on Thursday than Mac did, but Friday was an obvious difference. Mac suggested Mr. Smith was
   "always getting on them" and "didn't like them much."

   What days did you and your teacher disagree above?   M   Tues   Wed   (Th) (Fr)

   Notes. _Mac and their teacher agreed with each day but Thursday and Friday, but Mac thought Thursday was_
   worse than Mr. Smith did and that Friday, Mr. Smith thought the day was not as positive as Mac did. Mac
   admits being mad and that maybe their ratings were not as accurate as they usually would be.

4. **Now, use your SMARTS skills (circle the best response).**
   What was your day like when you followed your goal on the days listed above?

   - My day was worse
   - My day was just okay
   - My day was the same
   - (My day felt a little better)
   - My day was a lot better

(continued)

FIGURE 9.7. Mac's SMARTS Phase III Processing: Data Assessment and Goal Reformation Guide.

What is your day like when you do not follow your goal on the days listed above?
- My day was worse
- My day was just okay
- My day was the same
- My day felt a little better
- My day was a lot better

Suggested Processing Questions (Ask students to reflect on these or discuss as a group.)
- *What do you think your teacher was noticing about your goal performance?*
- *What have you learned from any challenges this week?*
- As a follow-up to any challenges, ask: *What did you notice about your pulse/heart rate/body temperature?*

5. **Evaluate goal progress (circle the best response).**
   Based on this data, circle your next action:
   - I will keep my current goal and try again.
   - I will update my current goal and try again.
   - I will choose a completely new goal and try again.

6. **On a new self-monitoring form (see Chapter 8 for Forms 8.2, 8.3, or 8.4, depending on students' grades and development) write out your new goal and be sure it:**
   - **Is focused on your classroom behavior**
   - **Is written in observable and measurable terms**
   - **Includes a form for both you and your teacher for next week**

7. **On the following scale, circle how confident you are that you will stick to your goal.**

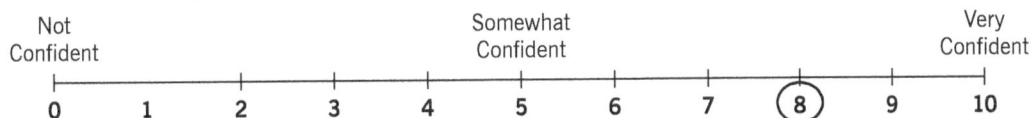

Not Confident   Somewhat Confident   Very Confident

0   1   2   3   4   5   6   7   (8)   9   10

8. **On the following scale, circle how ready you are to rate your daily goal performance.**

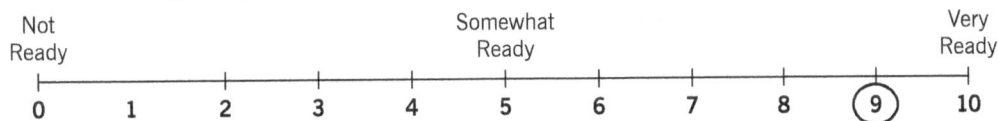

Not Ready   Somewhat Ready   Very Ready

0   1   2   3   4   5   6   7   8   (9)   10

FIGURE 9.7. *(continued)*

side and wants to see you meet your goals. Let's look at this next question: What was your day like when you followed your goal on the days listed above? (*Open-ended question*)

MAC: It felt a little better. Not great, but a little. (*Change talk*)

ALEX: Right on. What is your day like when you do not follow your goal on the days listed above? (*Open-ended question*)

MAC: Just OK.

ALEX: Can you share anything you learned from this week about your goal or monitoring? (*Open-ended question to elicit change talk*)

MAC: Yeah, I learned that my teacher isn't just watching and waiting for me to do something bad. He actually sees me trying to work on my goal. I didn't know that, and it feels good. (*Change talk*)

ALEX: I am glad you were able to see that. (*Affirmation*) How does this relate to your future work on your goal? (*Open-ended question to elicit change talk*)

MAC: I am going to keep trying. (*Change talk*) Maybe I can reach out to my teacher with questions on bad days. (*Change talk; Ability*).

ALEX: That sounds like a great idea! (*Affirmation; Support self-efficacy*) So, do you feel like you want to change your goal at all?

MAC: No, I want to keep trying to work on it!

In reviewing the consistency between Mac and their teacher's ratings, notice how Alex uses affirmations and questions to elicit change talk. In particular, Alex focuses attention on Mac's relationship with their teacher. Through simple reflections and questions, Alex builds Mac's sense that their teacher is on their side and wants them to be successful.

ALEX: Right on, Mac. On a scale of 1 to 10, with 1 being not confident and 10 being very confident, how confident are you that you will stick to your goal this week?

MAC: I think 10, very confident.

ALEX: (*nods*)

MAC: Hmm, maybe an 8.

ALEX: Why would you say 8 over, say, a 6 or 7?

MAC: (*shrugs*) I know I can work on my goal, but it's sometimes harder to reach. I can see some good things I did this week, and it

> ### MI and SMARTS Strategy
>
> Be sure to gauge or inquire about your students' responses to their confidence and readiness ratings. These data can also be used as progress-monitoring tools for your students' levels of engagement. If ratings indicate high levels of readiness and confidence, this change talk will predict stronger goal performance. If these ratings are low, explore why students would not select a different rating.

makes a difference. Like I get into fewer arguments and get less annoyed when I find ways to stick through it. (*Change talk; Ability*)

ALEX: You are confident you can do this because you already see the difference it's making for your own happiness, and you like having fewer hassles. (*Reflection*) I appreciate your honesty, Mac. (*Affirmation*)

MAC: You're welcome!

ALEX: Now, on that same 1–10 scale, how ready are you to rate your daily goal performance?

MAC: Oh, 9. I want to fill out the paper, but I forget a lot.

ALEX: I am proud of you for recognizing the positives of keeping track and noting that you forget. (*Affirmation; Support self-efficacy*) Do you want to think of some ideas that might help you remember? (*Asking permission*)

MAC: Sure, that would be good.

ALEX: Some students find it helpful to put a sticky note on their desk to remind them. What do you think of that?

MAC: Maybe I could do it, but I am nervous someone might see. Can I put it inside my desk or pencil case? (*Change talk; Ability*)

ALEX: That sounds like a good alternative. (*Affirmation*) What about talking to your teacher about occasional reminders?

MAC: That would work. I want to remember on my own, but that could be helpful too. (*Change talk; Ability*)

ALEX: Alright, let's try that this week.

> **MI and SMARTS Strategy**
>
> Mac should redraft a goal for the following week using Form 9.2, Goal Assessment and Reformation Guide, and can either keep the goal or adjust the goal. In your conversations, revisit SMARTS self-regulation strategies or return to earlier lessons that reviewed replacement strategies as a way to help your student identify a skill that can help them in the following week to achieve their goal.

This last section of the conversation is really intended to solidify the plan for the coming week, gain Mac's commitment to persist, and problem-solve any potential barriers. Notice how Alex asks for permission before jumping in to solving the problem of Mac forgetting to do the ratings. This builds the alliance and communicates clearly that these are Mac's choices about how they want to proceed.

SUMMARY

The Phase III processing activities are possibly the most important component of the SMARTS intervention. This is where students, with the help of a trusted adult, will review their progress and consider it alongside their goals and their own teachers' feedback. Practicing over time, students do get quicker at these steps and tasks. If at first it is hard for students, being patient and helping them understand the data and graphs will go a long way as they become experts at their own process. Over time, the data can also give both you and the student a sense of the success of the SMARTS plan, where they might need to revisit some of the SMARTS training or revise SMARTS goals, and whether or not SMARTS is helping them to reflect on their own progress.

To competently prepare and conduct the SMARTS processing phase with your students, here is a summarizing checklist of the forms needed and their purposes to complete Phase III's processing.

- **Form 9.1 (SMARTS Phase III Graphing Form).** This form is utilized to visually represent the daily percentages for students to compare their ratings against their original goals, prior performances, and teachers' data.
- **Form 9.2 (SMARTS Phase III Data Assessment and Goal Reformation Guide).** This form enables students to compare their own ratings with their original goals, prior performances, and teachers' data to understand their progress.
- **Forms 8.1, 8.2, and 8.3 (self-monitoring forms).** Once students have reviewed their data and reformulated their goals, Phase II repeats with the same form that students and teachers used to collect goal-progress data. (These forms are introduced in Chapter 8.)

Phases II and III then repeat iteratively. Goals can change, of course, because we encounter new challenges each day. Be flexible with students and help them identify areas that they want to improve upon, and guide them to consider how they want to improve their school experiences or challenges that they are having with peers and teachers. Finally, maintain the students' self-monitoring and teacher-monitoring sheets; they provide a record of the students' longitudinal progress.

In the next chapter, we explore modifications to SMARTS, including how to integrate external rewards, how to involve positive peers in the self-monitoring process, how to use SMARTS to communicate student progress with their families and caregivers, and how to fade SMARTS for a student who appears to have accomplished a degree of consistently with meeting their goals and may no longer need SMARTS as a targeted support. Don't worry, though; if they are successful, then they have learned the strategies ensconced in SMARTS and will continue to use those strategies for the rest of their lives in school and beyond.

SMARTS Phase III Processing: Self-Monitoring and Teacher Feedback Graphing Form

Directions: Using the week's Self-Monitoring and Teacher Rating forms to graph both your and your teacher's ratings on your progress.

1. Use the total number of Y (2), S (1), or N (0), or the total number of ☺ for each of the self-monitoring days for *both* your sheets and your teacher's rating sheets.
   a. If a day of self- or teacher data is missing, do your best to complete your rating and request that your teacher complete theirs.

   b. If absent for that day, leave that day blank.
2. Estimate the percentage for each day by dividing the total number of marks by the total possible (see the key below for different self-monitoring forms for students in grades K–3 and 4–5).

3. Place an *x* in the approximate place that corresponds to your percentage for each day.
4. Connect all of your *x*'s by drawing a line between them.
   a. Tip—use different-colored pencils or pens for your ratings and your teacher's ratings.

Date	Day 1	Day 2	Day 3	Day 4	Day 5
100%					
90%					
80%					
70%					
60%					
50%					
40%					
30%					
20%					
10%					
0%					
Notes:					

Kindergarten Form

Daily Score	Percentage
1/9 =	11%
2/9 =	22%
3/9 =	33%
4/9 =	44%
5/9 =	56%
6/9 =	67%
7/9 =	78%
8/9 =	89%
9/9 =	100%

Grades 1–3 and 4–5 Forms

Daily Score	Percentage
1/14 =	7%
2/14 =	14%
3/14 =	21%
4/14 =	29%
5/14 =	36%
6/14 =	43%
7/14 =	50%
8/14 =	57%
9/14 =	64%
10/14 =	71%
11/14 =	79%
12/14 =	86%
13/14 =	93%
14/14 =	100%

FORM 9.2

SMARTS Phase III Processing:
Data Assessment and Goal Reformation Guide

Name_____ Today's Date _____

1. Look at your data (SMARTS graphs and percentages)

Circle days where the data show you met your goal.　　**M　Tues　Wed　Th　Fr**

Notes. _____

_____

_____

Circle days where the data show you did not meet your goal.　**M　Tues　Wed　Th　Fr**

Notes. _____

_____

2. Look at your teacher's data (SMARTS graph and percentages).

What days did your teacher rate you met your goal?　　**M　Tues　Wed　Th　Fr**

Notes. _____

_____

_____

What days did your teacher rate you low on the goal?　**M　Tues　Wed　Th　Fr**

Notes. _____

_____

_____

3. Compare your data with your teacher's data.

What days did you and your teacher agree?　**M　Tues　Wed　Th　Fr**

Notes. _____

_____

_____

What days did you and your teacher disagree?　**M　Tues　Wed　Th　Fr**

Notes. _____

_____

_____

(continued)

4. **Now, use your SMARTS skills (circle the best response).**
   What was your day like when you followed your goal on the days listed above?

   - My day was worse
   - My day was just okay
   - My day was the same
   - My day felt a little better
   - My day was a lot better

   What is your day like when you do not follow your goal on the days listed above?

   - My day was worse
   - My day was just okay
   - My day was the same
   - My day felt a little better
   - My day was a lot better

   Suggested Processing Questions (Ask students to reflect on these or discuss as a group.)
   - *What do you think your teacher was noticing about your goal performance?*
   - *What have you learned from any challenges this week?*
   - As a follow-up to any challenges, ask: *What did you notice about your pulse/heart rate/body temperature?*

5. **Evaluate goal progress (circle the best response).**
   Based on these data, circle your next action:

   - I will keep my current goal and try again.
   - I will update my current goal and try again.
   - I will choose a completely new goal and try again.

6. **On a new self-monitoring form (see Chapter 8 for Forms 8.2, 8.3, or 8.4, depending on students' grades and development) write out your new goal and be sure it:**
   - **Is focused on your classroom behavior**
   - **Is written in observable and measurable terms**
   - **Includes a form for both you and your teacher for next week**

7. **On the following scale, circle how confident you are that you will stick to your goal.**

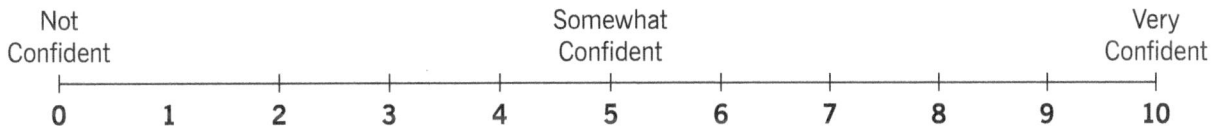

Not Confident				Somewhat Confident						Very Confident
0	1	2	3	4	5	6	7	8	9	10

8. **On the following scale, circle how ready you are to rate your daily goal performance.**

Not Ready				Somewhat Ready						Very Ready
0	1	2	3	4	5	6	7	8	9	10

PART III

NEXT STEPS

CHAPTER 10

SMARTS Modifications and Next Steps

The SMARTS approach to self-monitoring for elementary students can be a valuable tool for promoting self-awareness, self-regulation, goal-directed behavior, and generating a spark that could promote a life's worth of personal growth. Using the SMARTS approach to create a simple and effective self-monitoring program for elementary students will certainly require your expert consideration of a student's age, their developmental stage, and their learning style and needs. We also are firm believers that no one should blindly apply a single intervention in a systematic and blanketed style for all students needing support just because doing something is better than doing nothing. Whether that intervention is SMARTS, Check-In/Check-Out (Hawken et al., 2015), or any other targeted intervention approach, a blanket application across all students in need of targeted support that does not directly reduce the risk factors affecting them or build buffering skills that address the underlying problems will not help. However, we feel that the science supporting self-monitoring as well as the procedures for Phase I: SMARTS Student Training will provide the basic skills to efficiently engage in Phase II: SMARTS Self- and Teacher Monitoring and Phase III: SMARTS Processing Self- and Teacher Data. And, as stated in our theory of change, practice makes perfect; that is, students may find the process challenging, but keep at it, make it matter for students and your school (i.e., by following up with teachers to be sure they are contributing to student ratings as well as making sure students complete ratings themselves), and the SMARTS process will become second nature for students in no time.

It is likely that modifications will be made to the SMARTS process as we have described here in these pervious chapters, dependent upon your students' needs and abilities. To be sure, the lessons provided in Chapter 7 are targeted at older elementary students, but with basic modifications, they can be made applicable and useful for younger students in your building. The scientific literature is replete with examples from studies with students of all ages. We believe the basic framework in the hands of a capable facilitator will set students up with the training, skills, and practice needed over time to develop mastery in the self-monitoring process. It is impossible to discuss all modifications, next steps, and future applications of the SMARTS approach, but herein we discuss obvious modifications that we have encountered in our time working with SMARTS. These include using external rewards; involving peers, teachers, and families; adjusting the frequency of self-monitoring goals in Phase II or Phase III; and then fading the SMARTS intervention. We also discuss future directions, including using technology to facilitate self-monitoring. Specifically, this chapter provides an overview and details on shaping SMARTS to work for you and your students:

- *Customization is key.* The SMARTS approach to self-monitoring must be tailored to each student's age, developmental stage, and learning style. Avoiding a one-size-fits-all application ensures that interventions directly address the unique needs and challenges of individual students.
- *Balanced use of external rewards.* Although the SMARTS program promotes intrinsic motivation, the strategic use of external rewards can help engage students initially. It's crucial to balance these rewards to avoid diminishing long-term motivation.
- *Involving peers, teachers, and families.* Engaging peers, teachers, and families in the SMARTS process can enhance its effectiveness. Collaborative efforts ensure that students receive consistent support and encouragement across different environments, reinforcing the skills learned in the program.
- *Gradual fading of the intervention.* Successful implementation of SMARTS should lead to the gradual fading of the program as students internalize self-regulation skills. Carefully planning the transition from external supports to self-sufficiency is crucial for maintaining long-term behavioral change.

We also provide a list of frequently encountered questions and answers in Table 10.1 at the end of chapter to guide you in any common questions you may have about the implementation of SMARTS in your school.

BOOSTING SMARTS
BY USING EXTERNAL REWARD SYSTEMS

SMARTS and the intent of any self-monitoring program is to promote the conditions and the tools for students to be more internally motivated to display and adopt or present acceptable behaviors at school. These approaches aim to empower students to take charge of their learning and behaviors by monitoring goal progress, reflecting on that progress, and making the necessary adjustments to facilitate success. Although intrinsic motivation is often considered the ideal driver for sustained improvement and engagement, the use of external rewards to motivate students to participate in SMARTS can be an added strategy that will boost the effect of SMARTS and help students move from being externally motivated to internalizing some of the essential skills and practices embedded in SMARTS.

External rewards can take the form of tangible items, praise, recognition, or privileges. We are fans of all of these and recommend they be used to prime students and get them engaged in the SMARTS intervention. We are fans of rewards that are meaningful to students—and if those rewards have a social component, then they are likely to benefit students in other ways. According to SDT (Deci & Ryan, 1985), external rewards can foster a sense of competence and autonomy. Our biggest tip here is to make sure the rewards are tied to performance of (1) the group's expectations for each other and (2) the individual student's goals. By associating the rewards with Phase I's positive group training experiences or Phase II and Phase III's self-monitoring goal attainment, students are more likely to perceive self-regulation as a positive and personally meaningful endeavor that is worth pursuing. Rewards are particularly beneficial for younger students who are working on their regulatory skills (Haines et al., 2015).

While external rewards can be effective in the short term to get students engaged and follow rules during Phase I's training or to recognize effort and success during Phases II and III's self-monitoring and processing stages, overreliance may undermine motivation. When the reward exceeds the effort or is excessively provided, studies have shown that those external rewards can diminish motivation to engage in tasks.

The goal is to create a balanced approach to maximize the use of external rewards while reducing the drawbacks. Here are some suggested tips to create a balanced approach within the SMARTS framework:

> **Motivating Students with SMARTS**
>
> The SMARTS program aims to foster intrinsic motivation in students for self-regulation, but strategic use of external rewards can effectively engage students and help them internalize key self-monitoring skills.

1. Start with Phase I's group expectations and the SMARTS Jar reward-monitoring system. See Chapter 6 for more details about using the SMARTS Jar. Essentially, the goal is to set the parameters that encourage participation in Phase I's lessons, facilitate positive behaviors, and generate some enthusiasm for students who are not interested in participating in SMARTS at first. The best approach has been to set short-term (i.e., 2–3 weeks) and long-term (at the end of Phase I's training, after 6 weeks of Phase II and III's self-monitoring/data-processing meetings) goals that are selected by the students.

2. Utilize desirable social opportunities as rewards. Any reward that includes a social component is working with SMARTS to promote positive social interactions, teamwork, and a sense of community at your school. Here are a few social rewards we have used in past studies of SMARTS:

a. *Peer compliment train.* Encourage students to give each other compliments on their effort and performances. Start this by giving one student a compliment yourself as an example, and then they must pick the next student to compliment, and so on, until everyone has experienced a positive note about something they have done well, except you since you started it!

b. *Create leadership roles.* Carve out leadership roles for your SMARTS groups. These are social activities that can rotate. Divvy up activities between students—scribes to write words on a board during Phase I's training, a Phase III data-processing group leader who rotates each time students meet, a timekeeper for Phase I's training, a materials manager, a copy master to create copies of activity sheets or new goal sheets, and so on.

c. *Random acts of kindness.* In the case that students engage in a particularly supportive group, step outside the norm and take time to recognize those students in their classrooms in front of all their peers and teachers who are following your group. Be cautious here: Not all students appreciate being recognized in front of others. Use your judgment to determine if this is motivating to your students.

d. *Game time.* If students have been doing well but walk in one day and appear to be completely flat or demotivated altogether—don't worry, it happens—consider pausing the work and proposing a surprise game day for your group instead of doing SMARTS lessons. Encourage an inclusive game or one that has cooperative groups competing.

e. *Surprise rewards.* Again, if SMARTS students have been doing well but walk into your group one day and appear to have lost the wind in their sails, consider keeping a small snack for you all to have. Everyone needs a surprise snack.

f. *Lunch together.* If students need a motivator, then ask if they would like to invite a friend or peer to the group for lunch in your office or another area that would give them and their group mates some time together.

3. For SMARTS Phases II and III, consider encouraging students to successfully attain goals by using external rewards. Again, tying rewards to goals is a great way to promote autonomy. For example, encourage students by explaining that if they all attain their goals according to teacher- and self-monitoring data for the next week, then they can have a donut party or play a game instead of doing group the next week. Doing this for induvial students who need additional supports is OK as well, but if you can tie it to a peer, it is more beneficial, socially speaking.

BOOSTING SMARTS BY DIRECTLY INVOLVING PEERS

Directly involving peers in SMARTS can enhance its effectiveness. Often, when students are struggling with behaviors, their peers are the first to know. Prosocial and positive peers begin to recognize their peers with more challenging behaviors early in elementary school. Including a positive peer who is participating in SMARTS at any phase can be beneficial for a child who is struggling with challenges at school. This not only provides the SMARTS student with social opportunities to engage with prosocial peers, but it can also establish a SMARTS buddy system wherein they both can have an individualized SMARTS goal and help each other remember to rate or monitor their goals together or even share a goal if it makes sense to do so. In Phase I, peers can engage in the SMARTS student training as peer modelers, model the SMARTS skills for each other, or even create some role-plays to practice skills if that is agreeable to the peers. During Phase III, SMARTS peer dyads can provide each other with feedback as well.

BOOSTING SMARTS BY DIRECTLY INVOLVING TEACHERS

Involving teachers in the SMARTS program for elementary students is essential to its success. That said, we all know the busiest people in all school buildings are classroom teachers. They often lack the time and flexibility to engage in many activities, but there are other ways to involve teachers more directly in SMARTS. Hosting monthly check-in meetings to hone student feedback or sharpen the goals students are monitoring is one way of directly involving teachers. If a student has been referred for SMARTS from a schoolwide behavioral support team, then encourage teachers by telling them that the SMARTS data they are contributing to is not only providing important feedback to students during Phase III's data-review meetings but can also be used to inform the schoolwide behavioral-support team about whether the SMARTS intervention is helping the student.

Motivating Students with Peers in SMARTS

Involving peers and teachers directly in the SMARTS program can significantly enhance its effectiveness, with peers offering social support and modeling, and teachers providing essential feedback, goal-setting assistance, and data review to support student autonomy and success.

PROMOTING SMARTS STUDENT AUTONOMY BY ASKING STUDENTS TO PRESENT THEIR DATA

One of my (A. M. T.) favorite activities when working with SMARTS was to see students present their data in front of others. There were several ways this worked well. For students with IEPs and behavioral goals, we would have those students present their data.

It also made sense for some students who required a BIP to state important goals on that BIP and then ask those students to make them their SMARTS goals. The effect is that they are focused on what are presumably very important goals for them, and teacher data can also double as a monitor for that IEP requirement.

One way we have engaged teachers in the SMARTS process is also by developing a contract. At times, students struggled to get the goals correct or focused on a problem the teachers were seeing. Often in these examples, there can also be some friction between the SMARTS students and the teachers. Lesson 5 in Chapter 7 does directly involve teacher input into what students should focus on goal wise, but going one extra step and completing the SMARTS Student-Teacher Goal Input worksheet (Form 6.9) is another way to encourage teacher input in the process.

BOOSTING SMARTS BY DIRECTLY INVOLVING FAMILIES

There are several simple ways to involve families in SMARTS. The most obvious way is to include caregivers in the plan. As with any targeted intervention, this process should start with a notification to families and their consent to enroll a student in SMARTS. See Form 6.2 for a suggested parent letter about notification that their child is participating in SMARTS. Organizing a simple meeting or phone call to explain to the parents that SMARTS is a program that helps students learn important life skills is one way to honestly explain its benefits as a program that focuses on goal setting, monitoring progress, and learning self-regulation practices.

An obvious way to directly involve families in SMARTS is to seek their agreement to review the daily self-monitoring forms from students and teachers. These forms could also be signed by caregivers if the students and the caregivers agree it would be helpful. Returning the forms each day will be important to Phase II and Phase III's activities. Also, asking students to present their SMARTS data at a schoolwide behavior-support meeting or at their IEP meeting would also be a way to engage caregivers and share with them how their child is growing through SMARTS. Finally, if parents are experiencing challenges at home, coordination on SMARTS goals for self-monitoring between home and school might also be a collaborative way to work with families. Perhaps the goals your SMARTS students need to work on at school could also work well at home, or you can support SMARTS goal attainment at home by engaging parents in SMARTS and extending its activities to include the home. By involving families in SMARTS, we create a collaborative partnership between home and school and foster a unified approach to support students' growth and development.

Involving Family and Caregivers in SMARTS

Involving families in the SMARTS program can enhance its effectiveness by creating a collaborative partnership between home and school, where caregivers are engaged in reviewing self-monitoring forms, participating in meetings, and supporting goal attainment both at school and at home.

ADJUSTING THE FREQUENCY OF PHASE II OR PHASE III

Adjust the Frequency of Phase II and III to Meet Student Needs

The frequency of Phase II and III processes in SMARTS may be necessary for some students, particularly those needing more frequent self-monitoring and data review. Although SMARTS is designed for small groups, with slight modifications, it can also be effectively implemented with individual students.

Not all behaviors are the same, just as no two students are the same. It may be necessary to make modifications or adjustments to Phase II and Phase III's processes in SMARTS in the case that a student is not being successful as shown by the data over time. There is not a magic number or a formula to know when we need to do this or how frequently we might need to adjust the daily self-monitoring or the weekly data-review meetings, but for some students, they will require more frequent self-monitoring of their behavioral goals. Where students need more frequent goal monitoring, it may also be beneficial to build in an additional meeting each week to review their self- and teacher ratings on their goal performances.

USING SMARTS WITH A SINGLE STUDENT VERSUS A GROUP

SMARTS was designed as a small-group intervention, but we have also implemented SMARTS with students who do not do well in group settings. There are modest changes that need to be made to each lesson for training, but after the training, Phases II and III lend themselves nicely to offering single students access to SMARTS.

FADING SMARTS

As with all social and behavioral interventions in school settings, they are designed to be easily accessed and implemented, but we would expect that students will not need them indefinitely if they are successful. As such, it is important to employ evidence-based approaches to fading any particular intervention to ensure a smooth transition from external support to a smooth, self-sufficient, and internally motivated student. By gradually reducing the external guides and supports and maintaining positive behavioral change, we can facilitate long-term self-regulation. Here are several practices shown to be important for fading any targeted interventions in school settings:

Fading SMARTS for Successful Students

Gradually fade SMARTS for successful students by reducing external supports. For example, alter or reduce feedback, cues, and reinforcements while encouraging students to internalize self-regulation skills.

1. *Communicate about the right time to fade.* A plan for how a student will begin to fade SMARTS is a great place to start. Recognizing that a student is doing better is a good place to start. There are some students who will not want to give up the weekly meetings and associated events. For students who are motivated by adult attention, they might really miss the time with you as the SMARTS facilitator. If they are peer motivated, they may also miss the interactions from SMARTS meetings. However, it is important for those students to recognize that SMARTS was always there to create skills for them and that they will always own those skills. That is, encourage these students to continue setting goals and using the SMARTS systems for self-monitoring their progress.

2. *Determine the right time to fade SMARTS.* Again, there is no magic number for when this should occur, but in general, the student and teacher data should display a consistent pattern of stability and agreement before fading. Consistency and stability is largely dependent upon the student, and their behavior and other factors are beyond our capacity to predict.

3. *Gradually reduce the feedback.* If you are meeting with SMARTS students once per week, then start by pushing this back to every 10 days, and then 2 weeks, before closing your group down. Alternatively, you can create a goal-monitoring sheet that includes students monitoring their goal progress only once per day instead of multiple times per day.

4. *Reduce external cues.* If a student is relying on teachers and others to monitor their progress, begin to reduce these external reminders. Encourage students who are successful at their goals to internalize the process of reflecting and monitoring their performance.

5. *Reduce reinforcements.* In the case that you are relying on reinforcements for your SMARTS group, slowly begin to reduce the occurrences of these reinforcements.

6. *Utilize peers or social supports.* Peers or other forms of social support can be helpful when fading SMARTS. Peers can provide encouragement, accountability, and feedback in place of structured SMARTS Phase II and III meetings.

FREQUENTLY ASKED QUESTIONS: STUDENTS, PARENTS, TEACHERS, AND STUDENT-SUPPORT SMARTS IMPLEMENTERS

Providing a list of frequently asked questions (FAQs) for a targeted school-based intervention like SMARTS is crucial for ensuring that all stakeholders—students, parents, teachers, and school-support personnel—will understand their roles and responsibilities, the program's objectives, and how it will be implemented. This clarity helps facilitate smoother implementation, promotes consistent support, and aligns expectations across

TABLE 10.1. Frequently Asked SMARTS Questions and Answers for Students, Parents, Teachers, Principals, and Student-Support SMARTS Implementers

The SMARTS questioner	The SMARTS question	The SMARTS answer
Students	What is SMARTS?	SMARTS is a program designed to help you learn important skills like setting goals, keeping track of your progress, and managing your challenges in a positive way.
	What will I do in Phase I?	In Phase I, you'll participate in 10 lessons where you'll learn to identify challenges, set goals to improve upon, and develop skills to manage and regulate your behavior.
	How do I self-monitor my goals in Phase II?	During Phase II, you'll check on your goals daily, rating yourself on how well you think you've done. Your teacher will also rate you on the same goals.
	What happens in Phase III?	In Phase III, once per week, you'll review the data you've collected all week alongside your teacher's data and see if you've met your goal. You'll decide if the goal needs to change or if a new goal should be set considering the data that you have reviewed.
	Will I work with other students?	Yes, you may work with peers during the lessons, and sometimes you might have a buddy who can help you stay on track with your goals if that is helpful to you and your teacher agrees.
Parents	What is the SMARTS program?	SMARTS is a self-monitoring and regulation-training program designed to help elementary students develop important life skills such as goal setting, self-monitoring, and self-regulation.
	How will SMARTS help my child?	The program aims to empower your child by teaching them how to set goals, monitor their behavior, and make positive changes, which can lead to better behavior at school and at home.
	What is my role in the SMARTS program?	You can be involved by reviewing and signing your child's daily self-monitoring forms, attending meetings, and supporting the goals set in SMARTS both at home and at school.
	Will I be informed about my child's progress?	Yes, you'll be kept informed about your child's progress through regular updates, and you may also be asked to attend meetings to discuss their development.
	Can SMARTS goals be aligned with home behavior?	Yes, SMARTS goals can be adapted to address challenges at home, creating a consistent approach between school and home.

(continued)

TABLE 10.1. *(continued)*

The SMARTS questioner	The SMARTS question	The SMARTS answer
Teachers	What is the SMARTS program?	SMARTS is a self-monitoring and regulation-training program aimed at helping elementary students with challenging behaviors develop skills like goal setting, self-monitoring, and self-regulation.
	How does SMARTS integrate into my classroom?	In Phase II, students will self-monitor their goals daily in the classroom, and you'll be asked to rate their performances on the same goals. These data will be reviewed together in Phase III.
	What is my role in the SMARTS program?	Your role includes participating in SMARTS by providing feedback, rating students' goal performances, attending review meetings, and possibly collaborating on goal-setting with the students.
	How often will I need to meet with the SMARTS team?	You'll participate in monthly check-ins and review meetings in Phase III, but your daily role involves providing ratings for students' goals.
	How can SMARTS benefit my students?	SMARTS can help students become more self-sufficient in managing their behaviors, leading to a more positive classroom environment and better academic and social outcomes.
Principals or administrators	What is SMARTS?	SMARTS is a self-monitoring and regulation-training program designed to help elementary students with challenging behaviors develop self-management and self-regulation skills through a structured, three-phase approach.
	Why should our school implement SMARTS?	SMARTS helps students improve their behaviors, enhance their learning experiences, and develop essential life skills, ultimately contributing to a more positive school environment and better academic outcomes.
	How is SMARTS structured?	SMARTS consists of three phases: • *Phase I:* Training, including a pre-meet lesson and nine lessons to identify problems, set goals, and learn self-regulation skills. • *Phase II:* Daily self-monitoring of goals by students, with teachers also rating student goal performances. • *Phase III:* Data-review and goal-reformation meetings to assess progress and refine goals.

(continued)

TABLE 10.1. *(continued)*

The SMARTS questioner	The SMARTS question	The SMARTS answer
Principals or administrators *(continued)*	What is the role of the principal in SMARTS?	As a principal, your role is to support the implementation by ensuring that staff are trained, resources are available, and the program is integrated into the school's broader behavior-management strategies. You may also facilitate communication between teachers, support staff, and families.
	How can I support teachers and staff in implementing SMARTS?	You can provide professional development opportunities, allocate time for SMARTS-related activities, and encourage collaboration among teachers, counselors, and other support staff. Regular check-ins with staff can help address any challenges and reinforce the program's goals.
	What should I do if a student is not making progress with SMARTS?	Work with the SMARTS team, including teachers and support staff, to review the student's data and consider adjustments to the intervention, such as increasing the frequency of monitoring or modifying goals.
	How can I involve families in SMARTS?	Encourage communication with families about the program's objectives and their children's progress. Support the involvement of families in reviewing self-monitoring forms, attending meetings, and reinforcing SMARTS goals at home.
	How will SMARTS impact overall school culture?	SMARTS can contribute to a more positive school culture by promoting self-regulation, responsibility, and goal setting among students. As students learn to manage their behaviors, overall classroom management and the learning environment are likely to improve.
	How do I assess the effectiveness of SMARTS at our school?	You can assess effectiveness by reviewing student-progress data, gathering feedback from teachers and staff, and monitoring any changes in overall school-behavior reports or disciplinary incidents.
	How can SMARTS be sustained long term?	To sustain SMARTS, ensure ongoing training for new staff, integrate the program into schoolwide behavior-support strategies, and periodically review and refine the program based on data and feedback.

(continued)

TABLE 10.1. *(continued)*

The SMARTS questioner	The SMARTS question	The SMARTS answer
SMARTS implementers (you!)	What is the SMARTS program?	SMARTS is a structured program designed to help elementary students with challenging behaviors learn self-monitoring, self-regulation, and goal-setting skills through a three-phase approach.
	How can I support the implementation of SMARTS?	You can support SMARTS by helping to facilitate the program, providing training, working closely with students during Phase I, and guiding the data-review process in Phase III.
	What is involved in each phase of SMARTS?	Phase I includes lessons on identifying challenges and setting goals; Phase II involves daily self-monitoring and teacher ratings; and Phase III is a review and goal-adjustment process.
	How do I know when a student is ready to fade from SMARTS?	A student is ready to fade when they show consistent improvement in their behavior, as evidenced by stable data and feedback. You'll gradually reduce supports and help them internalize the skills they've learned.
	Can SMARTS be adapted for individual students?	Yes, SMARTS can be tailored to fit the needs of individual students, including those who might struggle in group settings, ensuring that the program meets their specific behavioral goals.
	What is the role of peers in SMARTS?	Peers can play a supportive role in SMARTS by helping each other with goal setting and self-monitoring and by providing feedback during the process, which can enhance the program's effectiveness.

the board. By addressing common questions and concerns, the FAQ list enhances communication, minimizes confusion, and ensures that everyone involved is well-informed, which ultimately supports the success and effectiveness of the SMARTS program. Table 10.1 (pp. 239–242) is a list of FAQs that we have encountered over the years. We admit that this is not an exhaustive list of all issues or questions you may encounter for SMARTS, but we feel it will be a good resource to draw from in case you do have questions.

SMARTS AND TECHNOLOGY: THE FUTURE OF SELF-MONITORING

As we've said, SMARTS is a process and never a product—just like you and your students' development. To that note, and at the time we are writing this manual, we are fine-tuning tools to better facilitate SMARTS self- and teacher monitoring and data graphing via a website and application (*https://smartsweb.missouri.edu*). Future SMARTS users, should they choose, can use the website to access all SMARTS lesson plans and related activity worksheets for Phase I. The website also includes some videos to enhance student trainings. Using the website, SMARTS Facilitators can work with students to create student cases, input goals, invite teachers to rate student goals, set reminders for teachers to rate goals, and create pop-up reminders for students to rate their own performances if students in a school have access to a tablet or device during the instructional day. Even if students do not have access to tablets or devices during the day, SMARTS students and facilitators can use the website to enter goals and then print out goal sheets to be rated in class each day and then entered into the website at a later time. The SMARTS website will help facilitators monitor those goals using a web-based application during Phase II. The website can create graphs and permit teacher and student notes and also includes other functions, such as a dashboard for SMARTS Facilitators. The dashboard is helpful to summarize who is and who is not accessing the website and rating themselves. It can also summarize all teachers at a school who are high raters for SMARTS students and provide a list of noncompliers so you as the SMARTS Facilitator can have conversations with those teachers and encourage them to participate.

SUMMARY

Writing this manual has provided us with an incredible journey to reflect on the unbelievable number of teachers, students, and student-support staff in numerous schools where we have tested and tried different aspects of what we have described here. It fills us with immense pride and satisfaction to think that this approach may be used to promote and support the autonomy of students who may have been struggling with prior school-personnel efforts who sought to control or manage those students' behaviors rather than teaching them to manage their own behaviors. Embracing the principles of autonomy support, we have seen both teachers and students flourish and take ownership of their own paths. Cultivating these skills in students will instill in them self-regulatory muscles that they will use in the many years to come, both in school and life beyond.

Thank you for your SMARTS!

References

Allensworth, D., & Kolbe, L. (1987). The comprehensive school health program: Exploring an expanded concept. *Journal of School Health, 57*(10), 409–412.

Bandura, A. (1977). *Social learning theory.* Prentice-Hall.

Bandura, A. (2005). The primacy of self-regulation in health promotion. *Applied Psychology: An International Review, 54*(2), 245–254.

Black, P., & William, D. (1998). Inside the black box: Raising standards through classroom assessment. *Phi Delta Kappan, 80*(2), 139–148.

Bloom, B. S. (1968). Learning for mastery. *Evaluation Comment, 1*(2), 1–12.

Boutelle, K. N., & Kirschenbaum, D. S. (2012). Further support for consistent self-monitoring as a vital component of successful weight control. *Obesity Research, 6*(3), 219–224.

Bowen, N.-K. (2006). Psychometric properties of the Elementary School Success Profile for children. *Social Work Research, 30*(1), 51–63.

Briesch, A. M., Briesch, J. M., & Chafouleas, S. M. (2015). Investigating the usability of classroom management strategies among elementary schoolteachers. *Journal of Positive Behavior Interventions, 17*(1), 5–14.

Briesch, A. M., & Chafouleas, S. M. (2009). Review and analysis of literature on self-management interventions to promote appropriate classroom behaviors (1988–2008). *School Psychology Quarterly, 24*(2), 106–118.

Bruhn, A., Gilmour, A., Rila, A., Van Camp, A., Sheaffer, A., Hancock, E., . . . Wehby, J. (2022). Treatment components and participant characteristics associated with outcomes in self-monitoring interventions. *Journal of Positive Behavior Interventions, 24*(2), 156–168.

Bruhn, A., McDaniel, S., & Kreigh, C. (2015). Self-monitoring interventions for students with behavior problems: A systematic review of current research. *Behavioral Disorders, 40*(2), 102–121.

Bruhn, A. L., Woods-Groves, S., & Huddle, S. (2014). A preliminary investigation of emotional and behavioral screening practices in K–12 schools. *Education and Treatment of Children, 37*(4), 611–634.

Busacca, M. L., Anderson, A., & Moore, D. W. (2015). Self-management for primary school students demonstrating problem behavior in regular classrooms: Evidence review of single-case design research. *Journal of Behavioral Education, 24,* 373–401.

Butryn, M. L., Phelan, S., Hill, J. O., & Wing, R. R. (2007). Consistent self-monitoring of weight: A key component of successful weight loss maintenance. *Obesity, 15*(12), 3091–3096.

Carr, M. E., Moore, D. W., & Anderson, A. (2014). Self-management interventions on students with autism: A meta-analysis of single-subject research. *Exceptional Children, 81*(1), 28–44.

Ceci, M. W., & Kumar, V. K. (2016). A correlational study of creativity, happiness, motivation, and stress from creative pursuits. *Journal of Happiness Studies, 17,* 609–626.

Centers for Disease Control and Prevention. (2014). *Whole School, Whole Community, Whole Child (WSCC).* www.cdc.gov/healthyschools/wscc/index.htm.

Chafouleas, S. M., Riley-Tillman, T. C., & Sassu, K. A. (2009). Self-monitoring within a three-tiered model: Extending a behavior strategy for all students. *School Psychology Review, 38*(2), 250–258.

Christenson, S. L., Thurlow, M. L., Sinclair, M. F., Lehr, C. A., Kaibel, C. M., Reschly, A. L., . . . Pohl, A. (2008). *Check & Connect: A Comprehensive Student Engagement Intervention Manual.* Institute on Community Integration, University of Minnesota.

Cicchetti, D., & Cohen, D. J. (Eds.). (2006). *Developmental psychopathology: Theory and method* (2nd ed., Vol. 1). Wiley.

Cleary, T. J., & Zimmerman, B. J. (2004). Self-regulation empowerment program: A school-based program to enhance self-regulated and self-motivated cycles of student learning. *Psychology in the Schools, 41*(5), 537–550.

Committee for Children. (2002). *Second Step: A violence prevention curriculum.* Author.

Davis, J. L., Mason, B. A., Davis, H. S., Mason, R. A., & Crutchfield, S. A. (2016). Self-monitoring interventions for students with ASD: A meta-analysis of school-based research. *Review Journal of Autism and Developmental Disorders, 3,* 196–208.

Deci, E. L., Koestner, R., & Ryan, R. M. (1999). A meta-analytic review of experiments examining the effects of extrinsic rewards on intrinsic motivation. *Psychological Bulletin, 125*(6), 627–668.

Deci, E. L., & Ryan, R. M. (1985). *Intrinsic motivation and self-determination in human behavior.* Plenum Press.

Deci, E. L., & Ryan, R. M. (Eds.). (2004). *Handbook of self-determination research.* University of Rochester Press.

Dishion, T.-J., McCord, J., & Poulin, F. (1999). When interventions harm: Peer groups and problem behavior. *American Psychologist, 54*(9), 755–764.

Dunlap, G., dePerczel, M., Clarke, S., Wilson, D., Wright, S., White, R., & Gomez, A. (2009). Choice making to promote adaptive behavior for students with emotional and behavioral challenges. *Journal of Applied Behavior Analysis, 42*(1), 185–201.

Durlak, J. A., Weissberg, R. P., Dymnicki, A. B., Taylor, R. D., & Schellinger, K. B. (2011). The impact of enhancing students' social and emotional learning: A meta-analysis of school-based universal interventions. *Child Development, 82*(1), 405–432.

Embry, D. D. (2002). The Good Behavior Game: A best practice candidate as a universal behavioral vaccine. *Clinical Child and Family Psychology Review, 5*(4), 273–297.

Fantuzzo, J. W., Polite, K., Cook, D. M., & Quinn, G. (1988). An evaluation of the effectiveness of teacher- vs. student-management classroom interventions. *Psychology in the Schools, 25*(2), 154–163.

Fuchs, D., & Fuchs, L. S. (2006). Introduction to response to intervention: What, why, and how valid is it? *Reading Research Quarterly, 41*(1), 93–99.

Gifford-Smith, M., Dodge, K. A., Dishion, T. J., & McCord, J. (2005). Peer influence in children and adolescents: Crossing the bridge from developmental to intervention science. *Journal of Abnormal Child Psychology, 33,* 255–265.

Greiner, J. M., & Karoly, P. (1976). Effects of self-control training on study activity and academic performance: An analysis of self-monitoring, self-reward, and systematic-planning components. *Journal of Counseling Psychology, 23*(6), 495.

Gresham, F. M., & Elliott, S. N. (1993). Social skills intervention guide: Systematic approaches to social skills training. *Special Services in the Schools, 8*(1), 137–158.

Haines, J., Haycraft, E., Lytle, L., Nicklaus, S., Kok, F. J., Merdji, M., . . . Hughes, S. O. (2019). Nurturing children's healthy eating: Position statement. *Appetite, 137,* 124–133.

Haines, S. J., Summers, J. A., Turnbull, A. P., Turnbull, H. R., III, & Palmer, S. (2015). Fostering Habib's engagement and self-regulation: A case study of a child from a refugee family at home and preschool. *Topics in Early Childhood Special Education, 35*(1), 28–39.

Hallahan, D. P., & Sapona, R. (1983). Self-monitoring of attention with learning-disabled children: Past research and current issues. *Journal of Learning Disabilities, 16*(10), 616–620.

Hanson, C. L., Olsson, E. M., Palermo, C., & Coulter, R. W. (2017). Adolescents with type 1 diabetes: The role of self-monitoring. *Diabetes, 66*(Suppl. 1), A139.

Harris, K. R. (1986). Self-monitoring of attentional behavior versus self-monitoring of productivity: Effects on on-task behavior and academic response rate among learning-disabled children. *Journal of Applied Behavior Analysis, 19*(3), 417–423.

Harris, K. R., Danoff Friedlander, B., Saddler, B., Frizzelle, R., & Graham, S. (2005). Self-monitoring of attention versus self-monitoring of academic performance: Effects among students with ADHD in the general education classroom. *Journal of Special Education, 39*(3), 145–157.

Hattie, J., & Timperley, H. (2007). The power of feedback. *Review of Educational Research, 77*(1), 81–112.

Hawken, L. S., O'Neill, R. E., & MacLeod, K. S. (2015). *The behavior education program: A check-in, check-out intervention for students at risk* (2nd ed.). Guilford Press.

Hawkins, J. D., Kosterman, R., Catalano, R. F., Hill, K. G., & Abbott, R. D. (2008). Effects of social development intervention in childhood 15 years later. *Archives of Pediatrics and Adolescent Medicine, 162*(12), 1133–1141.

Hawkins, J. D., & Weis, J. G. (1985). The social development model: An integrated approach to delinquency prevention. *Journal of Primary Prevention, 6*(2), 73–97.

Henry, L., Reinke, W. M., Herman, K. C., Thompson, A. M., & Lewis, C. G. (2020). Motivational interviewing with at-risk students (MARS) mentoring: Addressing the unique mental health needs of students in alternative school placements. *School Psychology Review, 50*(1), 62–74.

Herman, K. C., Reinke, W. M., & Frey, A. J. (2020). *Motivational interviewing in schools: Strategies for engaging parents, teachers, and students.* Springer.

Herman, K. C., Reinke, W. M., Frey, A., & Shepard, S. (2014). *Motivational interviewing in schools: Strategies for engaging parents, teachers, and students.* Springer.

Huang, F. L., Reinke, W. M., Thompson, A., Herman, K. C., & County Schools Mental Health Coalition. (2019). An investigation of the psychometric properties of the early identification system–student report. *Journal of Psychoeducational Assessment, 37*(4), 473–485.

Individuals with Disabilities Education Act, 20 U.S.C. § 1400 (2004).

Kamphaus, R. W., & Reynolds, C. R. (2007). *BASC-2 Behavioral and Emotional Screening System.* Minneapolis, MN: Pearson.

Kazdin, A. E. (2017). *Encyclopedia of clinical psychology.* Wiley.

Kolbe, L. J. (2005). A framework for school health programs in the 21st century. *Journal of School Health, 75*(6), 226–228.

Koziol, N. A., Hanley, G. P., Fisher, W. W., & Kuhn, M. (2017). Increasing academic engagement in inclusive settings: The effects of self-monitoring and performance feedback. *Journal of Emotional and Behavioral Disorders, 25*(4), 218–229.

Kulik, C. L. C., & Kulik, J. A. (1988). Timing of feedback and verbal learning. *Review of Educational Research, 58*(1), 79–97.

Kusche, C. A., & Greenberg, M. T. (1994). *The PATHS curriculum*. Developmental Research and Programs.

Lane, K. L. (2007). Guidelines for selecting rating scales for progress monitoring and academic assessment. *Assessment for Effective Intervention, 32*(4), 225–241.

Lane, K., Bruhn, A. L., Eisner, S. L., & Kalberg, J. R. (2010). Score reliability and validity of the student risk screening scale: A psychometrically sound, feasible tool for use in urban middle schools. *Journal of Emotional and Behavioral Disorders, 18*(4), 211–224.

Lear, J. G. (2007). Health at school: A hidden health care system emerges from the shadows. *Health Affairs, 26*(2), 409–419.

Lee, S. H., Simpson, R. L., & Shogren, K. A. (2007). Effects and implications of self-management for students with autism: A meta-analysis. *Focus on Autism and Other Developmental Disabilities, 22*(1), 2–13.

Lipnevich, A. A., Preckel, F., Kandler, C., Heinlein, J., Dresel, M., Boehme, K., & Roberts, R. D. (2011). Effects of feedback on achievement: A meta-analysis. *Psychological Bulletin, 137*(3), 518–555.

Maag, J. W. (2019). Why is the good behavior game used for bad behavior?: Recommendations for using it for promoting good behavior. *Beyond Behavior, 28*(3), 168–176.

Miller, W. R., & Rollnick, S. (2013). *Motivational interviewing: Helping people change* (3rd ed.). Guilford Press.

Miller, W. R., & Rollnick, S. (2023). *Motivational interviewing: Helping people change and grow* (4th ed.). Guilford Press.

McDougall, D., Heine, R. C., Wiley, L. A., Sheehey, M. D., Sakanashi, K. K., Cook, B. G., & Cook, L. (2017). Meta-analysis of behavioral self-management techniques used by students with disabilities in inclusive settings. *Behavioral Interventions, 32*(4), 399–417.

McDougall, D., Skouge, J., Farrell, A., & Hoff, K. (2006). Research on self-management techniques used by students with disabilities in general education settings: A promise fulfilled? *Journal of the American Academy of Special Education Professionals, 36*, 73.

Nelson, J. R., Smith, D. J., Young, R. K., & Dodd, J. M. (1991). A review of self-management outcome research conducted with students who exhibit behavioral disorders. *Behavioral Disorders, 16*(3), 169–179.

Nelson, R. O., & Hayes, S. C. (1981). Theoretical explanations for reactivity in self-monitoring. *Behavior Modification, 5*(1), 3–14.

Ninness, H. C., Fuerst, J., Rutherford, R. D., & Glenn, S. S. (1991). Effects of self-management training and reinforcement on the transfer of improved conduct in the absence of supervision. *Journal of Applied Behavior Analysis, 24*(3), 499–508.

Ozkan, S. Y., & Sonmez, M. (2011). Examination of single subject studies conducted on individuals with disabilities by using self management strategies: A meta analysis study. *Educational Sciences: Theory and Practice, 11*(2), 809–821.

Panadero, E., & Jonsson, A. (2013). The use of scoring rubrics for formative assessment purposes revisited: A review. *Educational Research Review, 9*, 129–144.

Patterson, G. R., Dishion, T. J., & Yoerger, K. (2000). Adolescent growth in new forms of problem behavior: Macro- and micro-peer dynamics. *Prevention Science, 1*(1), 3–13.

Pendergast, F. J., Ridgers, N. D., Worsley, A., & McNaughton, S. A. (2017). Evaluation of a smartphone food diary application using objectively measured energy expenditure. *International Journal of Behavioral Nutrition and Physical Activity, 14*, 1–10.

Reddy, L. A., Cleary, T. J., Alperin, A., & Verdesco, A. (2018). A critical review of self-regulated learning interventions for children with attention-deficit hyperactivity disorder. *Psychology in the Schools, 55*(6), 609–628.

Reid, R., Trout, A. L., & Schartz, M. (2005). Self-regulation interventions for children with attention deficit/hyperactivity disorder. *Exceptional Children, 71*(4), 361.

Reinke, W. M., Herman, K. C., & Sprick, R. (2011). *Motivational interviewing for effective classroom management: The classroom check-up.* Guilford Press.

Romer, D., & McIntosh, M. (2005). The roles and perspectives of school mental health professionals in promoting adolescent mental health. In D. L. Evans, E. B. Foa, R. E. Gur, H. Hendin, C. P. O'Brien, M. E. P. Seligman, & B. T. Walsh (Eds.), *Treating and preventing adolescent mental health disorders: What we know and what we don't know* (pp. 598–615). Oxford University Press.

Rutherford, R. B., Quinn, M. M., & Mathur, S. R. (Eds.). (2007). *Handbook of research in emotional and behavioral disorders.* Guilford Press.

Ryan, R. M., & Deci, E. L. (2000). Self-determination theory and the facilitation of intrinsic motivation, social development, and well-being. *American Psychologist, 55*(1), 68.

Sanford, A., Christenson, S. L., & Dimmit, C. (2011). Rating scale measures: A guide to their development and use. In A. Thomas & J. Grimes (Eds.), *Best practices in school psychology IV* (pp. 223–238). National Association of School Psychologists.

Shapiro, E. S., & Cole, C. L. (1994). *Behavior change in the classroom: Self-management interventions.* Guilford Press.

Shapiro, E. S., Durnan, S. L., Post, E. E., & Levinson, T. S. (2002). Self-monitoring procedures for children and adolescents. In M. R. Shinn, G. Stoner, & H. Walker (Eds.), *Interventions for academic and behavior problems II: Preventative and remedial approaches* (pp. 433–454). National Association of School Psychologists.

Sheffield, K. I. M., & Waller, R. J. (2010). A review of single-case studies utilizing self-monitoring interventions to reduce problem classroom behaviors. *Beyond Behavior, 19*(2), 7–13.

Shute, V. J. (2008). Focus on formative feedback. *Review of Educational Research, 78*(1), 153–189.

Siceloff, E. R., Bradley, W. J., & Flory, K. (2017). Universal screening of behavioral and emotional risk in schools: A multi-informant approach. *Journal of Emotional and Behavioral Disorders, 25*(1), 24–36.

Simpson, T. L., Kivlahan, D. R., Bush, K. R., & McFall, M. E. (2005). Telephone self-monitoring among alcohol use disorder patients in early recovery: A randomized study of feasibility and measurement reactivity. *Drug and Alcohol Dependence, 79*(2), 241–250.

Skinner, B. F. (1953). *Science and human behavior.* Simon & Schuster.

Smith, T. E., Thompson, A. M., & Maynard, B. R. (2022). Self-management interventions for reducing challenging behaviors among school-age students: A systematic review. *Campbell Systematic Reviews, 18*(1), e1223.

Snyder, M. (1974). Self-monitoring of expressive behavior. *Journal of Personality and Social Psychology, 30*(4), 526–537.

Sugai, G., & Horner, R. H. (2009). Responsiveness-to-intervention and school-wide positive behavior supports: Integration of multi-tiered system approaches. *Exceptionality, 17*(4), 223–237.

Sugai, G., & Simonsen, B. (2012). *Positive behavioral interventions and supports: History, defining features, and misconceptions.* Center for PBIS & Center for Positive Behavioral Interventions and Supports. www.pbis.org/resource/positive-behavioral-interventions-and-supports-history-defining-features-and-misconceptions.

Tannenbaum, S. I., Yukl, G., & Wolff, S. B. (2015). Rethinking individual contributor roles in organizations: The underlying processes and outcomes of taking charge. *Academy of Management Review, 40*(1), 20–43.

Thompson, A. M. (2012). *A randomized trial of the self-management training and regulation strategy (STARS): A selective intervention for students with disruptive behaviors.* Unpublished doctoral dissertation, University of North Carolina at Chapel Hill.

Thompson, A. M. (2014). A randomized trial of the self-management training and regulation strategy for disruptive students. *Research on Social Work Practice, 24*(4), 414–427.

Thompson, A. M., Herman, K. C., & Reinke, W. M. (2020). The role of mental health in education: A dynamic systems approach to school-based mental health. *Journal of School Psychology, 82*, 1–15.

Thompson, A. M., Stinson, A. E., Sinclair, J., Stormont, M., Prewitt, S., & Hammons, J. (2021). The mediating role of autonomy, relationships, and social competency in the Self-management Training And Regulation Strategy (STARS): A randomized control trial. *Journal of Society of Social Work Research.*

Thompson, A. M., & Webber, K. C. (2010). Realigning student and teacher perceptions of school rules: A behavior management strategy for students with challenging behaviors. *Children & Schools, 32*(2), 71–79.

Thompson, A. M., Wiedermann, W., Herman, K. C., & Reinke, W. M. (2021). Effect of daily teacher feedback on subsequent motivation and mental health outcomes in fifth grade students: A person-centered analysis. *Prevention Science, 22*, 775–785.

U.S. Department of Health and Human Services, Substance Abuse and Mental Health Services Administration. (2016). *Safe Schools/Healthy Students (SS/HS) initiative.* www.samhsa.gov/safe-schools-healthy-students.

Van den Berg, R., Ros, A., Beijaard, D., & Verloop, N. (2006). The impact of a comprehensive feedback program on student teachers' teaching skills, self-assessment, and perceptions of feedback. *Journal of Teacher Education, 57*(3), 263–282.

Weber, K. P., Fallon, L. M., Hughes, M. T., Schumm, J. S., Park, J. H., & Sanchez, F. (2016). The effects of self-monitoring on behavior skills in elementary physical education. *Journal of Applied Behavior Analysis, 49*(4), 827–842.

Zimmerman, B. J. (2008). Investigating self-regulation and motivation: Historical background, methodological developments, and future prospects. *American Educational Research Journal, 45*(1), 166–183.

Index

Note. *f* or *t* following a page number indicates a figure or a table